THE POLITICAL THEORY OF NEOLIBERALISM

CURRENCIES

New Thinking for Financial Times

Melinda Cooper and Martijn Konings, Editors

The Political Theory of Neoliberalism

THOMAS BIEBRICHER

Stanford University Press

Stanford, California

STANFORD UNIVERSITY PRESS
Stanford, California

Printed in the United States of America on acid-free, archival-quality paper

Library of Congress Cataloging-in-Publication Data

Names: Biebricher, Thomas, 1974– author.

Title: The political theory of neoliberalism / Thomas Biebricher.

Description: Stanford, California : Stanford University Press, 2018. |
    Series: Currencies | Includes bibliographical references and index.

Identifiers: LCCN 2018016758 (print) | LCCN 2018019839 (ebook) |
    ISBN 9781503607835 | ISBN 9781503603646 (cloth : alk. paper) |
    ISBN 9781503607828 (pbk. : alk. paper)

Subjects: LCSH: Neoliberalism. | Political science—Philosophy. |
    Neoliberalism—European Union countries. | European Union countries—
    Politics and government. | European Union countries—Economic policy.

Classification: LCC JC574 (ebook) | LCC JC574 .B54 2018 (print) |
    DDC 320.51/3—dc23

LC record available at https://lccn.loc.gov/2018016758

Typeset by Kevin Barrett Kane in 10/15 Janson
Cover design by George Kirkpatrick

Contents

Acknowledgments

This book was written in 2016 and 2017, but its ideas and arguments have developed over several years, and earlier versions of some arguments have been presented at conferences, workshops, and seminars. I would like to thank the many people who have been willing to discuss neoliberalism with me and thus helped me develop my own views and positions.

In particular, I thank those who read parts of the draft manuscript: William Callison, Marius Kött, and Susanne Rühle. They provided important feedback and raised the kinds of skeptical questions one hopes for from readers. I very much appreciate the reviewers for Stanford University Press, who offered thorough and thoughtful engagement with my work; their comments and suggestions undoubtedly helped improve the book in many respects. I am particularly grateful for the feedback from Andrew Dilts and Yves Winter. Although Wolfgang Streeck and I agreed to disagree on the role of ideas in politics, his advice not to overestimate the importance of theories—and theorists—was well taken.

I am deeply thankful to have had the good fortune that the initial book proposal ended up in the hands of Emily-Jane Cohen at Stanford University Press, who was interested in the project from day one and steered it through its various stages with wisdom and understanding—and a strong and helpful opinion on a word limit. Working with her was as pleasant as it was productive.

viii Acknowledgments

Other people have supported this project in more indirect yet essential ways. Wendy Brown's encouragement rekindled and maintained my enthusiasm for the project when I had doubts about it. Rainer Forst's unwavering support and advice throughout the years were invaluable and gave me the opportunity to complete the project.

Finally, I thank my friends and family and, especially, my partner, Raphaela, for their love and support. This book is dedicated to our daughter, Lucía.

INTRODUCTION

The Political Theory of Neoliberalism

At some point during Bryan Singer's genre-redefining 1995 thriller, *The Usual Suspects*, the elusive villain Keyser Söze shares some of his wisdom with the audience: "The greatest trick the devil ever pulled was convincing the world that he doesn't exist." Something similar might be said about neoliberalism even if attributing infernal implications to it might seem a little far-fetched. The term is as ambiguous as it is contested. While some consider it to be synonymous with the unleashed forces of turbo-capitalism (Bourdieu 1998; Chomsky 1999), others think of it as a moderate version of classical liberalism's blunt imperative of laissez-faire. And while some note a decade-long march of victory of neoliberal policy regimes worldwide (see Harvey 2005), others disparage it as a figment of its critics' fevered imagination that does not even exist—let alone rule the world—and the term ought to be sent into semantic retirement. The latter perspective contends that neoliberalism is not only vacuous but has also become so politically charged that it serves as little more than a polemical tool for theoretical and political smear campaigns waged with denunciatory intentions. And to be sure, this is correct insofar as there are hardly any self-proclaimed neoliberals to be found. Since it was (re)introduced to academic and political discourse in the early 1990s, only its critics have used the term (see Boas and Gans-Morse 2009). At present there is a growing reluctance even on their side to make use of it

1

because it disqualifies any speaker as a potential ideologue with anticapitalist biases. If you call someone neoliberal, it suggests that you are unwilling to engage in reasoned argument and would rather resort to polemical name-calling. So even if neoliberalism ruled the world, it would be a neoliberalism without any neoliberals, and even its academic critics dare not speak its name—a truly devilish trick.

I first show that neoliberalism is far more than a chimera made up by its critics. Neoliberal thought developed as a response to the crisis of liberalism in the 1930s, and there is a common denominator to this body of thought, albeit a thin one. It is not a common set of doctrines but what I call the neoliberal problematic, which concerns the preconditions of functioning markets. This problematic characterizes the work of a number of thinkers who can be referred to as neoliberals in the proper sense of the term, such as the German ordoliberals Walter Eucken, Wilhelm Röpke, and Alexander Rüstow, but also Friedrich August Hayek, Milton Friedman, and James Buchanan.[1] They provide me with the reservoir of ideas that I scrutinize in part 1, the central part of the book.

Here, I reconstruct, analyze, and problematize crucial elements of the political theory of neoliberalism. Neoliberal thought contains a genuinely political dimension that is integral to the neoliberal problematic and far from just an annex to a creed of self-regulating markets. Part 1 is structured around four major categories in neoliberal thought: the state, democracy, science, and politics. Neoliberal positions with regard to these issues vary considerably to the point of being outright contradictory, and part of the rationale behind this study is to capture the resulting heterogeneities and tensions between the various perspectives, which are grouped in *varieties* of neoliberal thought.

Part 2 shifts the attention to the world of "actually existing neoliberalism" (Brenner and Theodore 2002) with a focus on contemporary Europe, for two reasons. First, I am interested in an analysis of the condition of contemporary neoliberalism: how neoliberalism has been transformed over the course of the recent string of crises and whether and how it is thus different from precrisis neoliberalism. Second, I focus on Europe because the European Union (EU) and the Economic and Monetary Union (EMU) together are easily the most advanced laboratory in regard to the development of neoliberal political forms. Here we find neoliberal ideas encapsulated not just in nation-state structures and international (trade) regimes but as a supranational federation (with a common currency), which is a configuration that many neoliberals have reflected on extensively as a potential institutional panacea for a neoliberal project, all respective difficulties notwithstanding.

Consequently, chapters 6 and 7 are devoted to a discussion of the workings of the EU/EMU, to what extent they conform to neoliberal tenets and neoliberal thinkers' views on the EU/EMU, as well as European integration more generally. Finally, based on preliminary arguments concerning the impact of ideas on political practices in general and particularly under conditions of crisis and genuine uncertainty, I argue that the Eurozone in its current institutional setup increasingly adheres to the precepts of *ordoliberalism* as one variety of neoliberalism. In this sense, we witness the ordoliberalization of Europe: Not only is competitiveness heralded as the aim of all reform efforts; the Eurozone now has a competitive order that forces all of its members into a particular form of competition with each other deemed desirable, which results in a generalized politics of austerity. Furthermore, the structural characteristics of this "economic constitution" implement much of the ordoliberal convictions with regard to the role of the state, democracy, and science in governing a market—albeit a market of jurisdictions. This form of governance is deeply skeptical of pluralist democracy, instead relying on a technocratic mode of policy making that borders on the authoritarian. If it is true that the sign of our times is the rise of authoritarianism, we should not mistake this to signal the end of neoliberalism. To the contrary, certain varieties of neoliberal thought have always contained an authoritarian dimension, which is now increasingly on display in its actually existing form in Europe and elsewhere. Neoliberalism, properly understood as capitalist markets embedded in authoritarian political forms, has far from run its course—it may have only just begun.

Let us begin with a closer look at the potential reasons for and against the continued use of the term "neoliberalism." I see two critical lines of argumentation. The first disapproves of the way the concept has been reduced to a "political swearword" (Hartwich 2009) and demands a less value-laden analytical vocabulary to describe politico-economic ideas, policies, or institutions. The second highlights the closely connected problem neoliberalism shares with plenty of other terms that ascend to the status of intellectual buzzwords for a while: Because of their very popularity and subsequent dissemination into various disciplinary contexts and usage, they dissolve into amorphous catch-all terms or empty signifiers (see Brenner, Peck, and Theodore 2010, 183–184). "Discourse" and "globalization" have had to endure a similar fate.

The charge that neoliberalism is merely the semantic weapon of choice wielded by anticapitalist forces and it should be abandoned to make room for concepts and analytical categories not considered politically suspect betrays a problematic assumption. It implies the possibility of a language that is un-distorted by political leanings and would offer an unbiased linguistic access to social reality. After all, only if there is an actual alternative to the allegedly polemical vocabulary of neoliberalism does the charge of its critics stick. However, this assumption is less than plausible. While twentieth-century positivism/critical rationalism as it is conceived of in the works of Karl Popper (who once was a member of the Mont Pelerin Society, a transnational network of neoliberals) may have dreamt of a fully transparent language that comes without any additional connotative baggage beyond its explicit meaning, few currently share this dream.

The likely rejoinder is to argue that philosophical reasons may not per-mit us to conceive of an unbiased language but that it makes an important difference whether we use more or less biased terms. So rather than speak of neoliberalism, we could simply refer to a market economy or just plain capitalism. Aside from the fact that even some first-generation neoliberals argued against the use of the term "capitalism" "because it suggests a system which mainly benefits the capitalists" (Hayek 2003, 1:62), a more general problem arises: cleansing social theoretical language of any biases comes only at the price of abstraction, which may leave us bereft of a vocabulary with any diagnostic potential. What is the intellectual value added when we describe societies as simply capitalist? That description was true a hundred years ago and even earlier. It is as accurate for a description of Sweden as it is for the United States—and almost all other existing economies. In other words, it is so true that it becomes trivial. However, social inquiry that does not aim at timeless nomological knowledge is well advised to take spatiotemporal context seriously and consequently requires terminological tools below the level of abstraction of "capitalism" and "market economies" to capture what is distinct about these contexts. Such diagnostic potential appears to be of considerable analytical and critical value for any endeavor aimed at capturing "what our present is" (Foucault 1989, 407), how it differs from the past, and how it might be different. Despite its inconveniences, neoliberalism can be considered a promising candidate in the search for a critical-diagnostic terminology applicable to the contemporary world—more promising, in my view, than alternatives such as late capitalism, post-Fordism, or advanced liberalism (see Barry, Osborne, and Rose 1996), which come with their own set of even graver definitional problems.

What are the definitional difficulties of neoliberalism; and are they unique to this particular term or a more widespread inconvenience associated with labels that refer to traditions and strands in political thought? Those opposed to neoliberalism because of its frequent polemical use in debates often link this polemical potential to the lack of definitive content of the term. Supposedly, it is the emptiness of neoliberalism that turns it into a perfect discursive weapon, rich in antagonistic connotations and very poor in solid content. There is no need to downplay these difficulties, which actually begin with the root term of neoliberalism: "liberalism." Liberalism is a current of thought that, positively speaking, exhibits an enviable richness and has been described as intellectual home by a surprisingly heterogeneous group of thinkers. Less positively speaking, one could describe liberalism as a tradition of thought that is next to impossible to pin down to a definitional kernel (see Crouch 2011, 3). Consider that there are arguments made for an inclusion of the absolutist and semiauthoritarian thinker Thomas Hobbes in the liberal tradition. This is a clear indicator of how broad the liberal tent is, and we would expect that this translates, among other things, into difficulties with one of its genealogical heirs, neoliberalism. Beyond this common difficulty of labeling political genres, neoliberalism is laden with another complication rooted in the somewhat unique spatiotemporal dynamic experienced by its root term "liberalism." What I have in mind is the slow transformation of the term "liberalism" beginning at the end of the nineteenth century, especially in the Anglo-Saxon world. It is here in particular that liberal thinkers combined elements taken from this tradition with agendas of a more social-democratic or progressivist kind. The "new" liberalism of a John Dewey or a T. H. Green led to a profound shift in meaning of the term, particularly in the United States and Great Britain, which continues to cause trouble for a shared political language between the Continental European and the Anglo-Saxon world.² After all, this shift has left us with a constellation in which the left-leaning Continental European Social Democrat would be referred to as a liberal on the other side of the Atlantic, while a liberal in the Continental sense is probably considered a conservative in the American sense. This transatlantic divergence of meanings with regard to liberalism has left its mark on the usage of neoliberalism as well. Despite all the reservations noted, "neoliberalism" is an established term in European political discourse. But given the changed meaning of liberalism in the North American context, it comes as no surprise that neoliberalism can hardly be said to be a part of the repertoire of political discourse there. Audiences might wonder how neoliberalism can denote the very opposite of what they commonly view as liberalism. North American political discourse refers to the positions associated with neoliberalism in the European context as "libertarianism"—but the fate of the latter in European political discourse is the mirror image of neoliberalism in America: it is not a category of any significance in political discourse, its academic significance notwithstanding.

Should these terminological complications prompt us to abandon the concept of neoliberalism after all? My response is not to deny the difficulties of literally coming to terms with neoliberalism but rather to question the uniqueness of these problems and whether they should really be considered problems in the sense of avoidable mistakes resulting from faulty reasoning or something slightly different. The crucial point, in my view, is to clarify what we can hope to achieve with terms that designate anything from a political ideology, to an intellectual discourse, or a tradition of thought. Consider any number of examples from conservatism, liberalism, and socialism to critical theory, poststructuralism, or the "new materialism." In each case, it is impossible to draw lines with geometrical accuracy that would enable us to distinguish unequivocally between, for example, conservatism and its closest intellectual siblings and cousins from liberalism to authoritarianism. I have mentioned that liberalism is arguably the best case to illustrate the difficulty of defining intellectual traditions that evolve in complex patterns over time and geocultural contexts. Although any but the casual observer is aware of the fuzziness at the heart of all of these concepts, there are few calls to stop referring to liberalism or conservatism because of their terminological/conceptual deficiencies. After all, if the standard we aspire to in our use of these categories is to map the intellectual-political landscape with geometrical accuracy, then we would have to rid the cartographic toolbox of neoliberalism and practically any other term used to describe what are ineradicably heterogeneous strands and currents in thought and more or less congruent political positions. The fact that a call to retire all of these imprecise terms has not really gained any traction suggests that the tacit expectations with regard to these terms are not that they provide us with exact markers of the intellectual-political territory but that they offer us a broad sense of orientation in need of constant revision and questioning. The closer we scrutinize what a tradition presumably stands for, the clearer its ambiguities come into view. Conversely, the more we find out about a particular thinker, the harder it becomes to group that thinker into any one tradition in an unambiguous fashion. We should not view this as some kind of pathology but rather as business as usual for political theorists. Finally, this business that preoccupies so many studies in both the history of political thought and contemporary theory should not be seen as a dry exercise in intellectual stock keeping. On the contrary, this is an eminently political activity, and the political nature of constructing these traditions is, aside from the reasons already identified, the main source of the unabated controversy surrounding any one particular definition of, for example, conservatism that suggests thinker X is part of that tradition while thinker Y is not. Contesting a certain interpretation of conservatism and the respective representatives may not be the most important activity political theorists engage in. However, it is anything but a trivial matter how we define traditions and chart political and intellectual territory because these are the terms in which political contestations are being conducted. So while some may complain about the fuzziness of political labels and their contested nature, political theorists should be aware of their limits and dangers but still embrace them as an important medium of political contestation—and this includes a fortiori neoliberalism.

Having provided a preliminary defense of the use of the terminology of neoliberalism, I conclude with an outline and brief justification of the two major, and potentially controversial, assumptions and corresponding methodological decisions underlying this study.

First, I assume that an analytical distinction can be made between neo-liberalism as an intellectual project and neoliberalism as a number of con-crete political projects in various empirical settings. While I am ultimately interested in both the theory and practice of neoliberalism, the starting point and focus of this study is the theoretical level. This approach might be considered an "ideas-centered understanding of neoliberalism" (Cahill 2014, 32), which is met with criticism, especially by those who subscribe to a more materialist view and suspect neoliberalism's ideational dimen-sion to be of predominantly ideological significance (see Harvey 2005, 19; Mirowski 2013, 68). They point to the alleged chasm between neoliberal theory and practice and reprimand nonmaterialist accounts for their alleged disregard for the embeddedness of ideas in interest- and institution-based power structures that keep the former in place (see Cahill 2014). While I am not in principle opposed to studying "actually existing neoliberalism," the subject of part 2, I do see some problems with focusing exclusively on this dimension, because strictly materialist accounts come with their own set of difficulties. First, materialists routinely define some policy regime of, for example, privatization and marketization as neoliberal, but how would one arrive at such a definition without consultation of neoliberal texts and the ideas contained in them? For decades there was no neoliberalism, except in the form of an intellectual discourse, so taking the respective political prac-tices as a starting point is not a self-evident choice. Furthermore, the alleged discrepancy between neoliberal theory and practice is overstated in many materialist accounts, arguably due to a lack of interest in neoliberal theory, which is often summed up as the doctrine of "self-regulating markets." If this were an accurate interpretation, the divide between the two dimensions of neoliberalism would indeed be wide, but attributing an economistic view of market absolutism to neoliberal theory betrays a poor understanding of it.[3] Instead, neoliberal theory is deeply interested in the link between politics, society, and economics. Once we take it seriously as a body of thought in political economy, it becomes clear that there are notable correspondences between these designs and neoliberalism in practice. To be sure, it would be wrong to suggest that there is a 1:1 correspondence between neoliberal theory and practice, or that actors regularly and consciously aim to implement neoliberal ideas, or that the latter somehow realize themselves—I have no Hegelian inclinations. However, to infer from this that neoliberal theory is simply inconsequential is to have an impoverished understanding of political life deprived of its ideational dimension.[4] Finally, the price we would have to pay for not considering neoliberal theory in its own right but just an ideological veil of neoliberal practices is a political one. Imagine the response of a proponent of neoliberalism to the criticisms leveled at actually existing neoliberalism regarding, for example, its inequality levels or other problems. The answer would clearly not be that neoliberalism is to blame, but rather its poor and incomplete implementation keeps us from reaping the alleged rewards of thorough neoliberalization: The solution to society's problems remains *more*, not less, neoliberalism. The only way to preclude this exculpating argumentative strategy is to engage neoliberalism on the level of theories and ideas to show that the problem does not lie with selective implementation, unfaithful to the spirit of the respective ideas *but the very ideas themselves.*

The second methodological assumption concerns my mode of engagement with neoliberal thought. The purpose of this study is not only to reconstruct and analyze the political theory of neoliberalism but also to offer a critique of it. While others make the case for (a particular kind of) ideology critique of neoliberal theory (see Mirowski 2013), my critique has a slightly different thrust and is based on two equally important components. First, I distill the positive contents of neoliberal theory's political dimension and probe for internal inconsistencies and tensions within and between varieties of neoliberalism, as well as instances where if falls short of its own stated aspirations in what might be called an immanent critique. But as the time-honored discussions surrounding this mode of critique show, its strength lies in the fact that it engages its object on its own terrain and thus can never be off target, but its weakness flows from the same source. Accepting that terrain, the terms of engagement, excludes these from an immanent critique in its strictest form. Therefore, the second component is a focus on that which is *not* being said in neoliberal theory: that is, the assumptions and conditions presupposed and built into it, the resulting limitations and blindspots, and the implications and potential consequences of certain ideas were they to be put into practice. The result I hope to achieve is a rich and nuanced critique of neoliberal thought that is willing to give neoliberal theory its due: a critique that has no need to distance itself from each and every element of it to ensure the identity of some demonic "Other" that is neoliberalism and, conversely, the purity of the non-neoliberal that must not be contaminated by correspondences or partial agreements with it, let alone the outrageous idea of possibly learning something from its proponents. Thus, the critique I intend to develop is designed to be neither a refutation nor an unmasking in the sense of ideology critique but rather a *problematization* of neoliberalism's political theory in its various aspects.

CHAPTER 1

What Is Neoliberalism?

"Neoliberalism" is an inconvenient, albeit important, term for critical inquiries into the socioeconomic and political conditions of the capitalist present. Nevertheless, the problem remains that the potential usefulness of the term is greatly diminished because its meaning is unclear, or, possibly, as its critics believe, it has no meaning. Thus, it is no surprise that researchers who study neoliberal theory and/or practice feel compelled to offer a straightforward and unambiguous definition to preempt the charge of harboring an empty signifier floating around at the heart of their research agenda. However, this has led to a great number of studies that seek to define neoliberalism either through a set of specifically neoliberal policies like deregulation or privatization (see Chomsky 1999, 19; Larner 2000; Steger and Roy 2010, 14; Mirowski 2013, 333) or through some kind of conceptual kernel that supposedly represents its very essence (see Crouch 2011, vii; Mudge 2008, 706–707). However, these efforts are plagued by difficulties: There is an ineradicable air of arbitrariness to the various policy lists, and the breadth and internal heterogeneities of "variegated" (Jessop 2016, 123) and "polymorphic" (Peck 2010, 8) neoliberalism seem to defy any attempt at developing "a generic and trans-historical definition of neoliberalism" (Hay 2007, 53)—and this applies not only to actually existing neoliberalism but to its discourse as well. Still, it is hardly a solution to postulate that there "are thus a number of distinct, but related neoliberalisms" (Roy, Denzau, and Willett 2007, 5), since this only exacerbates the problem by having to define each and describe the nature of the bond that relates them.

This, then, is the predicament in which any work on neoliberalism finds itself. The main task of this chapter is therefore to develop an understanding of neoliberalism that avoids the overly parsimonious fallacy of attempting to "transcendentally 'fix' neoliberalism" with reference to some essence or core (Peck 2010, 15)—an understanding that is sufficiently accurate to capture the internal heterogeneity without dissolving neoliberalism entirely into multiple neoliberalisms without any underlying unity. I choose the following conceptual strategy in this undertaking.

Given the marked absence of any self-proclaimed neoliberals today and the suspicion harbored by some commentators that neoliberalism may have never existed other than as "a figment of the fevered left" (Mirowski 2009, 426), I argue that a useful starting point to investigate the meaning of neoliberalism is to look at what those who actually referred to themselves as neoliberals associated with the term. In other words, the first step in gaining an understanding of the neoliberal project(s) is the reconstruction of the historical context of its emergence, which may be summed up as the crisis of liberalism. Neoliberalism must be understood, first and foremost, as a response to this crisis based on a diagnosis of the factors that led to its decline. Out of this I distill what I call the neoliberal problematic, which, in my view, strikes the right conceptual balance between the unity and the heterogeneity of neoliberal thought. Neoliberalism, I argue, was never emphatically "one," and the historical approach employed here has not been chosen in the hope of finding the single origin of neoliberalism, where its essence could be isolated from all contingent ingredients in pristine purity, because there is no such place. Despite the undeniable tensions within neoliberal discourse that characterized it even in its origins, what *did* unite those who called themselves neoliberals was a shared problematic that animated their efforts. The market lay at the center of this problematic, but the problematic was inherently political, as I show in contrast to the conventional economistic accounts of neoliberalism.

The Birth of Neoliberalism: The Colloque Walter Lippmann and the Crisis of Liberalism

It stands to reason that few if any of the participants of the Colloque Walter Lippmann anticipated that their meeting would retrospectively come to be considered as marking the birth date of an entire intellectual tradition when they gathered at the Institut International de Cooperation Intellectuelle in Paris during the last days of August 1938. The five-day colloquium had been organized to discuss the American journalist Walter Lippmann's book *The Good Society*, published in 1937. Lippmann attended along with twenty-five mostly European thinkers from various countries (see Reinhoudt and Audier 2018; Walpen 2004, 55–61). In the records of this meeting we first find the term "neoliberalism" connoting a common agenda and a shared project.[1] Of course, referring to the birth of neoliberalism and the records of the meeting makes it seem as if a single origin and a founding text by Walter Lippmann were, after all, available as core ingredients of a straightforward definition of neoliberalism, but the simplicity of the narrative and the metaphor is deceiving.

Neither is there a single origin of neoliberalism nor is there an "ur-text" authored by Lippmann or any other neoliberal.[2] In fact, while Louis Rougier, who was the official convener of the meeting, supposedly added the term "neoliberalism" to the records after the meeting, it is not clear whether there was a consensus to adopt this particular label during the actual discussions (see Burgin 2012, 73; Walpen 2004, 60). More complications to the alleged birth of neoliberalism could be added, the gravest of which was the impending World War II, which stopped the neoliberal project with its plans for a research center, regular meetings, and intensified network building in its tracks. It took almost a decade after the Colloque for a similar meeting to take place—the second birth of neoliberalism, if you will—in April 1947, when sixty participants gathered in Switzerland to form the Mont Pelerin Society (MPS), which, to this day, is considered to represent a "neoliberal international" (see Mirowski and Plehwe 2009), although the word "neoliberalism" never even made it into the society's official *Statement of Aims* that had been agreed on by the founding members.

Yet the Colloque still does mark a useful starting point for an examination of the neoliberal project because its agenda and that of the founding conference of the MPS, in combination with the writings of some of the participants, can help us reconstruct the context of the emergence of neoliberalism as an intellectual-political project and the rationale underlying it.

Lippmann's *Good Society* was a highly inconsistent treatise; however, its diagnosis and overall assessment of the times struck a chord with some of the leading future neoliberals. Lippmann depicted and dissected a classical liberalism in rapid decline and called for an effort to stabilize and consolidate the course of an intellectual tradition that was otherwise bound to tumble straight into oblivion. This was the catalyst for people like Hayek in London or Röpke in Geneva, who shared some of these worries, to call for a meeting to discuss not only Lippmann's book but the dire condition of liberalism more generally. Accordingly, the context of neoliberalism's intellectual inception can succinctly be stated as the crisis of liberalism.

So let us take a look at some of the main factors that could be considered symptoms of the possibly fatal crisis of liberalism. By the late 1930s proponents of liberalism—and not only them (see Polanyi 2001, 3)—had become convinced that the decline of the liberal age had been set in motion with the onset of World War I in 1914. The war was of course a catastrophic and deeply traumatizing event for (Western) civilization in any number of respects, but it dealt a particularly heavy blow to a broadly liberal worldview for two reasons. First, the mostly optimistic outlook on history shared by many currents of liberalism, including the more popularized versions, was shattered by the atrocities of a war fought with the utmost disregard for human life; the Western Front was described as "a machine for massacre" (Hobsbawm 1994, 25). The relapse into four years of barbarism made the talk of progress (through commerce) ring hollow if not outright cynical. The world seemed to have entered a period in which the notion of progress became elusive and was increasingly replaced by "a sense of catastrophe and disorientation" (ibid., 94).

Second, the war complicated the liberal position because up until this time, ideas about (socialist) state planning had been just that, *ideas* that could be dismissed as unrealistic and irremediably utopian. However, World War I proved that economies could be run to a considerable degree on the basis of centralized planning without collapsing—which became even more obvious during World War II. At least in certain currents of liberalism the prime argument against socialism before the war had been that it was not only undesirable but also simply unattainable. This position became much more difficult to maintain with planning taking place in the war economy. To some extent the famous Socialist Calculation Debate during the 1920s and 1930s, in which some representatives of the Austrian school such as Ludwig von Mises and Hayek participated, has to be understood as an attempt to prove that despite these seemingly promising experiences, experiments in planning without markets and market prices were still ultimately doomed to fail.

During the 1920s, efforts were undertaken to restore the liberal civilization of the nineteenth century (see Polanyi 2001), but at the end of the 1920s they proved futile, as liberalism suffered another severe setback in the form of the Great Depression. While liberals had tried to prove theoretically that socialism was bound to collapse in the Socialist Calculation Debate, capitalism actually did collapse in practice on an almost worldwide scale. Given the enormity of the economic and social devastation caused by the crisis, it is no surprise that a broadly liberal position in favor of capitalist markets as indispensable guarantors of growth and wealth lost much, if not all, of its appeal, especially among the masses hit by unemployment and thrown into poverty. Thus, the crisis and its socioeconomic fallout created major problems for liberalism, as the pressure on elected governments to get involved in active crisis management and alleviate at least the most severe social problems increased to a point where the respective demands became almost impossible to ignore. Two developments in particular signify this turn of the tide that is of crucial importance for the inception of the neoliberal project.

The first is the New Deal, which President Franklin Roosevelt had characterized as "liberal" and which attracted considerable ire from Lippmann. The reforms associated with this label not only manifested a significant buildup of the American welfare state at the federal level through the introduction of a social insurance system; it also represented a profound change in the overall philosophy of the state. The state explicitly adopted a new set of responsibilities toward its population that no longer pertained only to defending it against external enemies, enforcing the law, and providing a minimum of public infrastructure. It now included attending to socioeconomic welfare more broadly, especially with regard to the adverse effects of a capitalist economy (see Hobsbawm 1994, 96, 138–140). The stoic attitude of letting economic crises run their course combined with the denial of any more than rudimentary responsibility for social ills had fallen into disrepute over the years of crisis, and governments all over the North Atlantic world began to reconsider their role in regard to the economy and society. John Maynard Keynes's theories came to represent this changed attitude, which brings us to the next facet of the liberal crisis, the rise of Keynesianism.

As early as 1924 Keynes had famously proclaimed "the end of laissez-faire" in a lecture of the same title he delivered at Oxford. It may have been premature at the time, but the 1930s proved Keynes right, although "hegemonic Keynesianism" would not come to full fruition until the post–World War II era. Keynes essentially argued for an active involvement of the state in economic policy in its various aspects. The position shared by welfare economics and economic liberalism was that capitalist markets would more or less automatically recover from external shocks or crises and slide back into market-clearing equilibria, guaranteeing profits, growth, and employment. However, Keynes contended that it was possible for markets to get stuck in suboptimal equilibria where continued stagnation, unemployment, and deflation loomed large unless the state stepped in to jump-start the economy. This could be achieved through an expansionary monetary policy, such as lowering interest rates and thus reducing the price of money, but even more important, through public investment to boost aggregate demand and thus encourage the private sector to expand production and investment. As the Great Depression dragged on, Keynes's view that dysfunctional markets without built-in correctives could get locked into crisis conditions offered the basis for a plausible interpretation of the empirical evidence. Moreover, his work, culminating in the *General Theory of Employment, Interest and Money*, published in 1936, provided governments with a sorely needed set of policy instruments that allowed for a more hands-on approach to dealing with an ailing economy. The rise of this activist philosophy of government, which even justified running deficits under certain conditions to pump money into an economy in crisis, was an important factor in the formation of neoliberalism, although the relation between the various neoliberals and Keynes(ianism) is more complex than one might expect.[3] Overall, though, Keynes, and much more so Keynesianism as it was further developed by economists like Joan Robinson and Nicolas Kaldor, represented a veritable bête noire for liberalism in the 1930s and beyond (see Hayek 1978a). The rise of the former was inextricably tied to and gave a clear indication of the latter's decline.

The final development contributing to the liberal crisis was surely the most alarming for the participants of the 1938 Colloque: the ascendency of deeply antiliberal political forces from Bolshevik Communism on the left of the political spectrum to European Fascism and German National Socialism on the right, as well as plain "old-fashioned authoritarians or conservatives" somewhere in between (Hobsbawm 1994, 113).

Needless to say, the very existence of the Soviet Union, with its centrally planned economy, provided a challenge for those liberals who had been arguing that socialism could not work. While it was hardly a secret that the Soviet Union had evolved into a deeply repressive regime that persecuted individuals and groups, its apologists pointed out that it had weathered the storm of the Great Depression better than many other societies, which had, in turn, raised the interest in "planning" even in capitalist countries (Hobsbawm 1994, 96). In any case, as repressive or even outright totalitarian as the Soviet Union may have been, in 1938, there was no reason to assume that it and its collectivist economy would collapse anytime soon. If the experience of wartime socialism was a thorn in the side of liberalism, proving that planning could work on a limited scale, the Soviet Union was a massive spear and evidence that entire societies could be organized according to a centralized plan—albeit at the cost of basic rights and the loss of hundreds of thousands of lives.

Similarly, Europe in 1938 was the site of triumphant antiliberal forces almost wherever the eye could turn—but here they predominantly hailed from the right of the political spectrum. National Socialism had seized power in 1933 in Germany, forcing the Colloque attendees Röpke and Rüstow into exile, and Italian Fascism continued to reign. In Spain, Franco's Falange had defeated the republican forces in the civil war, and in other countries, such as Hungary and Finland, semifascist authoritarian movements and parties were not in power but gaining political ground. And like Soviet Communism, the Fascist and National Socialist regimes were far from crumbling; so for an observer of the liberal persuasion the overall scenery must have seemed rather apocalyptic. After all, while Communism and Fascism would not agree on much else, they were united in their fierce enmity of anything bourgeois or liberal (see Furet 1999): "For a generation liberalism in Europe seemed doomed" (Hobsbawm 1987, 333).

These are the most striking symptoms of the crisis of liberalism, and the neoliberal project must be understood as a reaction and response to what the neoliberals-to-be perceived as a crisis of truly existential proportions, one addressed in various sessions at the Colloque devoted to the factors responsible for the decline of neoliberalism (see Reinhoudt and Audier 2018). This interpretation of the neoliberal project as a reaction to the antiliberal syndrome just described provides us with the first clue for the clarification of the neoliberal project's content through an understanding of what it was opposed to, or, to use an expression coined by Michel Foucault, its "field of adversity" (2008, 106).

The Field of Adversity

There can be little doubt that the key intellectual and political adversary of neoliberalism was what the early neoliberals would call "collectivism," although they may also have used more specific vocabulary. In this choice of words an important positioning already becomes clear, foreshadowing a terminological strategy later to be found in many theories of totalitarianism. In this perspective, the political distinction of significance is not right versus left, or Communism versus Fascism, but rather totalitarianism versus liberalism, or collectivism versus individualism. In other words, while there may be some differences between Fascist and Communist regimes, according to the neoliberal view their crucial common denominator is that they are collectivist. The possibly best example of this position is, of course, Hayek's *The Road to Serfdom* (2001), originally dedicated to the "Socialists of all Parties." Animated by the concern that the Allies might win the war but lose the battle of ideas and thus resort to planning beyond the wartime economy, Hayek aimed mainly to show that the well-meaning advocates of modest planning were inadvertently playing into the hands of those with whom they were at war. What must be defended against collectivisms of all persuasions is "an individualist civilization" (Hayek 2001, 14) that is equally endangered by Fascism and Communism (ibid., 27). We can also include similar views of other Colloque attendees such as Lippmann and Rüstow. Furthermore, Eucken's fundamental distinction between a centrally administered economy (*Zwangsverwaltungswirtschaft*) and an exchange economy (*Verkehrswirtschaft*) introduced in his *Foundations of Economics* published two years after the Colloque, which he was barred from attending by the Nazis, indirectly confirms that the purposes of centralization in the first system are of no real significance (see Eucken 1951a, 119–132). Thus, the first thing to note with regard to neoliberalism's field of adversity is that neoliberals of the 1930s and 1940s were staunch anticollectivists and defined themselves predominantly against both National Socialism/Fascism and Communism.[4]

In some of the more recent scholarship on the origins of neoliberalism, it has been argued that this is noteworthy because it shows how the main targets of neoliberal criticism shift over the years and decades. Although contemporary neoliberalism may be strongly associated with the critique of the state in general and the welfare state in particular, this allegedly differs from the situation in its early days: "At this stage, neo-liberal authors focused their energies on opposing the socialist and fascist strands of this discourse [on planning]," writes Ben Jackson; "the chief enemy of the neo-liberals was not the nascent welfare state or even Keynesian economics" (2010, 140). This is an important point and a reminder of the difficulties involved in defining something that has a history and whose contours and the relative priority of its oppositions shift over the course of time. And, of course, Jackson has a point; after all, one session at the Colloque was even devoted to the question of whether and how liberalism might be able to fulfill its social obligations (see Reinhoudt and Audier 2018, 149–156). Today's readers might be surprised to learn that Hayek's somewhat infamous *Road to Serfdom* contains strong polemics against "planning" but also concedes that "to limit working hours or to require certain sanitary arrangements, is fully compatible with the preservation of competition. . . . Nor is the preservation of competition incompatible with an extensive system of social services" (2001, 39). However, these passages are difficult to reconcile with the overall claim of his book that even the most modest attempts at

planning are likely to lead a society down the road to serfdom. This tension
at the heart of Hayek's account was Keynes's single but rather devastating
point of criticism in a letter to Hayek: "You admit here and there that it is a
question of knowing where to draw the line. You agree that the line has to
be drawn somewhere [between free enterprise and planning], and that the
logical extreme is not possible. But you give us no guidance whatever as to
where to draw it" ([1944] 1980, 387).

To put the matter differently, while their relative importance as neoliberal adversaries certainly shifts over time, it is not possible to conceptually
separate the critique of the welfare state from the critique of totalitarianism
even in early neoliberal discourse.[5] Foucault may have overstated the case
by referring to an "illiberal" "economic-political invariant" underlying the
analyses of early neoliberalism (2008, 111), suggesting that all roads of planning ultimately lead into the abyss of totalitarianism. However, Lippmann's
equivocation of the "gradual collectivism" that he detects in the New Deal
with Fascism and Communism (1937, 106), as well as Röpke's criticism of
the Beveridge Plan's extension of the welfare state in Great Britain, paints
an ominous picture of the buildup of the welfare state that is reminiscent of
Hayekian imagery: "The welfare state not only lacks automatic brakes and
not only gathers impetus as it moves along, it also moves along a one-way
street in which it is, to all intents and purposes, impossible or, at any rate,
exceedingly difficult to turn back. . . . This implies growing centralization
of decision and responsibility and growing collectivization of the individual's
welfare and design of life" (1960, 162–163).[6]

To sum up this first point regarding the field of adversity, neoliberalism's prime antagonists are certainly Communism and National Social-
ism/Fascism, which the neoliberals view as nothing more than different
manifestations of the same basic collectivism-cum-totalitarianism. But
the point of the neoliberal conceptualization of this sector of the field of
adversity is to draw connections between those most extreme instantia-
tions of a politics of illiberalism and other phenomena that might be seen
as respective prestages, such as the welfare state and, more indirectly,
Keynesianism—and by extension those who would promote it, especially
trade unions. The welfare state and the omnipresent but poorly defined
planning associated with it supposedly represent collectivism *in nuce*—but

there is a certain range of positions among neoliberals with regard to the inevitability and irreversibility of the drift toward collectivism. Furthermore, the relative dangers of the welfare state also depend on its particular configuration (see, e.g., Hayek 2001, 125).

It is against these adversaries that neoliberalism positions itself, seeking to *revitalize* a broadly liberal agenda or at least certain elements thereof in the face of the 1930s illiberal zeitgeist. To be sure, the fact that neoliberalism is concerned with a revitalization of liberal ideas, which must have seemed like an almost quixotic undertaking at the time, is hardly surprising; it is common sense among most commentators who choose a broadly historical approach to outlining the neoliberal project (see, e.g., Turner 2007, 42; Peck 2008, 14; Burgin 2012, 65). The more interesting component of what might be called the neoliberal formula can be derived from another, closer look at the field of adversity.

Narratives of Liberal Decline

The early neoliberals, both at the Colloque and at the founding meeting of the MPS, were adamant that the decline of neoliberalism was not only the result of the rise of its external adversaries but also attributable to problems *within* liberalism that would have to be addressed if it were to regain the status of a contender in the battle of ideas. An entire session of the Colloque was devoted to the internal factors responsible for the liberal demise, and the MPS also discussed the preconditions for a liberal revival in 1947 (see Reinhoudt and Audier 2018, 119–128). Thus, it is hardly an exaggeration to say that neoliberalism was the outcome of a collective liberal soul searching seen as a prerequisite for the revitalization of ideas that a hundred years earlier had almost reigned supreme. While neoliberalism is an attempt to revitalize a broadly liberal agenda, it is not simply a revival of these ideas. To face the challenges of (gradual) collectivism, it would not suffice to simply recycle classical liberal ideas and call for a return to the fundamental truths of Adam Smith or Adam Ferguson.[7] Liberalism would have to undergo a proper modernization if it were to successfully engage Keynesian and collectivist ideas, as Hayek made clear in his opening statement at the MPS founding conference: "As I see our task, it is not sufficient that our members

should have what used to be called 'sound' views. The old liberal who adheres to a traditional creed *merely* out of tradition, however admirable his
views, is not of much use for our purpose. What we need are people who
have faced the arguments from the other side, who have struggled with
them and fought themselves through to a position from which they can
both critically meet the objection against it and justify their views" (1992,
240). Liberalism needed to be modernized in order to compete, or rather,
survive in the twentieth century, according to the large majority of Colloque
participants, so the neoliberal project could not be a solely restorative one.

What puts the "neo" into neoliberalism is obviously this modernizing
effort. But this presupposed, crucially, a critical *revision* of the old liberal
agenda and an analysis of its shortcomings and aberrations. In other words,
the full field of adversity, against which neoliberalism defines itself, *also*
includes wrongheaded strands of liberalism that developed over the latter
half of the nineteenth century. These were internal factors of liberalism's
decline, according to the neoliberal crisis narrative. Let us take a closer look
at this narrative through four overlapping versions from Röpke, Rüstow,
Friedman, and Hayek, all written some years after the Colloque but largely
congruent with what we know about the discussions in its context.

Wilhelm Röpke's version of the crisis narrative begins with a rhetorical question: "Could it possibly be, that far from being just a victim of the
societal crisis it [liberalism] could have contributed to it through its own
errors? And if this should turn out to be the case and the crisis of modern
society is also the crisis of liberalism, is there no room for hope that a
cleansing and inner rejuvenation of liberalism will also be a crucial contribution to overcoming the crisis of society in general?" (1950a, 14–15).
His examination of liberal decline operates on the basis of a distinction
between an "imperishable" core of liberalism that is maintained and built
on in a process of "rejuvenation from within" and "ephemeral" aberrations
(ibid., 9). Three main "internal" problems are identified in his account: first,
"the relation between liberalism and the functions of reason, second, its
relation to community and third, the relation to economic life" (ibid., 25).
The respective aberrations that have harmed liberalism are "rationalism,
individualism and economic liberalism" (ibid.). Consequently, Röpke warns
of the hubris of intellectualism and the dangers of individualism when they

lead to atomization of the individual in society. In regard to socioeconomic life, he bemoans liberalism's one-sided focus on narrowly economic issues (ibid., 29), discussed later at greater length.

Alexander Rüstow is the most outspoken critic of liberalism among the neoliberals. He attributes the decline of liberalism, "the dominant philosophy of life in the Western World during the nineteenth century" (1942, 268), to reasons very similar to Röpke's last point. "In practice, liberalism meant for the nineteenth century predominantly economic liberty, i.e., the freedom of the market system" (ibid.). Still, Rüstow offers a much more elaborate account of the roots of the problem: a misconception of markets based on certain religious beliefs. For Adam Smith, as well as his physiocratic precursors, the economy was supposedly based on a "beneficial automatism of the economic laws" that had to be respected, and consequently all efforts at intervening in and steering this economy, for example, in the form of mercantilism, came to be seen as misguided in the name of "'Laissez-faire! Laissez-passer!' which at the same time was a summons to honor God and an adjuration not to allow short-sighted human anxieties to interfere with the eternal wisdom of the natural law" (ibid., 269, 270). As a result of this misguided understanding of the economic sphere and the failure to comprehend its linkage with other societal spheres, "an unmistakable degeneration of the market economy set in" toward the end of the nineteenth century (ibid., 272). A revitalized liberalism would have to abandon this misconception and shed the religious beliefs that fuel it. What clearly emerges from this as another intellectual adversary of neoliberalism is the (non)politics of laissez-faire. This is a major point that has often been ignored until the more recent controversies over neoliberalism and the financial crisis, in which neoliberalism supposedly represented the belief in self-regulating markets (see Stiglitz 2008). However, when we look at the intellectual origins of the neoliberal project, it is impossible not to see how strongly the early neoliberals distanced themselves from the twin ideas of the politics of laissez-faire and self-regulating markets.[8]

Not just the ordoliberals but even the young Milton Friedman (1955) subscribed to the crisis narrative of a misguided nineteenth-century "liberalism, old style"; in his "Neo-liberalism and Its Prospects" he explicitly identifies with the neoliberal agenda: "We have a new faith to offer; it behooves us to make it clear to one and all what that faith is" (1951, 2). And just like Röpke and Rüstow he constructs the prehistory of neoliberalism as one of liberal decline: "The collectivist belief in the ability of direct action by the state to remedy all evils is itself however an understandable reaction to a basic error in the 19th century individualist philosophy. This philosophy assigned almost no role to the state other than the maintenance of order and the enforcement of contracts. It was a negative philosophy. The state could do only harm. Laissez-faire must be the rule" (ibid.). Here, laissez-faire is even accused of indirectly contributing to the rise of collectivism, so there can be no doubt that the "new faith" of neoliberalism will have to do without it.

It may be surprising to those who think of Hayek as the patron saint of quasi-libertarian "Austrian economics," but as Austrian as he may be, Hayek was just as adamant as Rüstow and Friedman that a modernization of liberalism would require a critical assessment of its own mistakes and aberrations, including the notion of laissez-faire: "Probably nothing has done so much harm to the liberal cause as the wooden insistence of some liberals on certain rough rules of thumb, above all the principle of laissez-faire," he writes in *The Road to Serfdom* (2001, 18; see also Hayek 1992, 238). And in an entry on "liberalism" written for an encyclopedia, Hayek sets the stage for his account by distinguishing "two distinct sources" that will lead to the establishment of two different traditions within the liberal tradition (1978b, 119). In contrast to the framing of Röpke, who distinguished between a truly liberal core and various excesses and aberrations that subsequently come to taint that core, Hayek's liberalism is divided into two rival strands from the beginning. The first is a more conventionalist tradition personified by the thinkers of the Scottish Enlightenment from Smith to Hume. The second is a "continental or constructivist liberalism" (ibid., 125), which finds its most typical expression in the rationalism of Descartes or the staunch anticlericalism and antitraditionalism of Voltaire and, in Hayek's view, is particularly prone to losing its liberal sense of direction. The history of the liberal decline following its mid-nineteenth-century heyday is narrated very similarly to the other accounts, but in Hayek's version it is not just the laissez-faire radicalism of a Herbert Spencer that is considered an aberration detrimental to liberalism in general. As noted previously, the work of the later Mill and particularly the thought of T. H. Green intellectually prefigure a convergence of liberalism with strands of socialism or progressivism that results in what Hayek calls "moderate socialism" (ibid., 130). Thus, in Hayek's interpretation the decline of liberalism is the result of a bifurcation of the tradition into a faction of laissez-faire proponents, on the one hand, and supporters of the quasi-social-democratic "new liberalism," on the other, be it Green's version in the United Kingdom or Dewey's liberal progressivism in the United States.

So what have we learned about the neoliberal project through an examination of how it defines itself against its various others? The list of "external" opponents is headed by the various collectivisms but also includes Keynesianism, a sprawling welfare state, and its supporters. To contend with the various manifestations of this antiliberal syndrome, liberalism would have to be revitalized, something that could not be achieved through a restoration of the liberalism of the nineteenth century. Inevitably, revitalizing liberalism meant modernizing it, and that would result in a newly fashioned *neo*liberalism. Still, the precondition for a successful revitalization would be a critical assessment and revision of the liberal agenda, various versions of which we have just encountered. In other words, the field of adversity is not limited to an external dimension but also contains an internal one in which the twin aberrations against which neoliberalism defines itself—laissez-faire liberalism and new liberalism—are also to be found.

The Neoliberal Problematic

While this first sketch of the neoliberal project is already of some use, the effort to capture what defines this project can be taken further by addressing the neoliberal problematic. If the chief adversary of neoliberalism is collectivism, and that collectivism, in turn, is opposed to the capitalist market economy, then it is no surprise that the defense of capitalist markets broadly understood is the centerpiece of neoliberal thought. This is rather uncontroversial and seemingly leads us into the familiar territory of neoliberalism as market fundamentalism and turbo-capitalism. Yet this is not the case. After all, the idea of self-regulating markets requires the notion of a politics of laissez-faire in the noneconomic sphere if it is to be consistent. But if we take seriously the way the founders of the neoliberal project distanced themselves from or outright rejected the idea of laissez-faire, then it becomes virtually impossible to characterize neoliberalism as the doctrine of self-regulating markets. The neoliberals are no market fundamentalists; on the contrary, in a certain sense the market turns into a problem for them, because in the light of liberalism's decline and crisis, simply watching the iron laws of economics unfolding automatically and autonomously is no longer a tenable position for them. Consequently, the neoliberal problematic *concerns the political and social conditions of possibility for functioning markets*, the latter being characterized by the integrity of the price system, which must operate unperturbed.

The common denominator of neoliberalism cannot be expressed positively in the form of a number of doctrines or theses. What all neoliberals share is the problem of how to identify the factors indispensable to the maintenance of functioning markets, since the option of simply leaving them to themselves is no longer on the table. Obviously, this still leaves room for a range of different responses or ways of framing solutions to the neoliberal problematic as well as changes over time. What exactly it is that ensures the functioning of markets is a matter of continued dispute between different neoliberal thinkers and varieties of neoliberal thought. Thus, this is a conceptualization of neoliberalism that is still broad enough to capture the heterogeneities of neoliberal thought, the varieties of positions, and the transformations that take place over time. Still, there is a thin common denominator in the form of a shared problematic, and in my view this strikes the right balance between the Scylla of overly parsimonious definitions of neoliberalism as the doctrine of x, y, or z and the Charybdis of dissolving it into a constantly shape-shifting multiplicity of loosely related neoliberalisms.

I have argued that the market becomes a problem for neoliberals, and this is true in the sense that it is no longer seen as a mechanism operating independently of its surroundings. But this implies, strictly speaking, that the actual problem, and thus the center of attention, shifts to those surroundings that become the real focus of neoliberal thought, which suggests that we should develop a more "decentered" account of neoliberalism, where markets may reside at the center but the neuralgic area of analysis for a critical understanding of neoliberalism is the infrastructural periphery of markets. Thus, what we have in neoliberalism is not a body of economistic thought that views markets as existing in some kind of vacuum. Rather, neoliberalism must be understood as a discourse in political economy that explicitly addresses the noneconomic preconditions of functioning markets and the interactive effects between markets and their surroundings. Neoliberalism is often portrayed as fixated on markets and the economy, and it would be absurd to claim this to be entirely wrong, so I also acknowledge the centrality of markets for neoliberal thought. However, once we consider the writings of these neoliberals, who did not necessarily see themselves as conventional economists (see Mirowski 2009, 427), it turns out that they give at least equal weight, if not more, to the analysis of noneconomic issues and how they relate to the economy and the operation of markets. It is to these questions about the infrastructure of markets that neoliberals devote ever-renewed efforts of analysis and critique. While their views of markets per se, their internal workings as well their various merits, remain fairly stable over time, it is the noneconomic side of their work that turns out to be the most dynamic because it is here that the actual neoliberal problematic is addressed over and over again from different angles and perspectives. James Buchanan sums it up well in his description of his intellectual trajectory: "I found myself becoming a political philosopher, in inquiry if not by profession" (Buchanan and Musgrave 1999, 22).

Indeed, addressing these questions obviously and inevitably leads into genuinely political territory, which is the reason I have argued that the neoliberal problematic is an inherently political problematic: For example, how does the social environment of markets have to be shaped, what kind of state action is required, and what are the effects of democracy on the politics needed for functioning markets? It would not be accurate to state that scholarship on neoliberalism has ignored its political dimension entirely, but aside from a few exceptions this research mostly concerns the politics of actually existing neoliberalism. We may know a lot about the economic dimension of neoliberal theory and what may be problematic about "market justice," but surprisingly little is known about its political dimension. However, the intellectual desideratum of a reconstruction and analysis of this still underresearched area is not the only reason and rationale behind the endeavor to examine what I call the political theory of neoliberalism. It may be this political dimension—and not the economics of neoliberalism—that will turn out to provide the opportunity for a critique that does not exhaust itself in attacks on the "fixation on markets" and the "greed and egoism" neoliberalism supposedly fosters. Changing our focus may reveal that the political preconditions and implications of neoliberalism as they are laid out in neoliberal thought are too high a price to pay—even if the economics of neoliberalism turned out to be sound and acceptable. A final reason that those critical of neoliberalism should be interested in its political dimension is that the neoliberals and many of neoliberalism's critics inhabit eerily similar ground in regard to certain political issues. Neoliberals are critical of various aspects of the state, democracy, and science; but the same can be said about many of its (left-wing) critics. So it would seem important to examine closely the various positions and critiques thereof, not only to find out where and how these critiques and their suggested alternatives differ but also to explore whether or not there is something to be learned from neoliberal critiques and whether it might not be possible to borrow certain of their elements and redeploy them for critical purposes of one's own.

PART I

The Political Theory of Neoliberalism

Part 1 is devoted to the reconstruction, analysis, and critique of key elements of the political theory of neoliberalism, in other words, the political dimension in neoliberal thought. This political dimension is not just an appendix to a body of thought otherwise devoted strictly to economic matters but a vital aspect of a collective intellectual endeavor to address the neoliberal problematic of identifying and securing the manifold conditions of possibility of functioning markets. The following survey of the political thought of neoliberalism focuses on four elements that are most closely related to this guiding problematic: the state, democracy, science, and politics.

The relevance of the first two is immediately evident: Can the state contribute to the conditions that enable functioning markets, and if so, how and what can it contribute? Conversely, why and how may the state undermine these very conditions, and how can this be avoided? Four varieties of neoliberal thought aim at either enabling or constraining the state by either focusing on state output (policies) or a recentering/decentering of state structure. The latter results either in diffusing state power in multilevel governance arrangements or forging a semiauthoritarian state, which proves how strong the tensions between varieties of neoliberal thought turn out to be in some cases.

The issue of democracy is most closely linked to that of the state, because the guiding question concerns mainly how democracy might complicate the tasks and limits assigned to the state by neoliberal thought. For the neoliberals, democracy in its contemporary form turns out to be one of the gravest impediments in addressing the neoliberal problematic, but their writings still exhibit a variety of specific critiques of democracy with different diagnoses (from "rent-seeking" and self-serving politicians to the ignorant masses) and, consequently, different remedies. These range from a "strong state" that fends off demands from a democratic public and pluralist parties, to a set of constitutional rules on debt and deficits, or a legislative chamber resembling a supreme court that is insulated from the dealings of ordinary parliamentarism. Finally, neoliberal writings even consider introducing more direct democratic measures to keep political elites in check.

The third element, science, may seem less self-evident but is not only of immediate concern to the neoliberal problematic but also directly related to the neoliberal views on state and democracy. The guiding questions here are quite similar to the others: How and what can social science contribute to the conditions of possibility of functioning markets? How may a misunderstanding of the proper mode of scientific reasoning and its limits as well as the proper role of science in regard to the state and (a democratic) society lead to the very opposite? Neoliberal thought on science can thus be divided into two broad and almost diametrically opposed varieties. One extols the powers of (economic) science if conducted properly according to the right methods and posits scientifically generated truth against (collectivist) prejudice and ideology. The other is mainly concerned about the dangers of "scientism" and warns of how a science of economics mimicking natural science would do harm to any neoliberal project, either through faulty methodology or an overly confident belief in the powers of human reason. The two varieties also differ about the role that science should play in regard to politics: While the first (best exemplified by the work of Eucken) promotes the model of scientific policy advice, gesturing toward a technocratic form of policy making, the second (best exemplified by the work of Buchanan) finds the idea of scientists offering their services to politicians who are considered to be mostly interested in their reelection to be thoroughly misguided.

Politics is the final and crucial element of a political theory of neoliberalism. The questions in this context are how neoliberals view politics and, in particular, how they conceive of a politics of neoliberal reform. In chapters 2,

3, and 4 we encounter a combination of critical analysis and reform proposals regarding state, democracy, and the role of science. Chapter 5 examines
how these reform proposals are to be implemented, a far-from-trivial issue
that presents neoliberal thought with a rather serious challenge.

This challenge is neoliberal thought's striking inability to theorize a
politics of neoliberal reform, at least not without violating the very assumptions that underlie its own analyses and critiques of the shortcomings
of democratic politics. Ordoliberals like Röpke tend to place their hopes in
the emergence of some guardian-like elite, which is—against all odds—willing and able to realize the public good as it is defined in ordoliberal terms.
Hayek (and some others) has to resort to entertaining the possibility of
a (transitory) dictatorship to implement neoliberal reforms. Buchanan is
incapable of explaining how self-interested politicians would ever pass his
favored reform proposals, which would hurt their own self-interest, and
explicitly suspends the assumptions of *homo economicus* to keep neoliberal
hopes (often bordering on the eschatological) for reform alive. Overall, this
is arguably the weakest link in neoliberal political theory.

CHAPTER 2

The State

In a recent contribution to the debate a rhetorical question has been raised: Is the state "the bête noire of neo-liberalism or its greatest conquest?" (Schmidt and Woll 2013, 112). It is a rhetorical question because, as Schmidt and Woll are well aware, for the neoliberals the state is undoubtedly both. The strategic centrality of the state to neoliberal theory and practice derives from its very ambivalence, since it is, simultaneously, *the* crucial instrument in creating the conditions for functioning markets (see, for example, Friedman and Friedman 1990, 28), but also, arguably, the greatest threat to them. Consequently, neoliberal thought invests a lot of time and space in determining the proper role for the state to play. Despite the significant overlaps that must not be disregarded, within the body of these elaborations and considerations we can detect differing and even contradicting emphases and logics and, accordingly, distinguish varieties of neoliberal thought with regard to the state. My aim is to distill the main strategies of conceptualizing the state and its proper role in regard to the economy and society and to group the variants of the respective arguments and positions to develop a comprehensive overview and a critical assessment of the varieties of neoliberal theorizing of the state.

The starting point of the discussion is marked by a fundamental yet thin agreement among the neoliberals: The state has positive functions to perform, and they are neither confined to guaranteeing private contracts or, more generally, enforcing the law, nor is it helpful to think about the role of government in quantitative terms of "more" or "less" (see Röpke 1950b, 228; Hayek 2001, 84, 195; Friedman 1951). The question is how to give a *qualitative* account of the state and its activities not only in the sense of a description of the status quo of existing states but, more important, in the prescriptive sense of outlining the contours of the ideal neoliberal state. The second commonality across all varieties of neoliberal state discourse is a metaphor or image regularly employed to satisfy this requirement in the most intuitively plausible way. Although it will become clear that it is insufficient to capture the intricacies of the neoliberal view of the state, it still forms a good baseline that we can refer back to on occasion. This master metaphor of neoliberal state discourse casts the state as an umpire or referee (see, e.g., Friedman 2002, 25; Buchanan 1975, 68, 95; Eucken 1949, 29). In other words, the main responsibility of the state is to enforce the rules of the game in an impartial and authoritative manner. Implied in this description of the state's tasks are the two sides of the same coin of state power mentioned previously: the need to enable the state and at the same time to restrict it in its actions. Without someone to enforce the rules in a competitive game, it is seemingly inevitably going to descend into chaos, which is supposedly not in the interest of anyone involved. Yet to keep the game from collapsing, it is equally important that the referee is somehow restricted to just this activity and refrains from suddenly grabbing the ball, scoring a point, and thus directly interfering in the process of the game. Thus, this imagery involves, on the one hand, drawing a line between the indirect structuring of the game through an enforceable framework of rules that still allows the players to choose their own strategies within the boundaries of these constraints and, on the other, directly intervening in the game to steer it in a particular direction.

Analysts of actually existing neoliberalism would be quick to point out that this may be an appealingly categorical distinction between the state's agenda and non-agenda, but it has, for better or worse, little bearing on neoliberal states in their actuality. However, it is already within neoliberal thought itself that the descriptions of stately tasks often point far beyond the stoic rulings of an umpire.

Keeping this in mind, we turn to the varieties of neoliberal state discourse based on two analytical distinctions that serve to structure our survey. The first is the distinction between state output and state structure, or to be more precise, argumentative strategies that focus on either one or the other. The second concerns strategies of restricting the state and its capacities and an emphasis on the positive functions the state must perform as well as the various prerequisites that allow it to deliver on these tasks. The combination of these two analytical distinctions results in a four-field matrix that yields the respective number of varieties of neoliberal state discourse.

A Positive Agenda for the State: Policy Principles and Goals

We begin with those strategies of neoliberal state theory that focus on the output of the state and emphasize certain goals that the state should pursue through a particular set of policies. In most cases this endeavor is framed as an identification of certain policy principles, but the principles are not always as principled as the reference to them as such would suggest. The works of Milton Friedman provide the first example of such an approach and serve as a good illustration of principles in name only, or at least mostly in name only. While Friedman very rarely came close again to the almost enthusiastic endorsement of the state's positive functions, in contrast to a politics of laissez-faire on display in some writings of the 1950s (see Friedman 1951, 1955), he maintained a commitment to the need for government to perform certain functions, not the least "to do something that the market cannot do for itself, namely, to determine, arbitrate and enforce the rules of the game" (2002, 27; Friedman and Friedman 1984, 17). However, Friedman realizes that the metaphor of the umpire leaves the state's agenda severely underdetermined, and he consequently embarks on an attempt to justify positive state action based on four principles. The state, or rather, "government," which is the preferred term used by Friedman and Hayek (see Hayek 2003, 1:48), is first and foremost in charge of providing internal and external security for its citizens, protecting them "from coercion" (Friedman and Friedman 1990, 29). Government thus provides a precondition for a certain kind of individual freedom understood as the absence of coercion. These first two principles appear unproblematic to Friedman. The fourth principle contains a justification for paternalist state action in regard to those who are incapable of "responsible" behavior. As controversial as this may seem, it is the third principle that preoccupies Friedman the most, not the least because it is most closely related to the economic sphere and the workings of markets: State policy in these matters is required, the principle states, whenever there are "neighborhood effects," or what is now commonly referred to as "externalities," accruing to individual or collective (economic) activities. The issue is well known and in Friedman's treatment covers everything from the use of non-priced natural resources like clean air and water to negative effects certain business practices or forms of organization (e.g., monopolies) may have on competitors and the general public. Here the state is called on to rectify things, but Friedman is keenly aware of the dangers this principle entails. The problem, not unknown in political theory, has some analogies to John Stuart Mill's famous harm principle. One major question implied by Mill's reasoning is where to draw the line between self- and other-regarding spheres. With respect to Friedman's neighborhood effects, the question becomes whether there is ever anything, especially in behavior in markets, that does not have positive or, more often, negative externalities. An expansive notion of neighborhood effects thus easily turns into a justification for a broad agenda for state policy that may also be mobilized to argue for the introduction of social policies, and a more encompassing welfare state more generally, as compensation for negative externalities experienced by individuals in the economic sphere.

The first point to note is that we have already left far behind the parsimonious metaphor of the umpire with a state now possibly involved in compensating for many externalities, mediating between conflicting claims, and inevitably affecting private actors through its own positive or negative externalities. The second point to note is the fate of Friedman's principles over the course of the discussion—especially with regard to externalities. Unwilling to retreat from the principle in general, Friedman offers a seemingly pragmatic solution and suggests that in every case, benefits and costs of governmental intervention need to be assessed, and only when the former outweigh the latter is the state to move forward with its actions (see Friedman and Friedman 1990, 32). This seemingly turns the matter from one guided by principles into a utilitarian calculus, which is confirmed when Friedman concedes that "our principles offer no hard and fast line how far it is appropriate to use government" (2002, 32). Neither do they provide clear criteria by which to judge specific policies and whether they are part of a legitimate governmental activity (Friedman and Friedman 1990, 33). The principles and duties of government, in which Friedman placed his hopes to identify the proper scope of action for the state, thus turn out to be rather elastic. While some may appreciate this as a welcome dose of pragmatism in dealing with the state, this can hardly be a consolation for a neoliberal interested in a clearly defined and demarcated state agenda.

The next example concerning a positive agenda for state policy based on principles and goals can be referred to as the politics of the competitive order, which casts the state as the creator and guardian of this competitive order and the resulting competitive markets. Especially in the early postwar years but also beyond, this notion is found across almost the entire spectrum of neoliberal thought. In his presentation at the Mont Pelerin founding meeting Hayek noted "that competition can be made more effective and more beneficent by certain activities of government than it would be without them," adding that "the purpose of a competitive order is to make competition work," not to restrict its effectiveness (1980, 110–111). The young Friedman equally affirmed the "goal of the competitive order" (1951, 3) as a description of the economic agenda of the state (see also Buchanan and Musgrave 1999, 84). However, the concept of the competitive order originated in the ordoliberal tradition and, more specifically, in the works of Walter Eucken. For him, functioning markets were characterized, first and foremost, by the existence of effective competition, so economic policy ought to orient itself toward creating truly competitive conditions. Eucken's solution is the aforementioned competitive order, which the state is to establish and enforce. The competitive order is based on six *constitutive* principles: a functioning price system, sound money, open markets, private property, freedom of contract, and unlimited personal liability (discussed in detail later). The state is to set up a legal-political framework in accordance with these principles and enforce it, which brings us again to the notion of the impartial umpire. Ordoliberalism along the Euckenian lines, in particular, has since the end of World War I accentuated the need for a systematic and strictly rule-based economic policy that defines itself explicitly against the supposedly experimental character of the economic policies of the day (see Eucken 1960, 55–58). Eucken calls for an approach to policy based on the notion of interdependent political, social, legal, and economic orders, which requires an extremely high level of cohesion in policy making that takes account of the complexities involved in this interdependence of orders. Eucken concludes that in such a precarious constellation the negative effects of ad hoc interventionist policies would be exacerbated and thus confirms the need for the state to focus on its role as the guardian of the economic constitution. Thus, Eucken's approach may seem more principled than Friedman's—after all, his posthumously published magnum opus on economic policy is called *Grundsätze der Wirtschaftspolitik* (Principles of economic policy). However, the principles *constituting* the competitive order are not the only ones relevant, and this will lead to a significant broadening of the state's agenda.

Upon establishing the competitive order, the state cannot rest on the laurels of its creation because it needs constant maintenance (and possibly even adjustment from time to time) to prevent markets from deteriorating. The four *regulating* principles are to inform the state's continuous actions in this regard. The ordoliberal conceptualization of the market order is that it is not self-sustaining but subject to constant dynamics of corrosion. This changes the imagery of the state from a detached judge to an activist policeman of the market on high alert, constantly monitoring the intensity of competition and considering remedial actions in case it is found wanting.[1] The constant threat to the competitive order comes from the vital interest of each and every market actor to avoid and evade the pressures of competition, in part through collusion in the form of cartels, oligopolies, or monopolies.[2] Accordingly, the first regulative principle Eucken lists concerns a proactive antimonopoly policy.

Aside from the detrimental effect of economic power on the competitive order, Eucken identifies other sources of problems that the other three principles are to address. The first is not surprising: it deals with the problem of externalities, which Eucken apparently does not consider to be as dangerous as Friedman does. Much more surprising are the other two principles: the third stipulates the need for fiscal redistribution to avoid an undue emphasis on the production of luxury goods, and the fourth considers the problems arising from an "anomalous behavior of supply" in labor during economic crises (see Eucken 1960, 303). This is the possibility that the falling price of labor power due to a recession does not lead to the unwillingness to sell this good at such a low price (which would make the price rebound over time) but rather to an expansion of supply—because employees still have to make a living and must work even more at lower wages. Eucken offers some factors that may mitigate the problem, but there may come a point when the state should introduce a minimum wage. Two points are notable about these principles. First, they look less like principles than specific policies or measures that respond to very specific (detrimental) conditions. Second, it seems that minimum wages, fiscal redistribution, and the fight against anything that reduces the level of competition in markets make up a state agenda that is not confined to enforcing the rules of the game but may lead in certain cases to direct intervention into the workings of markets—the minimum wage being the most obvious example. This may be considered an outlier within Eucken's overall framework, but the policy agenda beyond the politics of the competitive order narrowly understood also significantly broadens the scope of appropriate and required state action in the realm of social policy. It is not entirely clear how exactly Eucken's respective elaborations are to be interpreted, partly because the editor assembled these passages after Eucken's death. Still, the question is not whether Eucken endorsed certain elements of social policy, from social insurance schemes to workplace and labor-market regulations (see Eucken 1960, 312–324). Rather, the status of these elements is unclear. One way of reading Eucken's formulations of social policy as complementing the competitive order and being necessary even in the case of an otherwise perfectly ordered socioeconomic sphere suggests that this is a countervailing additional element needed to balance the politics of the competitive order (see ibid., 313, 318). But there is another way of interpreting Eucken based on his remark on social policy having to be considered part and parcel of the "politics of the economic order" (*Wirtschaftsordnungspolitik*), which suggests that social policy may ameliorate some of the social hardships of the market economy and may work against capital's severe exploitation of labor, but the overall effect that makes it an integral aspect of economic policy is its *contribution to economic competition*. As Eucken points out, a certain level of personal material independence is the precondition for labor power being sufficiently decommodified so it does not have to be sold at just any price and there is a real competition for human resources (ibid., 319); and "when labor unions contribute to a balancing of the situation of a monopoly of demand [for labor] and push through wages, that are on par with wages under effective competition . . . then they contribute to the implementation of the competitive order" (ibid., 323). Such praise for labor unions is rare among neoliberals, but Eucken views it warranted not so much for social concerns—Eucken is a fierce critic of what he would consider abuse of labor union power to prevent wage suppression—as in the light of their contribution to increased competition. Whether Eucken's assumptions about market correction, minimum wage, and fiscal redistribution are in fact correct and whether they lead to an increase in the overall level of competition may be doubtful, but what is more important for our purposes is that we can formulate a concluding assessment of Eucken's perspective on the principles and scope of state action.

The impression we get from the Euckenian agenda of the ordoliberal state may be described as principled but only if by principle we mean the maintenance of the competitive order. More appropriately, it might be called a teleological or goal-oriented approach, the maintenance of the competitive order being that telos or goal against which all others are relegated to secondary importance, as are concerns over the proper mode and domain of the policies pursued.[3] Whatever it takes to defend the competitive order is thus the proper description of the state's agenda according to Eucken. The second example of this approach comes from Eucken's fellow ordoliberals Röpke and Rüstow. Both are adamant in their support for the defense and strengthening of the competitive order through, especially but not exclusively, an aggressive stance on monopolies and other forms of economic power (see Röpke 1950b, 228, 234; Rüstow 1942, 281). However, they add another more specific goal to the state's actions, "liberal interventionism" (Rüstow 1942, 281), which consists of an "intervention for adjustment" in contrast to an "intervention for preservation" (Röpke 1950b, 187). What Röpke and Rüstow have in mind is a policy that facilitates structural adjustment processes rather than defends the status quo. This is a remarkable demand for a number of reasons, the first of which is the nonchalant appropriation of the label "interventionism," which is usually anathema for neoliberal thought, and the explicit embrace of the respective forms of state action. When Röpke and Rüstow spell out the various forms of such interventionism, they consider a panoply of measures, ranging from those indistinguishable from ordinary social policy and relief for those adversely affected by structural changes, to those aiming for the quickest possible reinsertion of requalified human capital into the labor market through training schemes. The ideas of Röpke and Rüstow are, to some degree, reminiscent of a labor-market paradigm now called "flexicurity." They share the flexicurity regime's peculiar ambivalence between considerations of social security broadly speaking and a truly accelerationist paradigm of capitalism. After all, these interventions may ameliorate the hardship of prolonged unemployment at the individual level, but they assume the ability and willingness of individuals to retrain throughout their entire career in order to replace devalued human capital through a more profitable stock. Furthermore, on the aggregate level these interventions are bound to result in an ever-faster structural change because as many impediments as possible are removed from labor. However, what is in question here is not the substantive normative desirability of "liberal interventionism" but the implications for the state agenda. First, the positive commitment to interventionism of any kind questions the state's alleged role as umpire because it is overtly intervening in the process of the socioeconomic game. Furthermore, if the state is to encourage and support socioeconomic change, how can the state detect the overall direction of such change? Such assessments are obviously fraught with serious difficulties, and a fellow neoliberal like Hayek would argue that the only entity capable of knowing about this direction—to speak metaphorically—is the market, which is one of the main reasons for state restraint in economic policy (see Hayek 2002). Conversely, if the state were endowed with such prescience that it can and "must anticipate the final outcome of large structural changes" (Rüstow 1942, 281), one might wonder why it should not be much more involved in economic matters more generally.

We have to conclude that the attempt to pin down state output to a specific positive agenda, based either on principles or specific goals, ultimately grants the state a much broader scope of activities in regard to both policy actions than expected from the commitment to keep the state to narrowly, or at least rigidly defined, goals and principles. Friedman's neighborhood effects,

Eucken's regulating principles and social policy, and the liberal interventionism of Röpke and Rüstow all provide significant loopholes for the expansion
of state activity that may prove impossible to curtail in the long run and thus
are fatal to the original endeavor of each of the four thinkers.

The final example of a positive agenda for the state may seem rather
curious at first but demonstrates that there is a considerable range of
answers and proposed solutions to the neoliberal problematic of preconditions for functioning markets. For Röpke and Rüstow liberal intervention to hasten the dynamic of capitalist reproduction is not the only and
possibly not even the most important issue on the state's agenda. In addition, they propose a politics of demassification or, to put it positively, a
so-called organic policy (*Vitalpolitik*). Only when markets are embedded
in a healthy demassified society are their corrosive effects contained and
their own continued existence ensured. We look briefly at the ordoliberal
account of the emergence and problems of mass society before discussing
the details of an organic policy.

Massification is a long-term consequence of its dialectical counterpart,
individualization or atomization, which creates the conditions for the formation of masses in the first place. This process is concomitant with industrialization, which erodes long-established more rural lifestyles and leads to
massive urbanization. Uprooted individuals find themselves in cities without
networks or social capital, as it would be called today, and thus form the raw
material for massification: "Individuals are randomly thrown together as if
they were grains of sand piled up into arbitrary heaps by the wind; they are
the masses of the urban centers. . . . The resulting simple aggregation of these
individuals left entirely to their own devices is what we call massification.
It is the leveling of the social pyramid, an atomization that is accompanied
by agglutination" (Röpke 1949, 243, 246). In the diagnosis of the ordoliberals these atomized city dwellers suffer from "under-integration," and while
mostly anonymous processes of capitalist industrialization are responsible for
this problem, the old "paleoliberals," as Rüstow would mockingly refer to the
nineteenth-century advocates of "laissez-faire" (1963, 12), are also to blame
for ignoring it in the name of unfettered individualism. Their view of capitalist development was blind to the corrosive effect it would have on individuals
and the highly problematic side effects of under-integration. Lacking a sense

of belonging and thrown back on themselves, individuals are vulnerable to offers of reintegration put forward by collectivist movements as they address the individual as part of a national community in the case of Fascism and National Socialism, or the laboring masses in the case of Communism. Because of the sociological blindness of early liberalism, collectivist movements could gain ever more momentum by mobilizing the masses with what Röpke views as an offer of "pseudo-integration" (1950b, 11), which is not to be mistaken for a sense of real community. But the vulnerability of those uprooted pertains not only to the spiritual dimension of what Rüstow sometimes describes with the Heideggerian term "thrownness" (*Geworfensein*) (2017a, 170), but it also has a socioeconomic aspect, proletarization. The masses have no alternative but to sell their labor power on the labor market because they do not have any (family) networks to support them or alternative sources of income in their new urban dwellings. They are thus dependent on either employment, whatever its form may be, or support by the state. Needless to say, the ordoliberals prefer people to work rather than rely on transfer payments, but it is worth noting that they problematize the effect of extreme commodification of labor power as workers are forced to work under poor conditions and engage in productive activities that they find dull and meaningless: "The day is taken up by work which mother and father do in different locations, under external instruction and command and with minimal personal initiative. It is divided up in such a way that its overall significance is by no means always clear" (ibid.). We must not jump to the conclusion that this is a kind of crypto-Marxist critique of capitalist conditions of production, but there is a critique of alienation (which does not have to be Marxist) contained in the ordoliberal critique of proletarization and massification more generally. However, as serious as the grievances about dependency on work and the ensuing alienation may be, the more serious problem is associated with the alternative to work in the form of a welfare state that subjects individuals through coercive insurance schemes and keeps them in a state of economic immaturity, if not dependence (see Röpke 1987, 71). It is the missing (economic) independence in both scenarios that the ordoliberals see at the heart of the phenomenon of proletarization. The unsurprising skepticism, if not severe criticism, of the welfare state already indicates that while massification/proletarization has an undeniable economic aspect, this grave "sickness of the social structure" (Röpke 1959b, 34) cannot be cured through conventional social policy of insurance and transfer schemes, and neither is it a matter of simply raising wages. This would treat it as a solely material problem, failing to appreciate the aspects that point beyond strictly economic conditions: the "spiritual" aspects of massification. What then is the solution? For Röpke, the answer is deceptively simple: "Massification is increased by whatever fosters concentration; demassification is increased by everything that benefits decentralization" (ibid.). Röpke is a strong proponent of political decentralization—at least in the abstract—but what he demands here is a more encompassing social decentralization that concerns housing policy, economic policy, cultural policy, and aspects of social policy. The massive processes of urbanization would have to be reversed by creating conditions in which it is possible and attractive for people to return to small-scale munici-palities and supposedly live happier lives. Here men and women can "regain the lost balance between individuality and collectivity in the small living circle filled with human warmth (family, municipality, church communities, neigh-borhood, small and medium companies, scientific, literary and artistic circles etc.)" (ibid., 35). Röpke does not refer to happiness but rather "inner stability" and "responsibility," which could be restored through demassification, but in Rüstow's version this is exactly what is ultimately at stake.

For him a politics of demassification is part of an even more fundamen-tal "organic policy" that should serve to increase the overall well-being of people, both material and spiritual: "which possible measures should be demanded, in order to complement mainstream social policy in such a way as to lead to a genuinely satisfying organic situation [*Vitalsituation*]—an organic situation in which the individual can feel content and happy. This is what I call organic policy [*Vitalpolitik*]" (Rüstow 2017a, 168). To be sure, decentralization is part and parcel of such an organic policy, and Rüstow il-lustrates the demand with a rather idealized view of rural life, where "people have their little house, their garden, their piece of farmland, and in their free time they and their families can occupy themselves usefully with work that they enjoy" (ibid.). But the organic situation Rüstow is concerned about clearly has a number of different dimensions. Organic policy should be sup-portive of families and a particular kind of parenting, must pertain to schools, and also concerns gender relations, as Rüstow urges in an unapologetically reactionary way that young women should be prepared to perform mainly their established roles as housewives and mothers (see ibid., 172–173). Organic policy is thus directed at man (and woman), and given the enormity of the task, it is no surprise that Rüstow envisaged a science of humankind that would have to inquire into the *conditio humana* and thus inform the multilayered effort of increasing people's well-being in a holistic fashion (discussed in chapter 4).

How should this agenda of decentralization/demassification, which expands in Rüstow's version into an organic policy, be assessed? Not surprisingly, the two ordoliberals have been harshly criticized for what appears to be a rather retrograde streak to this part of the state's agenda (see Hahn 1993). All too easily their vision of an optimally integrated society with an appreciable overall organic situation appears as a highly idealized picture of early capitalism, where artisans and small landowners lived a fulfilled and self-reliant life independent of both giant corporations and their means of production and a bureaucratic (welfare) state. But while there is undoubtedly a measure of nostalgia underlying both, especially Röpke's account, whose cultural pessimism is more pronounced than Rüstow's, we should note that many currents in environmental thought and many among those who search for viable pathways into postgrowth societies would also emphasize the importance of a decentralized way of life for both consumers and producers. Propagating the decentralized life may be nostalgic, especially given that in 2008 for the first time in history more than 50 percent of the world's population lived in cities. However, if current trends continue and this figure reaches 70 percent by 2050, life in ever-growing megacities, which is already difficult to sustain for the majority of its inhabitants, may become just as devitalizing as Rüstow suggests.

However, what is important to note is the striking difference between the economic sphere and the social environment of markets in both accounts. While liberal interventionism accelerates the dynamics of capitalism ever further and thus requires flexibility and mobility, organic policy aims to achieve the complete opposite with regard to the nonmarket sphere. Its aim is deceleration, stability, and integration if not an outright attempt to turn back time. The charitable interpretation of this constellation is to view it as a deliberative balancing of countervailing tendencies, which is precisely the precondition for markets to reproduce themselves in a sustainable manner. The uncharitable counterpart is to view it as a contradictory constellation where the two ordo-liberals fail to consider the diffusion of either of the two logics into the other, simply assuming that they will remain in balance.

Most important, if the aim of neoliberal theorizing of the state in this variety is the identification of tasks and principles that yield strict demarcation lines for state action, the agenda of an organic policy is the complete opposite because it is as expansive and poorly defined as one could possibly imagine.

We can now turn to strategies of limiting and restricting state action on the basis of certain principles or procedural/formal requirements with regard to its output.

Limiting State Action: Compatible Interventions, the Rule of Law, and Balanced-Budget Amendments

In the discussion of liberal interventionism there seemed to be no criterion limiting the nature of the intervention as long as it was intended for the purposes of adjustment. However, this is true only in Rüstow's version of the argument; Röpke offers such a criterion with an emphasis on limiting state action, as discussed in the following examples.

Röpke introduces the distinction between "'compatible' and 'incompatible' interventions" (1950b, 160) and offers two criteria that, supposedly, enable a clear assessment of any policy in question as to its status in this regard. First, in order to be considered compatible, an intervention must leave the internal workings of markets, especially the price mechanism, as undisturbed as possible.[4] In other words, the intervention should always resort to the most "indirect" means possible (Röpke 1963, 256). Second, an incompatible intervention "creates a situation which immediately calls for further and even greater intervention. . . . The result is an unending dynamic chain of cause and effect and everything begins to deteriorate" (ibid., 161). This suggests a straightforward litmus test for policies, limiting compatible ones to those that are unequivocally permissible. Yet when scrutinized more closely, Röpke's distinction is not so clear-cut as it may appear at first. Considering the second criterion, there may be the possibility of an interventionist spiral triggered by a particular one, but it seems there are many instances in which the decision to make further interventions remains a political one based on expediency and interest—at least, it is questionable whether the facts simply speak for themselves. Röpke's formulation of the first criterion does not yield a categorical distinction because the stated aim is to have the *least possible* influence on the operation of the price mechanism. So this is an argument based on "lesser evils," but is there a "red line" beyond which interventions become strictly impermissible? To be sure, Röpke offers illustrative examples to clarify matters. For example, the devaluation of a currency is preferred over exchange controls, and a rent ceiling is described as an incompatible intervention because it arguably necessitates further interventions (see ibid., 160–161). But this seems to indicate that unless the state is explicitly setting prices or simply prohibits certain economic actions/exchanges, the intervention must be deemed compatible. This is obviously a rather heterodox interpretation of the *topos* of the (in)compatible intervention, attributed to both Röpke and Eucken (see, e.g., Foucault 2008, 138–139), that is often presented as the panacea for *Ordnungspolitik*, offering an analytical device to demarcate permissible from impermissible state action. Still, there are considerable complications here. Not only is there no reference to this distinction in Eucken's work, which leaves room for many types of policies to safeguard the competitive order (see Kolev 2013, 62), but one of the few unequivocally incompatible policies in Röpke's sense is the minimum wage, which Eucken considers necessary under certain conditions. At least some of Eucken's politics concerning the regulatory principles are thus *not* covered, but the scope of compatible economic policy is in fact remarkably broad, which lends further credence to my rather heterodox interpretation.

Consider two examples of what is considered to be within the confines of compatible economic policy. First, Röpke notes that "it is certainly in accordance with the market economy, if the state with the means of compulsion at its disposal (especially taxation) carries out a readjustment of income levels in order to effect a more equitable distribution." Second, it is even market compatible "if the state itself manages individual enterprises or even whole branches of production and now appears on the market in the capacity of producer or merchant" (Röpke 1950b, 189–190). It is not even necessary to dwell on the question of whether fiscal redistribution and a mixed economy actually satisfy the criterion of leaving markets or their price mechanism undisturbed, which seems at least debatable. It is worth noting, first, the complications involved in applying Röpke's criteria, which leaves room for doubt whether they really provide the necessary analytical device to distinguish unequivocally between compatible and incompatible interventions in any given policy case (see Kolev 2013, 153). Second, even if this turns out to be the case, the range of permissible state action is surprisingly broad, covering a great variety of interventions short of explicitly setting prices.

The second example of a limitation of permissible state output underlies the entire political thought of Hayek. Hayek held a doctorate in law, so it may not come as a surprise that his attempt to limit state action is based on a particular interpretation of the rule of law. This *topos* is a complex one, and it is not possible to discuss all of its aspects here. I focus first on the argument that concerns the nature of law and later on the more state-structural elements that concern institutional constellations and the separation of powers. Chapter 3 addresses the ambivalent relation of the rule of law to democracy.

It is only a mild overstatement to say that, for Hayek, the decline of liberalism amounts to the decline of the rule of law, and vice versa, because "liberalism is . . . the same as the demand for the rule of law in the classical sense of the term" (1967a, 165). The reference to the classical sense of the term implies that there has been a degeneration or decline in the tradition and understanding of the rule of law, and much of his constructive endeavors in designing a neoliberal order can be understood as an attempt to restore the rule of law properly understood.

According to Hayek, the rule of law is not the same as constitutionalism (2009, 180). Aside from its separation-of-power aspect, the rule of law is first and foremost a "meta-legal doctrine" concerning "what the law ought to be" (ibid., 181). Law, in other words, is qualified by certain formal requirements that turn it into what in the German law tradition was called a law "in the material sense of the term"—not in contrast to its formal but to its procedural properties. What does this mean? Hayek is trying to argue, first and foremost, against legal positivists who contend that anything emanating from the locus of sovereignty—whether legislatures or kings—is ipso facto a law as long as it is in accordance with certain procedural requirements, which are much more demanding in the case of parliaments than absolute rulers. To the extent that this interpretation prevails, the rule of law lacks any meaningful rule according to Hayek, because there is no restriction on what the sovereign decides to write into law. Against this understanding Hayek mobilizes countervailing legal traditions that require certain formal characteristics for laws to be considered in accordance with the rule of law. For example, the law needs to be generally known, its content needs to be clear and understandable, it must not be retroactively applied, it must be abstract (referring to an unknown and unspecified number of individuals in the future), and it must be applied equally to everyone (see ibid., 182–184).

Before we take a closer look at these characteristics and the problems they may pose, it is important to note some differentiations that Hayek introduces. "Law," for Hayek, is a term too unspecific, because too many different legal norms are called laws, while only legal norms including the characteristics just named are laws in the proper sense, which he now terms *nomos* and describes as "laws of just conduct." This kind of law is contrasted with *thesis*, the law of organizations, which lacks the formal characteristics of *nomos*. In Hayek's narrative, *nomos* and *thesis* have become conflated because parliamentary legislatures historically came to be put in charge of formulating both the rules of just conduct and the organizational rules for the proper conduct of the state, which is an important source of the decline of the rule of law. In addition, and for reasons related to the democratic nature of parliamentary legislatures, *nomos* and *thesis* are not just conflated. *Thesis* expands at the expense of *nomos*, or, what Hayek seems to consider as rough equivalents, public law increasingly crowds out private law: "The progressive permeation of private law by public law in the course of the last eighty or hundred years, which means a progressive replacement of rules of conduct by rules of organization, is one of the main ways in which the destruction of the liberal order has been effected" (1967a, 168–169; see also Hayek 2003, 1:114). While it is tempting to probe this narrative further, we must turn to another differentiation that provides us with a clearer sense of the limits Hayek means to impose on state action. The differentiation in question is the one between the coercive functions of the state and its service functions, the latter comprising, for example, the social policies previously mentioned.

The limits of the rule of law apply only to the coercive powers of the state, "in which its actions are strictly limited to the enforcement of rules of just conduct and in the exercise of which all discretion is excluded." The service state, however, "has no coercive power or monopoly" but "enjoys wide discretion" in the use of the resources at its disposal (Hayek 1967a, 165–166). This raises a number of questions that we can begin to address based on the initial observation that Hayek's attempt to restore law apparently does not aim at restricting state actions in their entirety through the rule of law. In other words, there would still be room for *thesis*, since the service state must be interpreted as an organization pursuing particular goals, namely, the efficient provision of a certain service. If this is correct, then the assessment found in some of the secondary literature, according to which Hayek aims at the establishment of a "nomocracy" instead of a "teleocracy"—terms he has borrowed from Michael Oakeshott—though intuitively plausible, is not completely accurate (Hayek 2003, 2:15; see also Plant 2016). Of course, Hayek's main point is that the former order is by far the preferable one, not only for normative but also for functional reasons. However, since Hayek's work mentions service aspects of the state on more than one occasion, there also seems to be room granted to teleological, goal-oriented, state action. What ultimately remains surprisingly unclear or at least somewhat undertheorized, given that it is such a crucial point in Hayek's design, is the relation between the nomocratic and teleocratic aspects of state action and, relatedly, what this implies for the relation between legislature and government.

The service state is granted discretion in its action, but does this mean that the rule of law does not apply at all to the provision of governmental services? In this case the state would have carte blanche, which would be an unexpected result after all the efforts Hayek invests in a robust circumscription of the state's powers. In fact, Hayek does makes it clear that the service state may not discriminate against clients, but whether this is an effective safeguard hinges on the matter of equal treatment. Depending on the outcome of this discussion, services could still be offered in a selective manner and citizens may have only limited legal claims to them—the state would/ could act like a quasi-private person (see Hayek 1967, 175). After all, the restrictions Hayek introduces aside from no coercion and no governmental monopoly apply only to *financing* the service state through taxation. The latter is a compulsive power of the state, and therefore the limits of the rule of law apply, but what exactly does this mean?

To answer this question, we have to take a closer look at the characteristics of *nomos*. The most controversial ones are certainly the requirements of equality and generality. Their overall thrust is clearly to prevent some kind of legalized discrimination through laws that apply only to certain groups or individuals, but it is more difficult to spell out exactly what kind of treatment through state law would be prohibited. Hayek himself notes that "a law may be perfectly general in referring only to formal characteristics of the persons involved and yet make different provisions for different classes of people. Some such classification, even within the group of fully responsible citizens, is clearly inevitable" (2009, 183). This is a rather far-reaching concession because it suggests that differential treatment of some sort or to a certain degree is admissible and even unavoidable. Clearly, if, for example, a "law" introduced a tax for the population of just one particular location, it would fail Hayek's test of lawfulness, but there seems to be considerable gray zone this side of clearly discriminatory measures. Hayek argues that the degree to which the effect of a law on specific groups or individuals can be predicted, and in that sense lacks abstractness, may be a helpful indicator in this regard, and he also considers the idea that the legitimacy of a differential treatment may be confirmed by the affected group consenting to the measure. But ultimately he is forced into the noteworthy admission "that, in spite of many ingenious attempts to solve this problem, no entirely satisfactory criterion has been found that would always tell us what kind of classification is compatible with equality before the law" (ibid., 184). Hayek's candor is to be applauded, and given the enduring controversies in moral and legal philosophy over these matters, his assessment must be regarded as accurate. But this leaves a gaping argumentative hole at a neuralgic point in Hayek's design of the rule of law as an effective limitation on the powers of the state—and it leaves one wondering what his justification is for his position on the state's power to tax, which was our initial question. He writes that "the means should be raised according to a rule which applies uniformly to all. (This, in my opinion, precludes an overall progression of the burden of taxation of the individuals)" (Hayek 1967a, 175). Hayek is obviously entitled to this opinion, which suggests a flat-rate tax, but it seems that he lacks arguments to counter any opinions to the contrary.

In fact, James Buchanan has noted this argumentative insufficiency and provides the last example of limiting state action through principles or for-mal/procedural rules that focuses precisely on the issue of financing state action through taxation. Before we review Buchanan's specific solution to the problem, let me briefly contextualize it within his overall approach of constitutional economics. The "distinction between choices among rules and choices within rules" (Buchanan 1997b, 118) is fundamental to this perspective, as Buchanan almost exclusively focuses on the former level of choices that he describes as constitutional choices regarding the fundamental rules of the political and economic game, encapsulated predominantly in individual (property) rights to be enforced by the umpire state. This is the result of a hypothetical constitutional contract based on individual con-sent, which places Buchanan in the contractualist tradition from Thomas Hobbes to John Rawls, both of whom he draws on in his approach. But while Buchanan takes the specter of Hobbesian anarchy seriously, his contractual legitimation of the state departs from Hobbes's view in at least two major assumptions: first, Buchanan's broadly democratic commitments, at least to the extent that they do not conflict with his normative bases of a strict normative individualism; and second, the firm belief in the possibility of limiting state action: "We reject the Hobbesian presumption that the sov-ereign cannot be constrained by constitutional constraint" (Brennan and Buchanan 1980, 10). How to fashion such a constraint that proves to be effective is arguably the main focus of Buchanan's thought (1975, 13), and his answer is based on analytical distinctions that we are familiar with from Hayek's account. Buchanan distinguishes between the constitutional contract that must be guarded by what he calls the "protective" state, which operates according to the model of the umpire,[5] and the "productive" state, which results from a postconstitutional contract. The latter does not concern the enforcement of rules but the state's provision of public goods, which can in principle include everything that markets cannot produce efficiently. But even beyond that there is room for a particular political community to decide what the state should provide and to what degree, including certain social policies (Buchanan and Musgrave 1999, 83, 284). This distinction bears some obvious resemblance to Hayek's nomocratic state constrained by the rule of law and the service state that produces certain goods for its citizens, possibly in competition with private providers. As we have seen, this side of state action is only vaguely circumscribed in Hayek's account, and Buchanan also seems skeptical about the possibility of developing substantive constraints on the scope of productive state action. So like Hayek, Buchanan focuses on the financial base of the productive/service state, which in itself is located in the protective state dimension because it is dependent on the threat of coercion, the power to tax. As we have seen, Hayek also addresses the issue of taxation, but he does so in passing, and his call for a nonproportional tax is based on the shaky foundation of the generality/equality requirement of the rule of law. Unconvinced by what he thinks is a "dangerously arbitrary" demand by Hayek (Brennan and Buchanan 1980, 157), which is also ultimately ineffective as a constraint on the power to tax in general, Buchanan seeks to identify an alternative set of procedural rules that would act as an indirect limitation to the productive state through a constraint on the possibility to finance it.

The most promising set of rules to achieve this, in Buchanan's view, is a constitutional balanced-budget amendment, or what in the European context is commonly referred to as a "debt brake" (see Buchanan 1997a). Needless to say, this is a highly topical, and some would say rather pressing, issue since most members of the EU have passed such debt brakes as an element in more or often less autonomously chosen austerity politics in countries hit particularly hard by financial, economic, and sovereign debt crises. Similarly in the United States, while there is no federal constitutional balanced-budget amendment—at least not an effective one—austerity politics is being pushed down to the level of states and municipalities, the latter of which have effective debt brakes since they are legally prohibited from running deficits (see Peck 2014). The balanced-budget amendment is discussed later, but here I present some preliminary critical elaborations on the functioning of the amendment as well as its implications in Buchanan's version of the argument. I also point out a fundamental ambiguity pertaining to both a balanced-budget rule and a rule-based politics of neoliberal fashion more generally as we have encountered it in Eucken, Röpke, and Hayek.

How would the amendment work? Buchanan places particular emphasis on the fact that he proposes a rule for a balanced budget that "is procedural rather than substantive" (1997b, 126), which he considers of systematic and strategic relevance. A substantive rule prescribing which cuts to make and which taxes to reform would be an excessive intrusion into the decision-making autonomy of democratically elected representatives, and, strategically speaking, the transparency of the rule's winners and losers would make it excessively difficult to build a coalition in support of it[6]—although we will see that this is a problem that continues to haunt the procedural rule as well. Instead, Buchanan argues for a rule that essentially stipulates the nondebt financing of all state outlays. How much the state spends and what it spends the money on is not defined by the rule, and Buchanan thus hopes to dodge the charge that the amendment would inappropriately enshrine a particular substantive economic policy at the constitutional level. In his words, "the amendment requires only that congressional majorities, within the other constraints through which they are authorized to act, pay for what they spend, with 'pay for' being defined in a willingness to levy taxes on those citizens who make up the current membership of the polity" (ibid.). Conversely, if there is no willingness to levy taxes, expenditures need to be adjusted accordingly. I confront this notion with some preliminary observations on the use of rules in politics before returning to the issue of balanced-budget amendments and developing a more robust critique in chapters 3 and 5.

Buchanan offers a justification for rules that bind the political sovereign with reference to a familiar figure in economics, Robinson Crusoe. Crusoe needs to make full use of daylight to get necessary work done on the island, but he has the bad habit of sleeping in, so he constructs an alarm clock to wake him up early in the morning (see Buchanan 1975, 93). For Buchanan, this is a rational response because Crusoe acknowledges his limited self-discipline, and through an external enforcement mechanism rather than a plea to his inner strength, he manages to realize what ultimately is in his own interest as he himself perceives it in the evening and on the following afternoon—but not in the morning, when it actually matters. Accordingly, as a strategy for achieving one's goals, laying down a rule for oneself and making sure it is enforced is a strategy superior to what the literature refers to as "case-to-case-maximization." The typical argument for this stance draws on a traffic example. Waiting on a red light in the middle of the night with no other cars in sight reduces current utility, but in the long run the rule is superior. While a driver may not be harmed running a light each and every time, just one mistake in her discretionary assessment might cost her life (see Friedman 2002, 51–53). This sounds reasonable enough, but the plausibility may just hinge on the suggestive example Buchanan constructs. Consider Crusoe again; he is a subject prone to giving in to temptation (and also keep in mind that this weak and wayward subject represents democratically elected decision makers in Buchanan's account) and thus in need of strict rules for getting up early to prevent a pattern of sleeping in from commencing. However, what if he falls ill and is in desperate need of sleep but still rises in the morning, distrustful of his own (unconscious) motives and solely focused on obeying the self-set rules, only to find his health deteriorate from lack of rest? In this example, sticking to the rules obviously is not rational, especially in the long run. So what would be called for is obviously "smart" rule following, a measure of flexibility in the application of rules or, what in the Aristotelian tradition is referred to as *phronesis*. It is not the rules themselves that are beneficial; rather, it is these rules in combination with those who establish them and implement them appropriately that make them so. And this pertains to a sickly Crusoe as well as a crisis-ridden country swallowing the bitter medicine of austerity. So the analytical plausibility and the normative appeal of both a balanced-budget amendment and rule-based politics in general cannot be conclusively assessed before the respective assumptions about rule-following and rule-implementing *actors* are scrutinized more closely, which we return to in chapter 5.

Structural State Constraints: Horizontal and Vertical Separation of Powers

State output is one possible place to apply constraining devices; the structure and form of the state is the other. The classic (liberal) approach to limiting the state's abilities through a specific structural setup is, of course, the separation of powers between the various branches of government. On a given scale of the state, there ought to be checks and balances between the legislative, judicial, and executive branches, constituting the institutional dimension of the rule of law. Given that separation of powers is a standard element in the broadly liberal repertoire of devices aimed at curtailing state power through internal differentiation and careful distribution of various competencies, it is somewhat surprising that the principle is rarely discussed explicitly in the majority of accounts considered here. This may simply mean that the principle and its effects are taken for granted and its desirability as a structuring device is tacitly assumed. But the argumentative thrust in some neoliberal accounts suggests that their stance in regard to this principle is more equivocal than one would assume for a branch off the tree of liberalism.

Buchanan's and Hayek's accounts provide a more extensive treatment of the issue. Given its centrality for Hayek's political thought, it is not surprising that he offers the most elaborate ideas about what implementing the rule of law would require on the institutional level. *The Constitution of Liberty* contains three chapters on these ideas, in which Hayek traces the roots of the rule of law in various geographical and political contexts, from constitutionalism in the United States to the German *Rechtsstaat*, as well as the tendencies that led to its respective decline. As already noted, in Hayek's view, above all, the conflation of legislative and executive activities—making and implementing/enforcing the law—is to blame for this decline, and accordingly, the strictest possible separation of these state powers and their clear assignment to different branches of government is required. Hayek's reconstruction of the institutional dimension of the rule of law yields an arrangement that is mostly familiar from other representatives of the liberal tradition. Legislatures create proper laws in the Hayekian sense, and a separate body of actors, the executive, implements the laws and is strictly bound by them (at least whenever coercion is involved). Hayek acknowledges that a certain measure of discretion is involved in implementing laws, and the lawfulness of such discretionary action thus must be established through an independent court system and judicial review. Obviously, the crucial point in this way of separating the power of the state is to prevent their conflation and misappropriation, which is precisely what has happened according to Hayek, as well as Buchanan, who models the proper functioning of the separation of powers on the basis of his distinction between the protective and the productive state.

The productive state is associated with the legislative branch, whose task is to produce public goods and law in general. The protective umpire state, however, is encapsulated in the executive and judicial branches. The mode of operation of these is decidedly different because the enforcement/ application of rules involves what Buchanan describes as a truth judgment analogous to scientific inquiry, whereas legislation is first and foremost a matter of interests and (collective) choices (1975, 69, 95). If this fundamental difference is disregarded, the proper balance of governmental powers is in jeopardy. So what exactly is wrong with the contemporary manifestations of the separation of powers for Buchanan and Hayek?

Buchanan primarily highlights the dangers of the executive and judicial encroachment on the genuinely legislative function of lawmaking. The dispassionate referee more and more often modifies the rules and thus oversteps the internal boundaries set up to demarcate various powers, threatening to undermine the (self-)limitation of the state and its branches. "Few who observe the far-flung operation of the executive arm of the United States government along with the ubiquity of the federal judiciary could interpret the activities of either of these institutions as falling within meaningful restrictions of the enforcer. Ideally, these institutions may be umpires in the social game; actually, these institutions modify and change the basic structure of rights without consent of citizens. They assume the authority to rewrite the basic constitutional contract, to change 'the law' at their own will" (Buchanan 1975, 163).[7] Note that this imperialism of the two branches is not just a matter of appropriating more and more competencies in regard to a legislature that is the only branch legitimated to make and change law. The problem is also the mode in which law is "rewritten," for example, by a court. Either the court tries to emulate the operational mode of legislatures, making choices and considering interests, and thus functionally ceases to be a proper court of law; or it decides like a court generally should, according to Buchanan, on the basis of a quasi-scientific truth judgment and thus profoundly misunderstands or disregards the nature of legislative politics, which is not about truth but interests and choices.

In Hayek's view, the imperial thrust between the various powers is reversed. It is the legislative chamber that seizes more and more powers that properly belong to "government," that is, the executive branch of the state that comprises law enforcement and the service function of the state (Hayek 2003, 1:130–131). Hayek's explanation of this dynamic is not easily analyzed, but one enabling factor is undoubtedly the decline of the generality requirement of a law, which made it possible for legislatures "to command whatever they pleased simply by calling their commands 'laws'" (ibid.). Although this may enable legislative entropy, what would be the motive for parliamentary actors to seize more and more governmental powers? Hayek seems to hint at a dynamic that is self-amplifying once it is triggered. A governing assembly will come to think of itself as running the country "as one runs a factory or any other organization" (ibid., 143),[8] which means that its authority and responsibility are unlimited and its scope of action therefore ever expanding. This argument in itself seems rather weak, but it gains plausibility in light of Hayek's view of democracy; and since his remedy to the conflation of executive and legislative powers, and, by the same token, measures and laws proper, also has far-reaching implications for democratic processes and institutions, we revisit this issue in chapter 3.

Buchanan's solution to the problem of the *horizontal* separation of powers, a specific proposal beyond restoring a constitutional order that is now "in disarray," is not apparent—and the "constitutional revolution" needed to restore order once more points us in the direction of the *actors* that are to be the revolutionary subject of this transformation of rules (1975, 166). Still, while Buchanan seems to offer little guidance about how the *horizontal* confusion of powers he is diagnosing is to be addressed, his designs for a proper *vertical* separation of powers turn out to be much more elaborate.

At first glance, it would seem that neoliberals were exemplars of what the late Ulrich Beck referred to as "methodological nationalism," the implicit frame of reference in all political considerations being the nation-state. To a certain extent this is accurate and somewhat understandable, since at least the post–World War II era was arguably the heyday of this political form and the nation-state therefore was the scalar center of attention for neoliberals as for other political thinkers of the time.[9] However, one of the main strategies for constraining the state in neoliberal thought is the vertical decentering of the nation-state, both upward through the formation of a supranational federation and downward through devolution, thus turning the nation-state itself into a federal political unit. Attempting both simultaneously might even increase the overall feasibility of such transformations: "It could probably be tackled more easily if international federation were undertaken at the same time as a reorganization of the centralized states on a federal basis, just as, vice versa, the second process would be helped by the first" (Röpke 1959a, 46; see also Hayek 2001, 240). So while both logics of decentering the state are discussed in the context of each other in many versions of the neoliberal argument for federalism, I try to analytically distinguish between the two to clarify and to put the focus on the link between the national and supranational levels.

Let us first briefly look at the context of the earliest versions of the argument that can be found in the work of Röpke, Hayek, and, less prominently, Rüstow. World War II, either as a potentiality in its actuality or in its impact, leaves a clear imprint on these works, depending on the time of writing, in that one of the motives for endorsing a supranational structure is the hope to pacify interstate relations through it.

This is most pronounced in Rüstow's essay "Politik und Moral" (Politics and morality), which also offers the only truly cosmopolitan argument along strongly Kantian lines: In order to overcome the potential of armed hostilities that are a characteristic feature of an international state of nature and thus forces even moral collective actors into wars of self-defense, there is only one ultimate solution, to establish a "world government" consisting of a supranational "legislative, judiciary and executive" (1949, 587–588). Whether this demand can be plausibly based on Kant's writings is of no concern here, but just as Kant had argued that it is not just reason that drives humanity to unite in ever-more encompassing political communities but also nature, or, more generally, empirical forces, Rüstow is adamant that there are certain empirical phenomena and respective forces pushing toward some kind of world government that he views as imminent: "The certitude of this prediction is based on the atomic bomb" (ibid., 589). As far as Rüstow is concerned, the question is only whether world government will exist under American or Soviet hegemony if the Soviets were to acquire nuclear arms as well. This points us in the direction of another aspect of the historical context of the early arguments for a supranational federation, particularly prominent in the work of Rüstow but also in Röpke, who is highly ambivalent about European integration but endorses the establishment of a European federation that should serve in an alliance with the United States as a "defence against the imperialism of world communism" (Röpke 1959a, 51). Matters of war and peace thus figure in the neoliberal thought on federalism, but what turns out to be at least as important as limiting the state's ability to wage wars is to constrain it in its powers regarding the domestic economy and society.

If we follow Röpke, both tasks were achieved in the most efficient and peaceful manner through the gold standard in former times. His earliest works from the 1920s dealing with these issues still investigate the possibilities of reinstating a system of international free trade based on guaranteed convertibility of gold, which had been a key factor in developing a highly integrated world market leading up to World War I. However, as Röpke comes to realize over the course of the early 1930s, the gold standard and the other preconditions of what Polanyi called the "Hundred Years' Peace" are irretrievably lost through processes that Röpke will analyze in *International Economic Disintegration* (1942).[10] It almost seems, therefore, that Röpke considers a federation as only the second-best solution to the problem of limiting state power, but the shift toward federalist designs can also be interpreted as an element in the modernization process of liberalism that is constitutive of neoliberalism. The world of the 1930s renders futile any attempt to restore the world economy that rested on old liberal principles, techniques, and institutions, so new approaches have to be developed as functional equivalents of the gold standard, if the attempt at "reconstructing the world economy" is to stand any chance at all (Röpke 1950b, 242).

But while Röpke is a passionate supporter of federalism in general, the analytical refinement of his thought leaves a lot to be desired, which is at least partly attributable to one of the major sources of his passion for federalism: his experience of Switzerland. Röpke was able to relocate from his initial exile in Istanbul to Geneva in 1936, and although he could have returned to Germany after the war, he chose to stay in Switzerland, which is already an indication of the attachment he formed to his new home. It is only a mild overstatement to say that his view of federalism—even on the supranational level—is an extrapolation of the existing federalist arrangements in Switzerland. To be sure, this has the benefit of basing claims and assessments on the example of a functioning form of federalism, but at times it limits Röpke's supranational imagination and is based on an idealization of Swiss federalism that is oblivious to any possibly existing problems. Nevertheless, it is difficult to argue with the core assumption underlying

Röpke's postwar thought on federalism. The nation-state is doubly defi-
cient because it is too big and amorphous to generate the experience of real
political community for its members, and it is too small to address some
of the most pressing problems of today that are solvable only on a trans-
or supranational level. We already know that Röpke would like to see the
first problem addressed through a consequent politics of decentralization
and subsidiarity, so let us focus on the second. Especially in the European
context, any political form beyond and above the nation-state can only be
of a federalist nature: "the essence of Europe [is] unity in diversity, freedom
in solidarity" (Röpke 1960, 244). There may be few who would disagree
with this (normative) characterization, but it begs the question how exactly
this is to be achieved in a trans- and supranational setting. Needless to say,
the reference to a "balance between the dividing and the uniting forces" in
such a federation remains purely formulaic as well (Röpke 1959a, 44). Still,
this is not to suggest that Röpke's considerations on a European federation
are vague throughout, albeit edifyingly so. Wherever he is more candid,
though, the thrust of the argument is rather skeptical about the possibility
of such a federation. His readers are cautioned that federalism is not just
an administrative technique but that it is rooted in an entire philosophy
(Röpke 1953a, 10). Still, could these attitudinal and "spiritual" preconditions be disseminated throughout Europe?

Röpke is only certain that this will not happen through a kind of integration that EU scholars would refer to as "neofunctionalist" and that was arguably characteristic of early postwar integration patterns. To put it simply, the
idea was that integration/harmonization of certain economic sectors would
trigger so-called spillover effects, necessitating the integration of more and
more other sectors for purely "functional" reasons, ultimately leading to
political integration as well. Röpke, however, is adamant that economic integration presupposes the "spiritual-political integration of Europe" (1953a,
13). This still leaves the reader with the question of how to achieve this,
not the least because Röpke is deeply concerned over any transfer of power
from the national to the supranational level—which, to some degree, would
appear to be part and parcel of truly political integration (see Röpke 1960,
243). The solution to the conundrum comes in the form of a reference to
the Swiss example; yet this hardly appears to be a solution for the short and

medium terms, because the point about federalist Switzerland is that it has grown "slowly and organically" over centuries (Röpke 1953a, 12). But this means that Röpke ultimately remains deeply torn over the desirability and necessity of a federation. There is a keen awareness of the functional benefits of a supranational federation to rein in the powers of national sovereignty but also to enhance transnational political problem-solving capacities. However, he has little to offer about the specific characteristics of such a federation, and, even more calamitously, Röpke cannot propose a path that could be deliberately chosen and followed toward "spiritual-political integration" because his conception of a federation is so deeply wedded to the Swiss case and its allegedly organic development. This is not to say that there are not very good reasons to harbor reservations about the possibility of a normatively desirable form of European integration, but if he is right and "humanity has now finally reached the point where unless future develop-ment succeeds in extending beyond the conception of the nation . . . the resulting punishment will be the downfall of civilization" (Röpke 1959a, 43), then waiting patiently for the organic growth of Europeanist attitudes and political commitments is hardly a persuasive political response.

This would seem to lead to rather pessimistic conclusions about the future existence of some kind of federation that somehow needs to integrate economically and politically simultaneously, while fostering the respective political mentalities necessary to support these processes. But while it is unclear how this is supposed to take place, Röpke at least is certain about the utter impossibility of European supranationalism turning into a socialist superstate. This brings us to Hayek's considerations on federalism, which are initially designed to confirm this impossibility but also point beyond this specific goal.

In *The Road to Serfdom* Hayek addresses one possible socialist response to the liberal attempt to prove the functional unfeasibility of socialism on the nation-state level, the argument that socialism is internationalist and thus may be dysfunctional when implemented in a single country but feasible on the level of a supranational federation. Hayek's rebuttal follows the overall logic of his argument, according to which the variety of individual needs and wants makes central planning without the systematic use of coercion impossible, especially on a trans- or supranational level. Hayek states, "But one has only to visualize the problems raised by economic planning of even an area such as Western Europe to see that the moral bases for such an understanding are completely lacking. . . . To undertake the direction of the economic life of people with widely divergent ideals and values is to assume responsibilities which commit one to the use of force" (2001, 228–229). However, this is not yet the most illuminating insight Hayek develops. In an article on federalism, originally published in 1939, he introduces a logic of limiting nation-state powers that remains pertinent today. Hayek's argument begins with what is almost a reversal of Röpke's position regarding the primacy of economic and political integration. Economic integration may or may not presuppose political integration, but the latter, according to Hayek, is certainly inconceivable without the former. Protectionist policies internal to a political unit must lead to conflicts between territorially fixed groups, and Hayek assumes that this will lead to disintegrative pressures, which the central government cannot absorb in the long run. This leads him to the conclusion that a stable federation requires a common market without impediments to economic interactions and movement across borders.

What would this imply for the powers of nation-states making up this federation, which Hayek even imagines to have a common currency? It would dramatically diminish the economic policy options of states because they now find themselves in a situation in which they vie with one another both for natural resources and various types of more or less mobile financial, industrial, and human capital. More concretely, this means that "not only would the greater mobility between the states make it necessary to avoid all sorts of taxation which would drive capital or labor elsewhere, but there would also be considerable difficulties with many kinds of indirect taxation." The fundamental reason is that states "will lose their monopolistic position" (Hayek 1980, 261).

In this perspective, the power of the state that turns it into a potentially uncontrollable Leviathan is the result of its "market position." States can dictate the conditions of politics and the costs (taxes, fees) to their citizens, who are effectively at their mercy. It almost goes without saying that the remedy for this special kind of market failure for the neoliberal Hayek lies in creating competition for the individual state, thereby reducing its monopolistic powers. A market of jurisdictions needs to be established. The logic of markets and competition thus is inscribed into both the supranational and subnational decentering of the nation-state since, principally, a market of jurisdictions can be established at the nation-state, provincial, and even municipal levels in what today is commonly referred to as "competitive federalism." The crucial factor to establishing a truly competitive environment is, of course, the mobility of capital in the broad sense, which suggests that the smaller the units, the more effective the competition between them, so the main goal in such a strategy of constraining the state would be a devolution of powers to substate units.

Hayek notes the possibility of devolution in passing (2001, 240), but an "interstate federation," as he calls it (1980, 255), is an even more promising arrangement for a particular reason. Competition requires maximum mobility, which means that substate units need to be embedded in an encompassing structure, the nation-state, which guarantees this mobility at least to a certain degree. However, the history of substate federalism is mostly characterized by the gravitational pull at the national scale, leading to a recentralization of powers and reestablishment of a monopoly. It is the fact that this dynamic is not, and possibly cannot be, replicated in the same way that makes the relation between national and supranational scales uniquely suitable for Hayek's purposes. Nation-state governments, he argues, by and large are considered to be legitimized to engage in a wide variety of policies that shift and reshift burdens and benefits between groups and territories based on some kind of national identity that forms a bond between the members of the population. Such a broad mandate to shape the livelihoods of those subject to it, however, will never be given to a supranational government: "The central government in a federation composed of many different people will have to be restricted in scope if it is to avoid meeting an increasing resistance on the part of the various groups it includes." As a consequence, "a lot of interferences in economic life will become impractical" (ibid., 265, 266). It is tempting to explore the almost eerie similarities between such a federation that Hayek developed in 1939 and the Eurozone of today, as the former almost amounts to a blueprint for the latter (see Streeck 2017), discussed further in chapter 6. I now scrutinize the views and arguments of the neoliberal who has devoted the most systematic efforts to the analysis of federalism broadly speaking.

The constitutional balanced-budget amendment is certainly the best-known concrete policy demand associated with the name James Buchanan. Since the mid-1970s (and to a certain extent even before then) his interest was piqued by federalist designs as an alternative institutional/structural device to achieve the goals of the amendment—only far more effectively. In a paper written while on a research stay in St. Gallen, Switzerland, Buchanan lauds the country for its "effective federalism" (2001, 241), just as Röpke did fifty years earlier, although this is not the only reason for Buchanan's praise. As already mentioned, the primary value of federalism for Buchanan is the restrictions it places on the size of the public sector and the budget, a view supposedly confirmed by the Swiss experience. Buchanan is aware that an empirical case does not prove anything, and he is enough of a theorist to probe the characteristics of federalist arrangements on a strictly analytical level. As mentioned previously, the initial attractiveness of federalism sparking Buchanan's interest lies in its potential use as "an indirect means of imposing constraints on the potential fiscal exploitation of Leviathan. It may be that an explicit constitutional decision to decentralize and hence to disperse political authority may effectively substitute for overt fiscal limits" (Brennan and Buchanan 1980, 174). In his later work, he even contemplates federalism as "an ideal political order" (Buchanan 1995b; see also Feld 2014).

Compared to Hayek's, Buchanan's work on federalism is much more detailed and voluminous, but to Hayek's credit, many of the insights that Buchanan's investigations yield are already implied in Hayek's article from 1939. However, in contrast to Hayek, Buchanan is unwilling to rely solely on transnational solidarity remaining too weak to legitimate a full-fledged policy portfolio on the supranational scale, which would compensate for the reduced powers of the nation-state in a federation and thus nullify the intended effect. Instead, he places his hopes in some additional safeguards, particularly the guaranteed right for nation-states and substate units to secede and a particular distribution of the power to tax between the various levels of Leviathan. The former provision is a logical extension of the basic mechanics of competition, which require actual exit options to be effective, so we focus on the latter. In Buchanan's view the centralizing dynamic of federalist settings is not contingent on but driven by the strategies of rational (collective) actors that benefit from it (see Buchanan and Lee 1994, 222).

So how is it possible to prevent this dynamic from offsetting the desired effects of limiting the overall tax load and maintaining tax competition, for example, through a centralized tax that may even be redistributed to the subunits to compensate them for their lack of revenue due to competition? Needless to say, Buchanan considers sharing revenue either directly among the competing units or indirectly through a central structure in the way just described as undesirable because it decreases the incentive to compete and thus should be constitutionally prohibited.[11] However, *reverse* revenue sharing is introduced as the mechanism to ensure that competitive federalism even beyond the nation-state could emerge as a sustainable model resistant to the multiple dynamics that would undermine it. The name of the model is apt because reverse revenue sharing would maintain the revenue-sharing structures that exist in most empirical cases of federalist arrangements (on the level of nation-states) but would reverse the flow of revenue. While today substate units in many cases rely on funds raised and distributed at the national level, Buchanan wants to make national revenue dependent on the substate units and, accordingly, the supranational level on the national. In other words, even if there were a sense of transnational solidarity robust enough to legitimate policies involving (redistributive) expenditures on a large scale (which Hayek deems unlikely), only the funds authorized by nation-state governments could be spent on the supranational level. Furthermore, as long as the supranational level lacks the independent power to tax, the possibility of being subjected to what Buchanan calls exploitation through taxation by this level of government is simply nonexistent. Conversely, the units on the lowest level of government are free to tax their citizens as much as they can—even in a discriminatory way—because the disciplining force of mobility will rein in the small Leviathans whenever they overplay their hand, fiscally speaking. Again, it is tempting to inquire how the characteristics of this model compare to those of the EU and its fiscal arrangements, which is considered later.

First, let me introduce a few thoughts that serve to problematize the model(s) of fiscal federalism, nationally and supranationally, that we find in Hayek and Buchanan, although my main critique is that the strategy of depriving the state of certain powers through its decentering and competition between the constituent units is difficult to reconcile with the demands for a transformation of state structures that seem to point in almost completely the opposite direction considered here.

There is a vast literature on the effects and feasibility of competitive federalist arrangements on the national or supranational scale, most of which is empirical. While supporters question the possibility of maintaining the allegedly beneficial (fiscal) decentering of the state over time and resist recentralizing pressures, critics of competitive federalism often raise the issue of a pernicious race to the bottom with detrimental results for most, if not all, jurisdictions involved. However, it is safe to say that the evidence regarding both issues is inconclusive so far (see Feld 2014), not the least because so much depends on the specific setup of the arrangement in question. So let me stay at the theoretical level and follow the path of immanent critique based on just one consideration: Jurisdictional competition presupposes a market, and the functioning of this and any other market—according to the neoliberal problematic—is based on certain conditions of possibility. One essential condition for effective competition is the possibility of bankruptcy, or market exit. It was Michel Foucault who highlighted the difference between a liberal understanding of markets as sites of harmonious exchanges and an ordoliberal /neoliberal understanding that emphasized competition as the crucial aspect of markets, which implied an understanding of markets as sites of conflict that necessarily had to produce winners and losers to function properly (see Foucault 2008, 118–119). So the question is whether and to what extent this condition also applies to jurisdictional competition.

Let us imagine a territory divided into subunits sufficiently small to ensure reasonably low exit costs, which are another major precondition of competition. Now policy packages as well as the respective price tags begin to diverge to attract capital, with different jurisdictions pursuing different strategies. Under ideal conditions—which are about the opposite of what most people consider normatively ideal in this case—capital, including human capital, will flow effortlessly to the jurisdictions that offer the policy-price combination that corresponds most closely to the respective preferences (which can vary; not everyone likes to live in a low-tax environment). A number of different scenarios can be imagined for the next step in such a dynamic model.

The one that spells the least trouble for it, in my view, is one that Buchanan at least takes into consideration but would be strongly at odds with Hayek's assumptions: There is some volatility in the market initially, but after some time a dominant model emerges for all jurisdictions because it turns out that individual preferences are not that individualist and most people prefer some middle-of-the-road policy product at a reasonable price. Hayek must consider this an unlikely outcome given his insistence on the variety of values and preferences in a population that serve as the main normative argument against centralized planning. Still, let us assume that individuals (and even capital) do not have preferences that are strong and divergent enough to trump residual "locational rents" (the utility of remaining at home), and the market reaches a beneficial equilibrium. This would mean that competition is practically suspended and exists only virtually until a particular government tests the patience of its citizen-customers by offering an inferior policy product or preferences change and/or intensify. In my view, this scenario yields a sustainable arrangement, but it is one based on somewhat unlikely assumptions about the conformity of individual preferences and rests on actual competition being the exception and its virtual version the norm. Nevertheless, under certain conditions this appears to be a functioning arrangement to effectively limit state capabilities through the decentering of statehood.

The more probable scenario for the dynamics of the model, in my view, would lead to a different outcome that raises some doubts with regard to its a priori feasibility. Let us assume that preferences do diverge in a significant way and some jurisdictions do lose a significant amount of capital/people to other jurisdictions. Even if the less attractive units are not depleted of all capital instantaneously, a significant loss makes it even more difficult to provide "good policy at decent prices." This means that the relocation dynamics become self-amplifying, and then it is just a matter of time until jurisdictions have to declare insolvency, probably prompting all remaining inhabitants to leave if they can—the locational rents for staying are a minor factor at this point. So what happens to a jurisdiction depleted of capital and deserted by its inhabitants? The most plausible scenario is for it to be integrated into another jurisdiction. Over time this is bound to result in fewer and bigger jurisdictions, which means that competition will be reduced by the same degree because of rising exit costs and the potential detrimental systemic effects of sizable governments going bankrupt and because fewer competitors find it easier to cooperate at the expense of their citizens: "For reasons equivalent to those familiar in oligopoly theory, the potentiality for collusion among separate units varies inversely with the number of units" (Brennan and Buchanan 1980, 180). In short, competition undermines itself in such a setting. How does this change once the competing units are embedded in a provincial, national, or supranational setting? Either there is not much change because horizontal or vertical bailouts are prohibited and/or difficult to orchestrate if, for example, due to reverse revenue sharing, the higher governmental level is completely dependent on funds from the lower tier. Or there is horizontal revenue sharing and/or vertical redistribution of funds, which in all likelihood will keep even struggling political "enterprises" in the market if not guarantee the existence of the various units. This is not to say that the federal or even supranational unit could not try to "incentivize" lower-level jurisdictions to behave more competitively and be more efficient in their policy production, but unless there are legal grounds and the actual possibility for a jurisdiction to declare insolvency, the pressure of jurisdictional competition is relaxed to a considerable degree. Much more will have to be said on these matters once we focus on the EU and the question of whether competing units could and should declare insolvency or bail each other out, but we now move on to the last quadrant in the matrix of neoliberal varieties of theorizing the state, addressing structural changes to the state so it can perform its positive functions.

Recentering the State: Authoritarian Liberalism

The cliché understanding of neoliberalism suggests that it is the doctrine of self-regulating markets and the minimal state. However, a closer look at the texts proves that this is at least an impoverished understanding of neoliberal thought because what we find there, at least in one of its varieties, is actually the call for a strong state. Needless to say, this statement needs some explanation, but let us begin with those accounts that indeed demand the restoration or fortification of state power—the strong state—and inquire how they arrive at this assessment.

The ordoliberals most explicitly postulate the need for a strong state, which is arguably most surprising in the case of the early Rüstow, whose magnum opus *Freedom and Domination* contains a fundamental critique of domination that one would assume to apply as well to the state as a structure of domination. Nevertheless, in his view it is one of the gravest errors of classical liberalism to have promoted the ideal of a weak state that would still maintain its independence: "No one noticed . . . the obvious sociological truth that the strength and independence of a state are interdependent variables, and that only a strong state is powerful enough to preserve its own independence" (Rüstow 1942, 276). This is already a succinct summary of the ordoliberal position with regard to how the structure of the state and its relation to the state and economy have to be transformed so it can operate properly and thus provide a crucial precondition for functioning markets. What the ordoliberals and many of their fellow neoliberals object to, first and foremost, is a seeming conflation of state, economy, and society, resulting in what Eucken refers to as the "economic state" (*Wirtschaftsstaat*) deeply immersed in economic processes on behalf of various producer groups and acting, at least to some extent, at their behest (2017a, 56). The most fundamental concern underlying the ordoliberal assessment is that the state's various entanglements will ultimately lead to its dissolution and destruction: "Responsible government must examine carefully all the possible means of resisting this pluralistic disintegration of the state" (Röpke 1960, 143).

Before we scrutinize more thoroughly what exactly characterizes a strong state, we first note the empirical background against which the demand of an independent and strong state emerges in ordoliberal thought. This is, of course, the Weimar Republic on the eve of its descent into chaos and, subsequently, Nazi totalitarianism. While this is not enough to exculpate the ordoliberals straightaway, it does explain the shrill tonality of some of their contributions and the radicalness of some of their views. Or, to put it somewhat differently, lamenting the dysfunctionality of a democratic system and a corporatism/pluralism that left the state overextended and drifting is not easily dismissed as unfounded alarmism in the Germany of 1932, when Eucken and Rüstow first voice the demand for a strong, independent state.

However, it must be probed, whether or not there are also more systematic reasons that led the ordoliberals to this conclusion; otherwise, we run the risk of buying into the narrative expounded by contemporary defenders of ordoliberalism who argue that it may have exhibited some problematic tendencies in the prewar era (e.g., advocacy of a strong state), but the experience of totalitarianism and war converted it to the values of liberal democracy, to which later writings supposedly attest. It is certainly true that the vocabulary of later ordoliberal texts is somewhat toned down and the explicit call for a strong state disappears.[12] Nevertheless, Röpke's warning of a disintegration of the state is from the late 1950s, and the basic logic of the underlying argument for the strong state remains largely unchanged even in the context of the liberal democracy of the early Federal Republic of Germany. The other strategy of developing an apologia for the undeniable existence of calls for a strong state in early ordoliberalism takes on the following form: The ordoliberals did indeed call for a strong state, but despite the problematic connotations this demand may have nowadays, what they meant by it was simply a state that would not weaken itself through overextension. The state gains strength through both its refusal to accept responsibility for all of society's ills and a prudent policy of self-limitation along the lines of the principles and goals discussed previously. However, by involving itself in any number of socioeconomic matters, the "economic state" cannot plausibly refuse societal demands for state action. Inevitably it will fail at some of the problems it has been called on to solve, thus leading to a continuous corrosion of state authority because nothing is more undermining to the state than not being able so solve problems it has claimed responsibility for. This argument is certainly part of the neoliberal repertoire (see, e.g., Hayek 2003, 1:143; Röpke 1950b, 192), but does this exhaust the meaning of the strong state in ordoliberalism?[13]

Let us take a closer look. We have already seen that a strong state needs to sever the ties that bind it to societal interest groups and their demands; it needs to find the "strength to free itself from the influence of the masses and in some way distance itself from the economy" (Eucken 2017a, 68–69).[14] Assuming that the attempt at disentanglement was successful, how is the state to operate once it is liberated from the pressures of society? Eucken demands that the state should not act according to the will of others but according to its "own will" (ibid., 60), which suggests an organicist conception of the state as some kind of macrosubject endowed with a will of its own. This prompts the question of how the will of the state is formed independently of societal influences, and Eucken is adamant that the most important aspect of the formation of this will is the state's unity (ibid.). Along similar lines, Röpke even refers to a "monistic state" (1960, 142), which is consistent with the antipluralist thrust of the argument for a strong state. The strong state is thus characterized by an independent and monistic/ uniform will formation, and furthermore, it ought to exhibit a government endowed with the will to govern. What is needed is a "really strong state, a government with the courage to govern" (Röpke 1950b, 192), and leadership, if not a "'leader' [Führer], who will not shirk political responsibility" (Rüstow [1929] 1959, 101).

Let us note at once that Rüstow and Röpke more or less plausibly assume that such a state is compatible with a democratic system; nevertheless, what emerges quite clearly from the various statements of the ordoliberals is a conception of the state that can be called authoritarian without any significant stretch. It is authoritarian not so much because of its emphasis on state authority, which could be simply a conservative position, but because its postulate of a unitary will of the state and the concomitant hostility toward anything that could threaten it, especially the demands from particularistic actors and, it would seem, a separation of powers deliberately designed to diffuse this process of will formation.

As mentioned previously, the charge of authoritarianism is routinely deflected and relativized by contemporary defenders of ordoliberalism, but in my view there is indeed a systematic reason for this stance, which points beyond the traumatic experience of an imploding democratic system and a faltering state in the Weimar Republic. Remember that it is incumbent on the state to establish and watch over the competitive order, which includes a robust policy of tackling economic power in its various forms. What kind of state is required to succeed at these tasks? First, the politics of the competitive order are a highly sensitive field because, as Eucken (1960) emphasizes, the political, economic, and legal orders are interdependent, and whatever the state does has an impact on these interlocking systems, which exist in a fragile balance. Ideally, this impact, including various unintended consequences, is contemplated beforehand in order not to cause unwanted disturbances. But how could a state, at the whim of ever-changing societal influences, ever produce decisions and actions that satisfy the need for such a prescient and coherent policy? This is exactly the question that Eucken poses to his readers in *The Principles of Economic Policy*, which was first published in 1952 and does not differ in its overall diagnosis from Eucken's writings in 1932: "Everywhere there is the undermining of state authority through particularistic forces that represent particularistic interests. . . . A state with a unified and consequent will formation . . . is indispensable today. All economic policy is seemingly placed in jeopardy, because the state fails as an ordering power" (ibid., 329–330). So the first reason why a state should have an almost monolithic internal structure is the complexity of economic policy, even when the state is supposedly not intervening directly in economic processes. This complexity, combined with the incoherence of state policy resulting from unchecked influence of societal actors on the process of will formation, is bound to lead to chaos—as the Weimar Republic seemingly proved. The second reason is the state's responsibility to aggressively check economic power and actors who would attempt to convert this economic power into political power through the official democratic channels or backroom lobbying.[15] But this requires a state that is autonomous (independent in its decision making) and has the capability to implement its decisions even if this means that, for example, a consortium of firms that commands excessive market power has to be broken up. It is a state, to be more specific, capable of smashing even giant companies like Google or Microsoft as well as banking institutions "too big to fail," such as Goldman Sachs and Deutsche Bank—and it goes without saying that the same applies to unions to the extent that they hold market power.

It would seem that the promotion of an at least semiauthoritarian state defined by the characteristics just listed is a risky strategy for neoliberalism, whose prime intellectual and political opponent is after all collectivism-cum-totalitarianism. But an analysis of Röpke's and Hayek's work shows how they seek to demarcate authoritarianism and dictatorship from the totalitarianism they criticize.[16]

Let us begin with Hayek: "The difference between the two ideals stands out most clearly if we name their opposites: for democracy it is authoritarian government; for liberalism it is totalitarianism. Neither of the two systems necessarily excludes the opposite of the other: a democracy may well wield totalitarian powers, and it is conceivable that an authoritarian government may act on liberal principles" (2009, 90). Based on these two pairs of opposites, Hayek reshuffles the relations between political forms and ideologies. The result is an intimation of a slippery slope that does not lead from authoritarianism to totalitarianism but rather from democracy to totalitarianism. This becomes even clearer in his writings from the 1970s, where he states "that the predominant model of liberal democratic institutions . . . necessarily leads to a gradual transformation of the spontaneous order of a free society into a totalitarian system conducted in the service of some coalition of organized interests" (Hayek 2003, 1:2). Note that Hayek refers to the "predominant model" of democracy and not democracy per se; we later explore how he would like to see the democratic process reformed, but the crucial point is that he makes it quite clear that if he were presented with the choice between an unlimited democracy and a liberal dictator, he would not hesitate, because "it is at least conceivable, though unlikely, that an autocratic government will exercise self-restraint; but an omnipotent democratic government simply cannot do so" (ibid., 99). Therefore, "personally, I prefer a liberal dictator to a democratic government lacking in liberalism" (*El Mercurio* 1981, D9). The latter statement is not taken from Hayek's writings but from an interview he gave the Chilean newspaper *El Mercurio* during a visit to the country in 1981 when it was under the rule of Augusto Pinochet's military dictatorship. The dictatorship followed the democratically elected government of Salvador Allende, who was ousted in 1973 and whom Hayek characterized in the same interview as driven by totalitarian aspirations. While his defenders tend to downplay the two visits to Chile, including meetings with Pinochet and his defense of the dictatorship in the interview as a misguided assessment in the heat of the political moment,[17] allegedly proving once more that theorists often show poor judgment when it comes to real-life politics, the previous quotations prove, to the contrary, that Hayek's position on Chile's supposedly liberal authoritarian regime is in fact consistent with what he writes about such regimes and the totalitarian tendencies of democracy in *The Constitution of Liberty* and elsewhere.[18]

Among the neoliberals, it is not just Hayek who attempts to distinguish categorically between totalitarianism and dictatorship or authoritarian rule. Röpke sets up the various opposites in a similar fashion, although his wording is slightly different: "If the ancient, like the modern tyrannies, are clearly different from dictatorship, it is not less false to confound them with the idea of a government that is hierarchic, aristocratic or authoritarian or to set them up as the opposites of democracy" (1942, 247).[19] After all, "every well-knit state comprises some more or less powerful elements of a hierarchic and authoritarian nature, and it would serve no useful purpose to consider as characteristic of the modern 'ochlocratic' tyranny a peculiar form of authoritarian government like dictatorship" (ibid., 246). The difference is, according to Röpke, that the "modern usurpers" have invariably "risen from the masses" and their democracy, and thus he arrives at the same conclusion as Hayek: "The antithesis of tyranny is not democracy . . . but the liberal principle" (ibid., 248).

However, Röpke gives the argument an additional twist that reminds us of a particular aspect of the liberal crisis syndrome—the war economy—which, in some aspects, resembles a regime of central planning. Röpke contends that "the introduction of an authoritarian regime, such as has now happened under the overwhelming pressure of war in the countries most involved" (1942, 248) should not mislead commentators to believe they are on the path to socialism—which is a major concern underlying Hayek's *Road to Serfdom*. "To do so in peace time would in fact carry their political and economic life irresistibly down the slippery slope of collectivist authoritarian totalitarianism" (ibid.) Röpke maintains that there is no reason to believe that the same automatism would hold for wartime authoritarianism, which apparently can be reversed once the war is over. But with this last move Röpke of course blurs the neat demarcation lines that he tried to draw earlier, which is most obvious in his reference to a decidedly undifferentiated "collectivist authoritarian totalitarianism" but also implied in his version of a slippery-slope argument that suggests there is indeed a link between authoritarianism and totalitarianism, but only during peacetime.

However, even if Röpke did not end up undermining his own discursive strategy, what is problematic about the efforts to distinguish between totalitarianism and authoritarianism is not necessarily the distinction as such, which may be a useful means of differentiating, for example, between various regimes, as in the work of Juan Linz (2000). Rather, it is the implicit *normalization* of authoritarianism taking place as if it had absolutely nothing to do with totalitarianism. Normalizing authoritarianism means that Röpke and Hayek, to choose the most prominent examples, do not just argue that not every authoritarian regime amounts to a fascist or communist totalitarianism, which is at least a defendable claim despite the difficulties of developing mutually exclusive ideal types of totalitarianism and authoritarianism. They cavalierly discount the totalitarian potential of authoritarian rule and instead highlight the respective dangers supposedly inherent in contemporary democracy, suggesting that anyone holding liberal views, broadly speaking, would be better off or at least safer under authoritarian rule. What we thus have to conclude is that at least one variety of neoliberal thought is infused with what some may consider an odd kind of liberalism, one that shows authoritarian tendencies and thus may be called "authoritarian liberalism."

Interestingly, this is the title of an essay by the German constitutional scholar Hermann Heller, first published in 1933, and his use of the term referred to the thought of another constitutional scholar from Germany, Carl Schmitt (see Heller [1933] 2015). In 1932 Schmitt gave a talk in which he gave the following explanation for the ongoing crisis of the Weimar regime: "The present German state is *total due to weakness* and lack of resistance, due to its incapacity to resist the onslaught of parties and organized interests. It must give in to everyone, please everyone and act at the pleasure of even the most contradictory interests" (Schmitt 1998, 218). Schmitt recommends a vehement effort on behalf of the state to sever ties that bind it to the economic sphere and thus depoliticize the economy and simultaneously deeconomize the state; but "a state that is to bring about this new order ought to be, as was said extraordinarily strong" (ibid., 227). It may be a stretch to characterize Schmitt's work in general as authoritarian liberalism, but Heller's term indeed sums up the essence of this particular talk, which conceptualizes authoritarian political forms and market economies as mutually enabling. It does so on an argument that bears a striking resemblance to Röpke's, Eucken's, and Hayek's ideas with regard to the strong state and authoritarianism, who, in this particular respect turn out to have at least very similar intuitions, as does Rüstow: Schmitt's talk on

November 23, 1932, was aptly titled "Strong State and Sound Economy." Rüstow's first call for a strong state can be found in a talk he gave exactly fifty-five days before, titled "Free Economy—Strong State."

Needless to say, authoritarianism poses a serious challenge to notions of pluralist democracy, and I problematize the former accordingly in the following chapter. I now simply draw some critical attention to the fundamental tension that exists between the two strategies of neoliberal state theorizing. While the one can be summed up as an attempt to limit the (nation-)state and curtail its powers through a decentering of its structure along broadly federalist lines, it would not be much of a stretch to say that the other is all about recentering the state with a premium on unity to the point of an almost monolithic state structure, that is, the strong state. While the one can be understood as a critique of nation-state sovereignty, the other seems to be driven by the need to restore state sovereignty or at least state authority. How is this tension to be interpreted? The first response might be that both strategies can exist side by side and may even complement each other. The state must be empowered to perform its positive functions and at the same time limited through decentralization to ensure it is confined to these functions. Yet this is just a restatement of the fundamental challenge that presents itself to the neoliberal theorizing of the state.

Furthermore, it does not take long to realize that the two strategies cannot comfortably exist alongside each other. One of the major reasons for a strong state is the need for an impartial enforcing agent that cannot be manipulated by the actors it seeks to regulate. But even if we assume that the state has severed the ties to, for example, economic interest groups, it can still be disciplined by them in a federal context through the threat of exiting the jurisdiction in question. In a setting structured by the competition over various capitals under conditions of extreme mobility, this is a powerful threat, and it is difficult to see how an individual jurisdiction could maintain control over the framework of its competitive order. It would seem that the possibility of regime shopping leads to anything but strong states that can regulate their markets according to ordoliberal notions or produce the public goods its citizens agreed on in a postconstitutional contract à la Buchanan. The semi-monopolist whose economic power is to be curtailed by the state as guardian of the competitive order could simply move to another jurisdiction and still sell its products in the original one, so any enterprise unhappy with the tax and regulatory regime could set up in a particular jurisdiction. The only way to keep the effects of federation from turning the idea of a strong state in economic matters into a sham would be to have the guardianship of some kind of market order migrate upward to the supranational level. This would prevent the various jurisdictions from engaging in a competition that will have overall detrimental effects for the citizens of the various jurisdictions, but this demand is hardly to be found in the neoliberal writings. While Hayek does at least mention the possibility of some supranational framework for the common market, the main emphasis is on the supranational scale enforcing freedom of movement and economic interactions, thus only intensifying competitive pressures on the various jurisdictions. Röpke is vehemently opposed to any transfer of sovereignty to the supranational level whatsoever. It must be concluded that the demands for a strong state characterized by both capacity and autonomy, to put it in the terminology of Theda Skocpol (1985), on the one hand, and the decentering of the state through federalist arrangements, on the other, represent an antinomy in neoliberal state theorizing that is ultimately un-resolvable. This is a matter we return to extensively in the context of EU politics in chapter 7, where we will see that there *is* indeed a unique way of combining the two varieties.

CHAPTER 3

Democracy

The various neoliberal positions on limiting but also enabling the state through certain constraints on its outputs, internal restructurings, and relation to its environment obviously have implications for the respective perspectives on democracy that are the subject of this chapter. Democracy is an element of neoliberal political theory that deserves a discussion on its own terms. It is of fundamental importance for contemporary political theory, and at least some of the critical remarks directed at democracy in its current institutional shape are not easily dismissed as exclusively neoliberal ideology but resonate with concerns shared across a broad political spectrum. Finally, while the discussion of the state focused on rules, principles, and structural issues, an investigation of neoliberal views on democracy also shifts the emphasis from these rather static elements to the dynamics of (democratic) political life and the various actors that populate and dominate it.

I begin with the common denominator of neoliberal accounts of democracy—that it is a problem for functioning markets—and then highlight what I consider the two core contentions that structure the spectrum of various critical diagnoses. The first focuses on the pluralist aspect of contemporary democracy; the other, on the alleged excess of power accruing to democracy in its contemporary form. Both contentions are far from incompatible, but certain neoliberal positions lean more toward one side than the other, while others rest on both contentions in almost equal measure, which they consider as two sides of the same coin. Based on this survey of various diagnoses, I briefly look at the main damage that democracy supposedly does, according to the different interpretations, and discuss the various remedies proposed to alleviate the alleged pathologies of democracy. Here the varieties of neoliberal thought on democracy are most pronounced, with recommendations ranging from extending the sphere of markets at the expense of democratic decision making to introducing more direct democratic elements and thus complementing existing institutional arrangements.

Democracy and Its Problems: Majoritarianism and Limitlessness

Simply put, the common denominator of all neoliberal views on democracy is the conviction that it poses a more or less serious problem. It is a problem insofar as its mechanisms complicate the already challenging task of conceptualizing the proper role of the state in its relation to markets and society; but it also, more fundamentally, has the potential to plunge societies into chaos and/or transform them into machineries of massive exploitation and repression that ultimately come to resemble the collectivisms that the neoliberals so vehemently oppose. This is not to suggest that all of the perspectives discussed here demand the abolition of democracy, although some of the options seem to come close to it. But even those accounts that are, overall, most favorably inclined to democratic decision making offer trenchant critiques of democracy's (potential) pathologies that must be addressed to avoid dramatic consequences.

The first issue in need of clarification is what exactly "democracy" signifies in neoliberal discourse. The object of the neoliberal critique throughout is democracy in its *representative* variant, which obviously does not make the neoliberals unqualified supporters of the nonrepresentative version; in most cases this is assumed to make matters even worse. The point is that neoliberal critique indeed aims at democracy in its actually existing or predominant form as the various thinkers conceive of it. While other aspects of neoliberal thought are abstract and decontextualized—from Buchanan's models and formulas to Eucken's ideal types of economic orders—the discourse on democracy is almost always contextualized; it is not an engagement with theories of democracy but a diagnostic aimed at concrete democracies, their actual functioning and respective shortcomings.

In my reading, the neoliberal discourse on the problems of democracy is structured around two poles between which a spectrum of positions exists.[1] The first of these poles is best summed up with reference to the positions of Hayek, Friedman, and Buchanan and is constituted by two interrelated points. Hayek sums up both most succinctly by mobilizing another pair of opposites—or at least nonidentical phenomena—to make his case against contemporary democracy. On the one hand, he states, is the principle of constitutionalism; on the other is what he views as the contemporary understanding of democracy as "a form of government where the will of the majority on any particular matter is unlimited" (Hayek 2003, 1:1). There are two separate points to this, the *unlimited power* of democratic government and the *rule of majorities*, but before we take a closer look, we first examine Hayek's argumentative strategy.

While the neoliberal critique of democratic practices and institutions is almost always concrete, a crucial resource the critique makes use of is some kind of alternative account, which may be an abstract ideal that is nevertheless considered to have been implemented at least to a certain degree in the historical past, as demonstrated by Hayek. His framing of the problem is a narrative of decline operating analogously to the ones regarding liberalism and the rule of law that we have already encountered. In other words, Hayek is careful not to be painted into an unequivocally antidemocratic corner and casts himself as a supporter of "the basic ideal of democracy" (2003, 2:2), which, however, has become gravely distorted in its contemporary manifestations. The most pernicious distortion has given rise to the belief in democratic government as unlimited, which is not surprising in light of what we already know of Hayek's conceptualization of the rule of law and its decline.

But now we get a clearer of view of the historical developments and faulty assumptions he blames for this deterioration of democratic practices up to the current point. Both can be summed up in the notion of parliamentary sovereignty. For Hayek, this principle represents the various facets of democracy's decline. With the shift to democracy it was no longer considered important to have checks and balances or other limitations on government, contends Hayek, thus reproducing a familiar *topos* in the critical liberal discourse on democracy found also in Mill and others: the naïve belief that as long as "the people" rule, there is no need for other safeguards against the abuse of power. But even if the people were to make wrong or at least ill-advised decisions, the democratic doctrine would have been at a loss in attempting to rein in the popular will expressed in parliamentary decisions because it is tied to a misconception of sovereignty, according to Hayek. We must not dwell too long on this particular topic I have discussed more extensively elsewhere (see Biebricher 2014), but let us at least note that one of the multiple layers in Hayek's critique of democracy is a critique of a certain understanding of sovereignty. The notion that "there must always exist an ultimate 'sovereign' source of power from which law derives" is no more than a "sophism" that informs the democratic self-aggrandizement (Hayek 2003, 1:28), which contends that parliamentary sovereignty by definition cannot be held in check because then parliament would not be truly sovereign. But this is to misconstrue the matter in Hayek's view because in a constitutionalist setting sovereignty is not located in any one place; as a matter of fact, it disappears. "If it be asked where under such an arrangement 'sovereignty' rests, the answer is nowhere—unless it temporarily resides in the hands of the constitution-making or constitution-amending body. Since constitutional government is limited government there can be no room in it for a sovereign body if sovereignty is defined as unlimited power" (ibid., 2:123). For Hayek, "sovereignty," as it is commonly used, is a metaphysical concept, which may be an accurate assessment, but it is still doubtful whether it can be simply conjured away as he suggests.[2]

To summarize, the combination of trust in the inability of democracy to do any harm to the people with a mistaken view on sovereignty and increased governing through legislatures leads to the conviction that "the representative assembly is not only the highest but also an unlimited authority" that cannot and must not be curtailed in its reach (Hayek 2003, 2:3). Furthermore, and this is already familiar terrain for us, it has immunized itself against any attempts at limiting it to certain forms of action—that is, the rule of law—by moving from the (properly democratic) view that "only what is approved by the majority should be binding for all, to the belief that all that the majority approves shall have that force" (ibid., 6). With these shifts, the wheels are set in motion toward the slow but steady transformation of contemporary democracies into totalitarian societies, which prompts Hayek to submit "that if democracy is taken to mean government by the unrestricted will of the majority I am not a democrat" (ibid., 39). And as is befitting for someone who had a keen sense of the power inherent in language and particular terms, Hayek proposes that true democracy should be renamed "demarchy," which is the "ideal of an equal law for all" (ibid., 40), thus avoiding the confusions in our politico-economic language he sees looming in this and many other cases.

Buchanan and Friedman share these Hayekian grievances to a large degree, albeit with slightly differing nuances and emphases. Buchanan's concern over a democratic state/government cutting the ties through which it could be controlled and held accountable only intensifies over the course of his oeuvre. Starting from a public-choice perspective that rigidly applied methodological individualism to the government and state apparatuses, Buchanan conceptualized all of these as strictly interpersonal relations, thus almost dissolving government and state into the former: "'Government' as such, cannot exist, and 'governmental outcomes' may exhibit relatively little internal consistency or stability" (Brennan and Buchanan 1980, 29). This makes for all kinds of dysfunctionalities, such as massive incoherence of government policy, but from the analyses of public-choice theorists emerged an archipelago-like image of the state that made it rather implausible to harbor fears about its transformation into a totalitarian state subjecting society to its will.

This changes with Buchanan's switch to the concept of Leviathan in the early 1980s. Up to that point, Buchanan had concurred with the public-choice mainstream that the motive of securing reelection on behalf of politicians in a democracy constrained these political actors to a significant degree. This does not mean that the outcomes were necessarily "efficient"; yet the state could hardly be considered despotic, but neither was it to be seen as a benevolent guardian of the common good. It is only the latter assumption that is retained in the framework of Leviathan. The Leviathan state is analyzed as if it were a monolithic kind of government. Of course, this creates problems for a methodological individualist such as Buchanan, who even admits a "methodological 'leap to Leviathan'" (Brennan and Buchanan 1980, 30), which he still maintains to be a defendable one. None of the elected and unelected state personnel has any intention of further-ing Leviathan's interest (or the public's), but the resultant of all individual actions always points in the same direction: the urge to maximize revenue. Leviathan has thus inherently expansive tendencies, and Buchanan concludes that this dynamic is no longer effectively curtailed by electoral controls; an increasingly unaccountable democracy with unlimited power thus turns into Leviathan (see Buchanan 1975, 161).

But Buchanan also shares Hayek's reservations regarding the majority principle, as does Friedman. To a certain extent, the arguments are all varia-tions on the theme of a looming "tyranny of the majority," well known from any number of liberal and conservative critiques of democracy. Hayek insists on the will of the majority to be expressed in abstract rules only, but he also emphasizes that "the argument for democracy presupposes that any minority opinion may become a majority one" and opposes strongly the idea that just because a particular opinion has the backing of 51 percent of the people, it must be considered better or superior to others. If anything, Hayek states, they are likely to be inferior to those that "the most intelligent members of the group will make after listening to all opinions" (2009, 96), not least because majority decisions will often contain compromises made to gain that majority. However, he believes that if there is anything to be said in favor of democracy, then it is the fact that built into it is an institutionalized competition of opinions in which minorities may eventually even convince the majority. Hayek assumes that only through such small dissenting elites are societies as a whole exposed to new ideas and over time advance. Ac-cording to Hayek, this is, of course, hampered by a notion of democracy that fetishizes the majority principle. Moreover, all three thinkers problematize the basic experience of being outvoted and relegated to a minority that has to comply with the majority's decision on a certain matter.

Hayek's concerns are fueled by the value subjectivism he inherits from the marginalist Austrian Carl Menger, leading him to the conclusion that democratic decision making had best confine itself to matters on which there is substantive agreement in the electorate. Buchanan's reservations are based on the Wicksellian point that the unanimity rule would ensure a Pareto optimum in political decision making because no policy could be adopted that would not improve some or all positions, or at least not do any damage.[3] Normatively speaking, this would be the ideal rule for politics, and it is only for reasons of feasibility that Buchanan accepts the majority principle, reluctantly acknowledging "the normative strength that majority rule has in public attitudes" (Buchanan and Musgrave 1999, 118). Friedman makes his case against majority decision making that subjects the minority to "conformity" by explicitly juxtaposing it to markets where one is never outvoted. "That is why it is desirable to use the ballot box, so far as possible, only for those decisions where conformity is essential" (Friedman and Friedman 1990, 66). Implicit in this statement is a suggestion about how the deficiencies of democratic decision making may be overcome: through the use of markets, discussed in more detail later.

I conclude the exposition of this pole of the neoliberal critique of democracy by noting some broad similarities between the points raised here and critiques of democracy voiced from the other end of the political spectrum that concern especially the legitimacy of the majority principle. Claus Offe, to choose but one prominent example, has shown that the majority principle involves a number of inherent problems and is premised on a number of preconditions in order to be normatively acceptable (see Guggenberger and Offe 1984). One of the inherent difficulties is the problem of quantitative decision-making procedures being unable to account for the *quality* of the votes—the intensity of the preference expressed in them. Should a majority of 52 percent with hardly a real interest in a particular matter really be able to force their decision on a minority of 48 percent who passionately disagree? One of the fundamental preconditions is similar to the point made by Hayek previously: A minority that has no chance of ever becoming the majority (e.g., "structural minorities") can legitimately contest the use of the majority principle in regard to their rights. Similarly, all decisions that would be irreversible or only reversible at prohibitively high costs should in principle not be made according to the majority principle, because even if the current minority opinion becomes the majority, the original decision cannot actually be reversed. My point is simply that the critique of the majority principle in itself is not an exclusive concern for neoliberals, and there is even a degree of overlap, albeit a very small one, between the reasons given, for example, by Buchanan or Offe to support this critique. However, while there may be agreement that something is problematic about the majority principle or its preconditions, the conclusions drawn and remedies prompted by this diagnosis differ fundamentally.

Let us turn to the other core contention of the neoliberal critique of democracy, which we glimpsed in the previous discussion of the strong state, and now it becomes clear that what actually stands in the way of such a state is democracy, or at least a certain kind of democracy. The fundamental problem raised by this variety of criticism is the *pluralism* of contemporary democracy, the undue influence of actors pursuing particularistic interests in the political process and the distortions that result from this influence. The most vivid descriptions of the problem are found—as so often—in the ordoliberal accounts. Rüstow refers to the "pathological form of government . . . of pluralism" and the "decay of democracy" as the "state which begins to feed the beasts of organized business interests will finally be devoured by them" (1942, 277). Similarly, Röpke sees the "state become plaything and prey of the vested interests" and predicts that the "struggle among group interests . . . leads to the disintegration of the state" (1950b, 130–131). And not just interest groups but also parliamentary parties are to blame since they were transformed into "parliamentary agencies of economic pressure groups and were financed by them" (Rüstow 1942, 276), thus acting as relays for the demands of the former.

Eucken echoes the overall diagnosis, which for him is particularly worrisome because of the collusion of economic and political power bound to undermine the competitive order as economic power is translated into political influence, possibly leading even to political dependence on economic power: "Economic policy by the state and the representation of business interests here blend into a tightly coordinated unity" (2017a, 57). Eucken is an interesting case because contemporary defenders of ordoliberalism place a high premium on saving him from the charge of harboring antidemocratic sentiments. I have already described two strategies of exculpation with regard to the strong state. With regard to democracy, the most recent arguments defending Eucken are found in Viktor Vanberg (2014) and Daniel Nientiedt and Ekkehard Köhler (2016). Vanberg mostly reiterates the usual arguments softening the demand for a strong state, but even the former director of the Walter Eucken Institute expresses some skepticism with regard to Eucken's democratic bona fides. Nientiedt and Köhler resort to a different argument, according to which Eucken objected mostly to a particular kind of democracy, an identitarian one along the lines of Schmitt and Rousseau, exemplified in the economic state that merges state, society, and economy (2016, 1749). This is hardly a convincing interpretation because what Eucken objects to is the expression and furtherance of particularistic socioeconomic interests by private and state actors, which is typically described as pluralism. Note also that Carl Schmitt, in the talk mentioned previously and in *The Concept of the Political* (1932), describes and laments exactly the same processes that Eucken sums up under the term "economic state," which therefore could hardly characterize an identitarian democracy as Schmitt viewed and espoused it.

Another important factor suggesting that Eucken, in certain respects, is closer to Rousseau's and Hegel's views of state and democracy is that he clearly views the state as a potential guarantor of the common good, the general will that must prevail over particularistic wills, to use the vocabulary of Rousseau. Is this not exactly why the state has to free itself from the influence of various socioeconomic actors and the political parties that they steer like parliamentary puppets to further their necessarily *particularistic* interests? It is this thoroughly Hegelian task of the state defending the general interest against the antinomies of social life that elevates what it does, and thus also public power used in the process, to a different normative status, which is the answer to the question why state power is normatively different from private/economic power raised earlier.[4] Clearly, the general interest is hardly as substantive in Eucken as it can be made out in certain readings of Rousseau or Hegel; it solely pertains to the maintenance of the competitive order, which is in everyone's best interest—just not as Rousseau's *citoyen* but as a *consumer*. Did Eucken's views change after the war, as one of the apologia narratives states with regard to the strong state? It is hard to tell, because as Nientiedt and Köhler note, democracy is simply never mentioned in the postwar writings, which I find rather telling.[5] This is not to suggest that Eucken was simply an antidemocrat but that he was deeply skeptical of a pluralist understanding of democracy. Such an understanding does not demand that private actors or political parties pass a litmus test of acting only in the general interest—whatever it may be—but principally affords even the narrow-minded pursuit of particularistic interests prima facie legitimacy and thus conveys a decidedly liberal, but apparently not a very *ordo*liberal, understanding of democracy.[6]

In the ordoliberal, especially Eucken's, version of the argument against pluralism an additional and final factor comes into play that we should note, not least because of its significance for the various remedies suggested to cure the ills of democracy. Modern democracy is not only pluralist; it is also mass democracy. Groups pursue particular interests contrary to the general interest per se, but the masses are also a part of these endeavors in some way (see Eucken 2017a, 59). The problem is that the masses are not well equipped to comprehend the intricacies of either governmental order in general or economic policy in particular. Moreover, according to Eucken, who is the most adamant elitist among the ordoliberals, there is a "destructive power" to the masses, which tends toward "destroying especially those orders that actually function" (1960, 16, 14). For Röpke and Rüstow "massification" is also a key concept, but while they associate a number of social pathologies with the masses, they are much less inclined to suggest that the masses are epistemologically unfit to form a coherent and even reasonable political will (see, however, Rüstow 2009, 34). Although Röpke attributes such an "intellectual regression" only to "mass as an acute state" (1960, 53), mass as a "chronic state," which he analyzes with reference to José Ortega y Gasset's *Revolt of the Masses*, still poses dangers. Uprooted and estranged "mass man" is easy prey for demagoguery, propaganda, and advertisement and thus may still be turned into the pawn of some mischievous politico-economic cause, especially if the condition of massification becomes permanent (ibid., 56). Democracy, in sum, is likely to produce dysfunctional and even irrational political output/outcomes, and at its worst it turns into a catalyst for collectivist transformations.

While part of the problem of the pluralism the ordoliberals criticize is the *irrationality* of the masses, who may even be swayed to act against their own presumed best interests (i.e., a well-ordered economic sphere), the more contemporary version of the argument is concerned instead with the very *rationality* of actors ultimately leading to the decline of pluralist democracy. What I am referring to is the theorem of *rent seeking*, the basic logic of which is no different from the ordoliberal argument, albeit without the invocation of the state as the guardian of the common good to which, for example, Buchanan is vehemently opposed, and on the basis of a much more rigorous formalization through a model of human behavior. I briefly introduce this now notorious behavioral model of *homo economicus* before I return to it in a more extensive discussion later. The theoretical groundwork of Buchanan (and to a lesser degree, Friedman and Hayek) rests heavily on *homo economicus* as a rational utility maximizer and the application of this model to bureaucratic and democratic politics.

This application leads to a constellation in which private individuals and organized interests have a strong incentive to demand some kind of special treatment or an exemption from the rules (because individual utility is maximized if everyone else has to follow rules we do not have to follow ourselves) and accordingly approach the political system with such demands for "rents." On the supply side of the market for rents in a democracy are politicians eager to be reelected and thus incentivized to offer rents in return for presumed electoral allegiance from the respective groups/organizations that benefit from preferential treatment. What is problematic about this market on which, it seems, supply and demand for rents match in a happy equilibrium?

Buchanan raises two critical points against the "rent-seeking society" (Buchanan, Tollison, and Tullock 1980) that are of equal importance for his account of democracy. First, rent seeking is a classic case of individual versus collective rationality/efficiency: Along the basic lines of a prisoner's dilemma a (collective) actor in a democracy has to assume that other actors will lobby for their particular interests, which is likely to affect the first actor adversely, if only indirectly; that is, it is worse off, relatively speaking, if others gain some preferential treatment. If each actor acts rationally on an individual basis, then the outcome will be exactly what the ordoliberals have already decried, a political system besieged by special interests that clamor for improvements of their situation. Obviously, this description is easily articulable with the discourse on "ungovernability" that became a crucial *topos* in the neoconservative discourses of the 1970s and early 1980s in both North America and parts of Europe (see Crozier, Huntington, and Watanuki 1975; Offe 1984). An unruly and renitent post-1968 population that lacks the discipline and ego strength of former generations in the heroic age of capitalism demands more and more favors from the state and is less and less prepared to comply with societal rules.[7]

But apart from these neoconservative interpretations, the problem according to Buchanan is rather that individually rational behavior ends up creating a situation in which almost everyone is worse off than before, because even if they all get what they lobbied for, they will be put at a disadvantage in regard to every other group or category that receives some kind of rent. So if the rational-choice calculus is applied rigorously, it turns out that everyone is being hurt by pursuing his or her individual interest. Importantly, the main thrust of the argument is not directed at the selfishness of interest groups in the name of some common good. Rather, the logic of the situation, in which everyone has to assume that others are lobbying on behalf of their own group or organization, makes it imperative to seek to influence the political process if one is not to be put at a disadvantage through the relative improvement for others. While everyone would be better off not lobbying at all, it is a requirement of rationality to engage in it, if only prophylactically.

Thus, according to this reasoning, a rent-seeking democracy is inefficient and even more so to the extent that it is transformed into the model of Leviathan we are already familiar with: a government determined and able to raise revenue continually to increase the surplus that remains after all the public goods for society have been produced or paid for so it has financial resources at its disposal to finance genuine rents, thus burdening citizens with excessive taxes.

While the first problem of rent-seeking democracy has an almost tragic aspect to it, Buchanan's second line of critique points to straightforward exploitation through externalization, and there is nothing "tragic" about it in Buchanan's view. Who exploits whom? It is, first, political actors, both individual and collective (i.e., political parties), that exploit citizen taxpayers. Buchanan radically questions the power to tax and argues that as long as there is no earmarking of revenue raised and citizens cannot be sure that it is used for the production of public goods, it is hardly different from straightforward expropriation. How is this linked to an externalizing logic?

One way of describing the rent-seeking constellation is to liken it to a deal between electorally relevant social categories or organizations and political parties, in which the former trade votes and electoral support for rents that, most of the time, come at a cost. It is a deal that works for both sides, not least because, according to Buchanan, the costs are externalized and borne by the tax-paying citizenry. In light of these elaborations it becomes clear that the diagnosis of a "tyranny of the *majority*" as the crucial problem of democracy is at least ambiguous if not misleading. After all, according to Friedman, the (parliamentary) majority is actually "a majority composed of a coalition of minorities" (Friedman and Friedman 1984, 52) down to individual politicians who act as mutual enablers of generating rents through logrolling, vote swapping, and hammering out compromises. Moreover, which nonparliamentary groups are most likely to benefit most from rent seeking? Again, it is Friedman who makes the point, relying partly on Mancur Olsen's arguments from *The Logic of Collective Action*.

Small groups and minorities are seemingly weak, but they may actually be at an advantage in lobbying efforts. They are much easier to organize because they tend to be more homogeneous, and monitoring individual effort on behalf of the group is easier than in large heterogeneous groups. Furthermore, the smaller the group, the larger the individual spoils and, conversely, in case of reforms that threaten certain "privileges," the worse the damage: "But the minorities specially affected have strong incentives to mount a propaganda barrage to assure that the majority are not well informed" (Friedman and Friedman 1984, 7). Democracy amounts to the exploitation of the many by the few, is the irritatingly Marxist-sounding first conclusion of this line of critique. Exploitation in Marx's account was, among other things, based on a deceptive arrangement in which workers presumably were paid the equivalent of their labor power. Exploitation in Buchanan's account is also based on a deceptive arrangement called general taxation, and it works better the larger the population across which the costs can be spread, because invisibly small increases in the individual tax burden will already generate massive surpluses (which is, incidentally, another reason why Buchanan is opposed to the power to tax for supranational federations).

However, externalization of rent costs through taxation is still not the gravest problem democracy in its currently existing form generates, because as undetectable as a small tax hike may be for the average person, one would assume that people will eventually realize that tax volumes keep rising and will wonder why this is happening or will simply not vote for the government in the next election. In other words, the government has to resort to a more elegant form of deception about the costs of rents, which is also an externalization, and in this operation future generations are the victims of exploitation. This is of course just another way of saying that the smoothest way of financing rents is not through taxation but through running deficits and accumulating debt, possibly in combination with a mild degree of inflation, which tends to reduce both the real value of the debt owed and the real (financial) value of rents for groups. The lack of representation of future generations in present democratic decision-making processes is a perennial problem for democracies because the basic principle of autonomy, which requires that those affected by decisions and rules must have a say in the respective will-formation processes, is inevitably violated through debt or any other decision that has an effect on posterity, such as the decision to use nuclear power.

But Buchanan would probably argue that in the case of public debt, it is not a matter of an occasional exception to the principle of autonomy but a systematic and continuous practice of shifting financial burdens toward future generations. This directs the critical attention to a final profound deficiency of democracy, the short time horizon of democratic decision making. If it is indeed rational for politicians to think about the next election and radically discount any other effect decisions may have far beyond that temporal horizon, democracy is necessarily plagued by chronic short, termism, unable to develop and pursue long-term policies. We do not have to draw on public finance to see that this concern is pertinent, but we can point to climate change and the loss of biodiversity as problems that present almost insurmountable problems in the framework of democratic decision making as Buchanan describes it—and for the time being, the empirical facts unfortunately seem to be on his side in this regard. Whether we view this as a willful exploitation of nature and future generations who are deprived of living conditions similar to ours or to an almost tragic shortsightedness that is the aggregate result of seemingly rational individual behavior (there is at least a measure of rationality in discounting future effects because tomorrow an asteroid could hit the earth), the rent-seeking democracy is prone to producing normatively and functionally questionable outcomes, as long as it is not effectively curtailed in its seemingly unlimited Leviathan power, which is the link between the two poles of the discussion. Pluralism and rent seeking are phenomena that also occur in "limited democracies," as Hayek calls them; conversely, while a government may have in principle unlimited power, it may not necessarily make use of it to the full effect—at least this is what Hayek hopes. However, the combination of rent seeking and unlimited governmental power in a democracy leads to a spiral of ever more demands and ever more output. Although this would seem to characterize a responsive democracy, the neoliberals are convinced that it will have the various devastating consequences just sketched, not just for markets and their viability—although this remains the focus of the critique along the lines of the neoliberal problematic—but for the future of society and the world more generally.

Who are the culprits in the various accounts? Eucken and to a lesser degree Röpke would probably argue that, to a more or less significant extent, it is the masses that turn (pluralist) democracy into such a dangerous and rather dysfunctional governing arrangement; thus, they place themselves in a long tradition of rather conservative worries about some kind of "mob rule" or, to put it in more refined terms, ochlocracy. However, this is not the main thrust of the critique concerning the political actors that populate democracies, because Eucken and Röpke's more or less pronounced elitism suggests to them that, more often than not, the masses are the mostly passive object, not the subject, of political projects, thus echoing the claims of elite theorists such as their contemporaries Vilfredo Pareto or Gaetano Mosca, who attributed no independent political agency to the masses. The problem lies, rather, with interest groups of all kinds who seek to influence the political process on their behalf. By the same token it is political parties who are portrayed as either the parliamentary arm of lobby groups or a cartel of gatekeepers who have monopolized the process of political will formation and are thus in a unique position to benefit from the rent-seeking game down to the individual politician. It is—and this is an assessment that is shared by all neoliberals discussed here—relatively small groups who benefit at the expense of a large majority or the "common good," in the vocabulary of the ordoliberals.

In my view, this is a point worth noting, not only because this general diagnosis can easily be articulated with an antiestablishment populist project, but it also resembles in certain aspects a much more left-leaning critique of actually existing liberal democracy. To be sure, when those neoliberals who subscribe to these arguments make the point that minorities benefit at the expense of majorities, this can of course refer to groups who receive transfers through some kind of social policy financed by a majority, and it can also refer to policies of "affirmative action" that seek to improve access and inclusion for minorities. However, it seems to me that a generic leftist criticism of political parties acting as the parliamentary arm of Wall Street, trading haphazard regulation of financial markets for campaign donations and thus affording relatively small but powerful organizations, or one might even say a small financial elite, massive influence in the political process, is also easily accommodated by the neoliberal critique of rent seeking. More generally, it would probably be difficult to find anyone who is not more or less concerned about the political influence of lobby organizations, whether located on K Street in Washington or in close proximity to the EU institutions in Brussels. This does not imply that I find this line of critique entirely convincing and normatively acceptable, but at the same time, I find it hard to dismiss the concerns underlying it as completely unwarranted and mistaken. In other words, the sheer fact that the criticism comes from neoliberals does not automatically make it wrong. Still, what may give even those who are not dogmatically opposed to neoliberal thought more pause are the suggestions put forward in response to the normative and functional deficiencies that neoliberals detect, to which we now turn.

Dealing with Democracy: Between Restriction and Complementation

The first of four somewhat synthesized options to deal with the problems of democracy, introducing restrictions on state output and respective transformations of state structure, has already been discussed: most important are Hayek's rule of law and Buchanan's balanced-budget rule. With regard to Hayek, from a democratic perspective the problem is, first and foremost, that he pits popular sovereignty against the rule of law in a zero-sum constellation. To the extent that popular sovereignty asserts itself, the rule of law is diminished, and vice versa. This fundamental assumption leaves

Hayek unable to see the conceptual possibility that the relation between the two principles is not conflictual but is one of mutual presuppositions, as argued by Jürgen Habermas (1992), among others. In this interpretation, only a democratic opinion and will-formation process structured by the rule of law is a truly democratic one, and only those rules that a populace has given itself, or at least had a say in, can be just in the sense of the rule of law. Obviously, this conciliatory reconceptualization comes with its own problems, but, as stated very early on, the criticism of neoliberal theses must not be entirely confined to an immanent critique that accepts the neoliberal frame of reference. At times, it must also confront neoliberal positions with alternatives to throw into relief assumptions that have been taken for granted and reveal ensuing blindspots.

But the problem with Hayek's position is not just the conceptualization of the rule of law versus popular sovereignty but also the impression that he aims to marginalize one at the expense of the other. As we know, Hayek endorses the "basic ideal" of democracy, but it is doubtful what this ideal entails in light of his efforts to construct a Procrustean bed for democratically legitimated state action. Moreover, his characterization of demarchy as the normatively desirable form of democracy as "equal law for all" seems to add little to the requirement contained in his notion of the rule of law. In other words and contrary to what Habermas would argue, the modalities of the process out of which this *isonomia* emerges and to what extent the citizenry is involved hardly figures in this ideal.

James Buchanan's idea is to rein in the accrual of deficits and debt in order to finance rents with a balanced-budget amendment (possibly in combination with a federal reshaping of state structures). I have already problematized the potential rigidity of such a rule, but from a democratic point of view two other issues must be raised. First, remember that public debt can be interpreted as a shifting of financial obligations to future generations subject to the effects of a decision in which they had no say, so the problem is one of democratic representation. This seems plausible enough at first glance and can be easily moralized, as political and public discourse proves, with the recurring trope of "burdening our children and grandchildren with debt"—what person could support such a practice? It is not my intention to trivialize the issue of public debt but to add some important qualifiers to the argument that raise doubts about whether it is really a clear case of intergenerational misrepresentation. We must note the basic fact that wherever there is debt, there is someone holding that debt. What this means is that our children and grandchildren do not just inherit public debt; we also bequeath the bonds that correspond to these debts to them.

This makes the matter far more complicated because the argument about democratic misrepresentation rests on the following reasoning: Nonpresent persons need advocates who represent their needs and interests, but in the case of persons not yet born, these interests are difficult to ascertain. Yet we can safely assume that, ceteris paribus, they do not want to be born into debt bondage. Even if we accept this presumed interest, only a certain part of the future population will be opposed to accruing debt in the present; those who inherit the bonds cannot be attributed with an unequivocal interest in terminating a practice that they benefit from financially. The matter is thus turned from a generational conflict into a matter of class. Furthermore, the ceteris paribus condition does not hold in regard to the issue of debt and future generations. While members of future generations presumably would prefer not to be burdened with debt, the question is whether this attitude remains unchanged if the curtailment of public debt also implies, for example, a drastic reduction in investment in public infrastructure. Obviously, Buchanan's rebuttal would point out that there is no guarantee that money is spent to build infrastructure rather than to placate powerful interest groups or even to engage in veiled Keynesian politics of raising aggregate demand through public investment. The problem is that these distinctions are difficult to make because investment in public infrastructure may be all of these things at the same time; thus, it is difficult to write an exemption for public investment into the amendment that might not be turned into a loophole (see Buchanan 1997b, 132–133). This means, at the very least, that the presumed interests of future generations are less straightforward than they would seem, because an interest in no debt has to be articulated with an equally plausible interest in public infrastructure—which those future generations will have to rely on to some degree even if they can afford private services.

The second argument for the democratic merits of the amendment relates to effective popular sovereignty. What use is democratic autonomy, Buchanan may ask, if the power to choose politics that the citizenry endorses is undercut by a lack of financial resources to implement them? Or, even worse, what becomes of popular sovereignty when the threat of national default forces democracies to accept financial support through the IMF, World Bank, or the European Troika that comes with conditions that are largely nonnegotiable and override the likely discontent of citizens? Obviously, this point cannot simply be dismissed, if only because of the striking empirical examples of any number of countries that struggle with more or less serious sovereign debt crises. Nevertheless, while excessive debt is likely to cause such problems (not in each and every case, though, as the United States proves), deficits and debt in general are not, as proved by a brief look at the world around us in which they are the norm and do not inhibit democratic sovereignty. Again, this is not to trivialize public debt but to dedramatize it so it cannot be mobilized as a knock-down argument for an amendment that, in itself, is very likely to hamper democratic sovereignty. Such an amendment would deprive the state of financial resources needed to pursue certain political projects and instead prescribe rigorous expenditure cuts, that is, a state of permanent austerity. Buchanan would probably respond that this means to jump to conclusions because his version of the amendment simply stipulates that all expenditures need to be financed through taxes; therefore, the alternative to expenditure cuts is to raise taxes. However, this is hardly a convincing stance for a public-choice theorist, whose crucial point is that raising taxes comes close to political suicide in a democracy, which is the main reason that financing state outlays through deficits and inflation, which are not as easily detectable and more diffuse in their "cost" than taxes, is so much more attractive. If interpreted on the basis of Buchanan's own assumption, the balanced-budget amendment means de facto austerity politics and thus radically circumscribes democratic autonomy.

The last point builds on this conclusion regarding the likely effects of the amendment and concerns the question whether this is a matter to be codified on a constitutional level. What are the intentions behind the demand to enshrine a certain norm in the constitution? Most important, the constitutionalization of a norm manifests an attempt at depoliticizing a certain issue by codifying a respective norm on the highest and most durable level of juridical rules. To be sure, constitutional rules are still subject to controversy and conflicting interpretations, as the balanced-budget amendment would be, but the instrument itself is permanent; it cannot be removed through a simple parliamentary majority or an executive order. Therefore, to a large degree, its very existence is taken off the table of democratic contestation; thus, one could argue that constitutionalization equals decontestation. This is, of course, exactly the rationale behind Buchanan and others' demand that public finances need to be removed from democratic politics, at least to a certain degree, if they are not to be misused for rent-seeking purposes. However, the success of such a decontestation also rests on the issue/norm at stake being sufficiently uncontroversial and formulated at a relative high degree of abstraction. Is the amendment a norm that lends itself to successful and legitimate depoliticization?

As we already know, Buchanan argues that the formal character of the amendment ensures that no substantive economic policy is written into the constitution, but in light of what has been just argued concerning its likely austerity effects, this seems rather questionable. Furthermore, what kinds of political issues can be legitimately removed from democratic contestations because of the poor policy output this may produce? The strongest case for the depoliticization of certain issues through various forms of delegation (to institutions, agencies, or constitutions) has been made by Giandomenico Majone (1994), who bases his argument on a distinction between regulatory and redistributive politics. While the latter obviously produces winners and losers, the former supposedly provides Pareto-efficient solutions, for example, through the introduction of common product standards or a common currency policy that benefits everyone involved or at least puts no one at a disadvantage. These issues can and should be removed from majoritarian institutions, then, because they are in this sense sufficiently uncontroversial. The problem with the balanced-budget amendment is that it is impossible to portray it as a form of regulatory politics because it has many redistributive effects; therefore, even someone as sympathetic to a beneficial depoliticization as Majone would undoubtedly argue that this is a policy in need of continued democratic legitimation that must not be removed from the field of contestation. We revisit this issue in the context of the current European austerity regime but now turn to the remaining neoliberal options for remedying the ills of democracy.

The cliché understanding of neoliberalism suggests that its monotonous response to the problems of democracy is to strive for a replacement of its institutions and processes through market coordination. This is far from the only response on offer from neoliberal thinkers, but like many clichés this one also contains a kernel of truth, as the argument about the superiority of markets does occasionally surface, but it is much more nuanced than one might expect. We are already familiar with what is perhaps the strongest endorsement of markets in regard to democracy: Friedman's point that markets offer unanimity without conformity, while the opposite is supposed to be true for democracy. Let us examine the respective arguments more closely.

One way of making the case for the market is to describe it as superior with regard to the efficiency of preference transmission. In political markets "you almost always vote for a package rather than for specific items" (Friedman and Friedman 1990, 65). Furthermore, if you vote for one party or person, you cannot vote for another one as well, whereas in a market you could split the money you spend between various goods. Most important, you might cast a vote for the losing party or candidate and in an even more fundamental way may not get what you want because you are part of the minority, while in the market "a dollar vote is never overruled" (Buchanan 1954, 339). Aside from this set of issues, democracy may also produce decisions of inferior (individual) rationality because of the nature of its choice process. This argument can be traced back to Schumpeter's realist theory of democracy and points to the relative weight of the individual vote and the ensuing incentives to make an informed choice. After all, the value of anyone's vote in a mass democracy is infinitesimally small because it is exceedingly unlikely that it will be the decisive one. Given that it has such little value, why would anyone incur the costs of informing themselves when this does not increase the value of the vote, and why would citizens ultimately vote at all? However, markets require decisions and place the entire responsibility for them on the individual; therefore, an informed choice "pays off" (see ibid., 337). Finally, Buchanan also points out the deficits of democratic markets concerning the accountability of producers and the ability of citizens to control them effectively, because "political competition is intermittent" while the market is a continuous tribunal (1991, 97).

It would seem, then, that the support for markets as the more perfect democracy might follow directly from this juxtaposition of two coordinating mechanisms. Nevertheless, while Friedman favors market coordination over minority-producing democracies, even he assumes that there are matters in which conformity is essential, and "it is desirable to use the ballot box, so far as possible, only for those decisions" (Friedman and Friedman 1990, 66). In the case of Buchanan, who offers the most systematic comparison of both choice settings, all of the points just mentioned figure in the column of the market as well, but he also introduces some caveats about market choices, which are not likely to produce "greater *social* rationality" (1954, 341). Neither does he support a wholesale shift of matters to the market but offers only considerations about various reasons to explain why some matters should be decided in some but not other settings. He notes that in a democracy, "voting choice provides individuals with a greater sense of participation in social decision-making, and, in this way it may bring forth the 'best' in man and tends to make individuals take somewhat more account of the public interest" (ibid.). This is a rather surprising appraisal of the "republican" aspects in democratic decision making, but it would be too easy to attribute it solely to the immaturity of the young Buchanan of 1954, not yet sobered in his views by the radical realism of public-choice theory, as the following sections will show. In any case, the neoliberal assessment of the relative merits are more nuanced than one might expect and hardly do we find the straightforward call for markets to replace democratic decision making, although the way they are juxtaposed is often highly suggestive to this effect.

Let us examine this argument critically and scrutinize its tacit assumptions about what democracy means. The obvious point to make about the market as a seemingly more perfect democracy is that despite all the advantages listed by neoliberals, it lacks a fundamental requirement of democracy: equality. While neoliberals tend to espouse only particular kinds of equality, the notion of (formal) democratic equality—one person, one vote—is hardly ever put in doubt.[8] Therefore, it is all the more surprising that someone like Friedman, who clearly wants to push the argument for the market (with all the qualifications mentioned previously), never even mentions the problem that purchasing power as the economic equivalent of the vote is distributed in the most unequal way. To be sure, political equality has always been and still is (perhaps even more than before) a myth that has to disregard lobbying or campaign donations rampant in contemporary democracies. But at the very least there is the commitment that every vote has equal value in an election, and there is nothing comparable in economic markets. In contrast to Friedman, other neoliberals note this fundamental difference, such as Röpke, who strongly supports the "'plébiscite de tous les jours' in which every shilling spent by the consumer represents a ballot-paper," but immediately adds the "disadvantage . . . of distributing the ballot-papers very inequitably" (1942, 253). And there are even hints at the possibility of addressing this problem by a redistribution of ballot-papers or, as Buchanan puts it, a change among individuals in the "power structure" of markets (1954, 341). But neither Röpke nor Buchanan pursues this systematically, which is perhaps not surprising given that this would lead them in the direction of a program of massive economic redistribution.

So while the market option as a remedy to the deficits of democracy must already be considered flawed (even by the neoliberals' own standards), two more points must be added to this discussion. First, it is important to note that the comparison of democracy and markets is skewed toward the latter because it extrapolates from a particular form of democracy to democracy in general. Consider the issue of the indivisibility of the vote, which forces citizens to spend their entire political capital exclusively on one option. There are plenty of municipal election systems today that offer a choice of splitting votes and expressing intensities (e.g., you can give a particular candidate three of seven votes you have and distribute the remaining four among other candidates representing other parties). Furthermore, votes for the loser of an election are entirely lost in winner-take-all/majority systems, while proportional representation systems capture at least some of the range of varying preferences among the electorate.[9] And while coalition governments may seem highly problematic because they possibly distort the preference transmission process, by the same token they could have the beneficial effect of offering the possibility of getting two or more goods—political parties—at once. In other words, the characterization of democratic markets may fit with the empirical characteristics of American presidentialism and British parliamentarism, but it is hardly representative of all democratic markets, which may display, for example, traits of consociationalism (institutionalized forms of power sharing).

The final point regards two additional assumptions about the meaning of democracy that are hidden in the favorable juxtaposition of markets and democratic procedures. The first is that democracy is improved when preferences are transmitted more accurately and individual citizens have a better chance of getting what they want. The worst that can happen in a democracy is that citizens are outvoted and thus do not get what they want. Only if this is rendered the most important issue in democracy can the market appear so much more desirable, because there we always get exactly what we want—if preferences are backed by purchasing power. Being in a minority should not be trivialized because, within certain limits, a government elected by a majority can use coercion to make the minority comply with a law. But I contend that underlying the neoliberal fear of being outvoted is a view of (democratic) "politics as zoo-keeping," as Benjamin Barber once called it, which is dominated by the concern to keep everyone safe from one another "rather than to bring them fruitfully together" ([1984] 2003, 3, 5). Democracy thus is always seen as a source of potential dangers, rarely as a context of cooperation, fostering mutual understanding and learning about ourselves and others by having our minds changed in the course of the democratic process. It may thus turn out that realizing our initial preferences is not the only issue of importance in a democracy; democracy could also turn out to be just as important as a context of discovery and reinterpretation of these preferences in exchange with others.[10] This is a more encompassing understanding of democracy that is more republican or deliberative, and while there is no doubt that such an understanding is not without problems, I bring it up here to expose the limitations of neoliberal views of democracy rooted in their fundamental assumptions about it.

Another limitation can also be identified by comparing this variety of neoliberal thought on democracy with republican/deliberative views. Note that the democratic citizen in these neoliberal arguments is typically construed as a consumer of politics. The consumer is not necessarily passive because there is demand for certain political goods. However, these goods are exclusively produced by political parties or other political actors and offered to consumer-citizens. The democratic virtues of the latter exhaust themselves in making more or less informed choices in picking one or another policy bundle that they can influence only indirectly through this

choice. For a deliberate and republican democrat this is a deeply impoverished understanding of democracy, especially the democratic autonomy
of citizens, which requires that they obey only the laws they have given
themselves. To be sure, this pathos of self-government must be adjusted to
the conditions of modern representative mass democracy, but for democracy
to claim legitimacy, it must provide citizens with a sense of coauthorship of
laws, through deliberation processes in the public sphere or other forms of
participation. This notion of coauthorship is completely lost once democracy is nothing more than a specifically ordered political market, in which
citizens choose and consume political goods, as suggested by the respective
arguments of neoliberals.

The third variety of solutions suggested to address the problems of
democracy might be summed up as the (semi)authoritarian option. This is
a solution that obviously targets the dysfunctionalities arising from an excessive pluralism that allegedly characterizes contemporary democracy, and it
is mostly but not exclusively associated with the ordoliberals, whose ideas
concerning a strong state are already familiar to us. The recurrent themes
here are the independence and unity of the state's will-formation process, and
while this may not necessarily have blatantly antidemocratic implications, it
seems rather clear that a depluralization of democracy is envisaged. Beyond
this general point Röpke and Eucken offer few specifics about what a less
pluralist democracy in the sense of a better insulation of the state in regard
to societal interest groups could look like. However, Hayek, who is not a
stranger to (semi)authoritarianism, sketches out one possibility.

The later Hayek became more and more disillusioned with actually
existing "bargaining" democracies, which he blamed for "the miscarriage
of the democratic ideal" (2003, 3:98–99); and in the third volume of *Law,
Legislation and Liberty* he puts forward a "model constitution" to address the
shortcoming. The core of Hayek's proposal is a rigid institutional separation
of powers, in keeping with his long-held ideas with regard to the rule of law.
Hayek sees a significant part of the problem in the confusion of tasks on
display in existing assemblies that both legislate and govern. In his model
constitution there is a strict separation between a governing assembly, the
members of which are elected on the basis of parties and existing election
systems, and a legislative assembly. It is this second chamber charged with

legislation proper that carries the transformative weight of the proposal. It is supposed to be an assembly composed of relatively mature citizens elected for a relatively long time (fifteen years) without the possibility of reelection but with a guarantee of being employed by the state in some apolitical position afterward. Hayek furthermore stipulates very specific electoral rules for this assembly charged with determining *nomos*, the abstract rules of just conduct that also bind the governmental assembly, suggesting that elections take place on the basis of age cohorts. This means that all citizens aged forty-five elect fifteen of their own cohort for the assembly to replace the fifteen sixty-year-olds whose term is over. The following year the same procedure takes place for those who turn forty-five.

Let us first understand the rationale of Hayek's proposal before the respective concerns are discussed. If the problem of parliamentary democracy is the combination of interest groups seeking legislative favors and politicians relying heavily on granting them to further their chances at reelection, then this vicious collusion of interests has to be somehow broken up. We already know a lot about how Hayek interprets the situation in unlimited democracies, and his main solution to the ills of this situation so far was the generality of proper law that would make it impossible to treat groups or individuals favorably. However, Hayek was aware of the problems in applying this criterion, so he introduces an additional safeguard that operates on the basis of a changed incentive structure: Since reelection is impossible and future employment secured, there is little incentive to formulate laws partial to a particular lobbying group. They may still aim to influence the legislators but will, in all likelihood, find it more difficult to sway them in a certain direction; at least this seems to be Hayek's expectation. Elections based on cohorts do not only ensure that there are no legislators under the age of forty-five; they also have a depluralizing function in Hayek's proposal. Remember that the main culprits in pluralism are vested interests, politicians, and political parties that end up operating as the parliamentary arm of these interests according to ordoliberals. Hayek imagines that each age cohort will have clubs divided into local chapters where the "class of 1984" can regularly meet until they vote for one of their own. In these clubs social conflict lines ought to be downplayed and the formation of political parties is discouraged: "If they [club meetings] should occasionally also become platforms for party debates, their advantage would be that those leaning towards different parties would be induced to discuss the issues together, and would become conscious that they had *the common task of representing the outlook of their generation* and to qualify for possible later public service" (Hayek 2003, 3:118; my emphasis). In a best-case scenario, the members of the legislature would think of themselves not as representing or expressing social cleavages as if they were party politicians but solely as representatives of their cohort, which would result in a thorough depoliticization of the chamber in the sense of pluralist democratic politics, or, as Hayek himself formulated it, "the dethronement of politics" (ibid., 128).

How is this model to be assessed? First, what are the chances of this attempted dethronement of politics, or what I call depluralization of democracy, being successful? Several considerations mostly concern the relation between the two chambers and the likely effects of the strict separation of powers. While some commentators are concerned with the *nomoi* placing the governmental assembly in a Procrustean bed, radically diminishing the state's steering capacity, others see the opposite effect to be more likely: a *nomos* that is too abstract and too formal to rein in governmental discretion and leaves ample room for the governmental assembly to implement and interpret these norms (see Plant 2009). Furthermore, it is not even clear whether the assignment of a certain issue to one or the other chamber can be decided on unequivocally, even by a Supreme Court, as Hayek suggests (Gamble 1996, 149). Most of these issues are ultimately related to an inconsistency at the center of Hayek's argument. He tries to shield the legislature against any particularistic influences so its members can frame laws that are truly general, which Richard Bellamy, following John Gray's influential reading, interprets to warrant a Kantian test of universalizability: but for the "Kantian test of universalizability to produce widely acceptable determinate outcomes it will be necessary to assume a common good among the members of the community" (Bellamy 1994, 432; see also Gray 1984, 65). At first, this conclusion is surprising because notions of the common good are anathema to most neoliberals and to Hayek in particular, who made the diversity of preferences among people a cornerstone of his critique of socialism. Yet it is rather unsurprising in light of Hayek's efforts to shield the legislative chamber from "distorting" influences that range from his "Rousseauean banning of factions" (Bellamy 1994, 432–433) from the legislature to the outright disenfranchisement of anyone receiving transfer payments from the state—which could mean a large proportion of the citizenry and would have included Hayek himself while he was a professor at a publicly funded university (see Hayek 2003, 3:120). This disenfranchisement together with the reduction of active voting rights to a single ballot at the age of forty-five usually draws the fiercest criticism from commentators, but it is still consistent with Hayek's idea of a demarchy as law that applies equally to all (within the same legal category), and we must not forget that restrictions on active and passive voting rights are not principally anti-democratic. Although some aspects of Hayek's ideas could at least be said to follow the same, albeit radicalized logic as existing restrictions, such as the requirement of maturity for voters, others pursue a goal inconsistent with his own normative political epistemology: the fostering of a certain degree of homogeneity inside the legislature. Hayek may not have been an authoritarian out of principle, and despite the reference to homogeneity, the parallels to Schmitt should not be overstated, but at the very least, the model of democracy he proposes is a deeply antipluralist one, and with its assumptions and implications, it threatens to undermine some of his own most fundamental commitments.

The final variety of amendments aiming at an amelioration of democracy's deficiencies may easily be the most surprising one, especially in light of what we know so far about the overall critical stance neoliberals take on democracy, as much as they may differ in their reasons and resoluteness. The specific proposal is to introduce more direct democratic elements, especially referendums, as a complementation of representative democracy. More broadly speaking, one could say that if we have just encountered the (semi)authoritarian option, then this could be called the populist option to remedy the pathologies of *representative* democracy. Even Hayek endorses the use of referendums, if only in passing. He views the use of referendums as a "complement" to judicial review by the courts in his ideal system of government as laid out in *The Constitution of Liberty*, where he characterizes it as "an appeal to the people at large, to decide on the question of general principle" (2009, 168). Referendums receive the most favorable discussion by Buchanan, who points out various merits in a paper written while on a research stay in Switzerland. Specifically, "direct democracy acts to reduce the special-interest legislation that becomes increasingly descriptive of modern indirect democracies," and in it "there could arise no fear of a quasi-permanent legislative or political class, composed of incumbents skilled in manipulating the interests of those groups seeking special favors from government, who provide the source of massive rents to the members of the class" (Buchanan 2001, 238).[11] Remember that neoliberals think that first and foremost "particularistic" organizations like political parties or lobby groups are to blame for the problems of democracy. Thus, the strategy of circumventing these organizations and establishing a direct link between electorate and government is not wholly implausible (and this thrust of the argument links it with the antipluralist strategies discussed earlier), except to those like Eucken and Röpke, who exhibit the most pronounced fear of the masses.[12] Even Rüstow gestures at the option of bypassing organized interests, suggesting that "a good democratic government distinguishes itself . . . by appealing directly to the people over the heads of parties and groups if necessary" (1963, 99; see also 69).

Still, the most populist credentials among the neoliberals, which correspond with his pronounced antielitism, belong to Buchanan (see Brennan and Munger 2014, 337). However, the direction of this populist thrust is somewhat underdetermined. Buchanan is to have remarked after returning from a trip to Great Britain that if he had been born there, he would have become a socialist, given the fortified class structure of that society. While many leftists may commend him for this statement, the vitriol aimed at the "normal 'parliamentary' process" and the "system" that is effectively "out of control of the electorate" (Brennan and Buchanan 1980, 25), single-mindedly focusing on its exploitation, is compatible not only with certain leftist critiques of liberal-turned-plutocratic democracy but also with the right-wing populism of the Tea Party and others who suspect the Washington elite of conspiring against the citizenry it represents in name only. The suggestion that there is a cartel of parties that together with varying lobbying groups has monopolized the political will-formation process lends itself as analytical and polemical ammunition for a wide range of political positions and causes that may share nothing but a more or less diffuse distrust in political elites and the political process. Similarly, referendums can be the more or less appropriate vehicle for any kind of political agenda, and as we will see in chapter 5, Buchanan is interested in it not only as a prophylactic instrument ensuring that "legislators, executives, bureaucrats, and judges will keep arbitrary actions within tighter boundaries when they are subjected to potential reversals through popular referenda" (2001, 240), but also as the potential vehicle of introducing the balanced-budget amendment.

We can conclude that there is a neoliberal stance on democracy that is overall skeptical of existing democratic arrangements for various and often overlapping reasons—many of which could be agreed on by representatives of other political positions as well. In many cases it is not so much the findings themselves with regard to democratic pathologies but rather their interpretation and respective remedies that seem at least debatable—even in the case of the direct democratic populist option. Furthermore, as we will see in chapter 5, the views on democracy introduce major tensions or lacunae in many varieties of neoliberal thought beyond the inconsistencies already discussed.

CHAPTER 4

Science

The assessment of the proper role, powers, and limits of science—particularly a science of economics or political economy—is of crucial substantive and strategic importance in addressing the neoliberal problematic. The question is, on the one hand, to what extent economics, properly understood, can make a positive contribution to dealing with this problematic and thus function as an intellectual resource in support of a neoliberal project. On the other hand, neoliberals are concerned about the dangers that an ill-conceived science of economics and, more generally speaking, a certain kind of rationalism may pose to a neoliberal project. Strategically speaking, the question is whether the benefits of enlisting the authority of science as justification and legitimation for neoliberal politics, and thus increase the chances of success of a neoliberal project, outweigh the risks of affirming the power and authority of science, when the main intellectual and political antagonist is a collectivism that describes itself as *scientific* socialism.

This core ambiguity within neoliberal thought forms the basic structure of the following discussion. First we look at the neoliberal view that tends to affirm the possibility of a true science of economics, its powers, and its positive contribution to addressing the neoliberal problematic. Friedman's, Rüstow's, and particularly Eucken's views can be grouped into this current within neoliberalism. While the other view does not outright deny the possibility of a science of economics, it does have a very particular idea of what it is, a science of spontaneous orders and/or the choices that constitute it. Furthermore, this view tends to highlight the limitations of such a science and warns of the damage that "scientism" and an undue emphasis on rationality may do to a liberal market society, broadly speaking. Here the protagonists are Buchanan, Röpke, and especially Hayek. We conclude by looking at the various positions with regard to the political significance of science: the role it should play and whom it should address. Here we can distinguish between those who either theoretically and/or performatively espouse the notion of scientists as political consultants and advisers, who offer their expertise directly to political decision makers, and those who opt for the electorate or the general public to be the proper audience of scientists–turned–public intellectuals. The range of positions extends between two almost diametrically opposed poles that are inhabited by Eucken, on the one hand, and Buchanan, on the other.

The Powers of Science versus the Fear of Scientism

We start by examining those neoliberals who highlight the powers of economics as science, albeit for profoundly different reasons. While Friedman lauds the predictive powers of economics along instrumentalist lines, Rüstow and Eucken make it a point to stress the truth value of economic insights based on the right methodology. So while all three are science enthusiasts, on a different level, they subscribe to opposing positions. Friedman's significance to the debate over economics as science seems almost inversely related to the volume of his contributions to it: Friedman wrote a single essay on the issue of method in economics in 1953, and over the decades at least thirty journal articles and countless book chapters have been devoted to it. His "Methodology of Positive Economics" begins with the distinction between a positive science of economics and a normative or regulative one. While one is concerned with the "is," the other's domain is the "ought." As the title indicates, the essay is devoted to the former, and this is anything but an arbitrary choice. Normative economics in one way or another is based on positive economics. And in Friedman's view most controversies in economic or social policy are not rooted in differences over normative economics that express people's differing ethical orientations but rather in disagreements over the effects of certain policies under consideration to achieve a goal, the normative value of which is not controversial.

A skeptic may wonder about the reliability of the knowledge generated in just about any social science given its unwieldy object domain—humans—and the difficulties that arise from a dearth of controlled experiments with those objects. But Friedman is unimpressed with these concerns and downplays the distinction between natural and social sciences to a matter of varying degrees of precision and accuracy. Specifically, he warns of drawing the wrong conclusion from the relative difficulty of testing substantive hypotheses in the social sciences that they should become more formal: "Economic theory must be more than a structure of tautologies if it is to be able to predict and not merely describe the consequences of action; if it is to be something different from disguised mathematics" (Friedman 1953, 11–12). This reminder already contains a succinct mission statement for a science of economics according to Friedman: Its central task is to generate hypotheses or theories that yield nontrivial *predictions* about yet-unobserved phenomena. This is important for two reasons. First, it is important for a science that wants to be politically influential, and second, it is the basis of a falsificationist method in which empirically false predictions imply problems in the theory that need to be rectified. This description of Friedman's view is largely uncontroversial, but the common ground between interpreters extends no further than this. I focus on two disputed and interrelated points in particular: the predictive emphasis in Friedman's view of science and the role that assumptions play in determining the quality of a theory or hypothesis. The issues at stake are the alleged instrumentalism and the antirealism of his metatheory of science. To begin with, Friedman seemingly reduces science to the sole task of making accurate predictions (ibid., 7). This is obviously difficult enough, but the problem may be not only that this mistakes what a science of economics is capable of achieving, as other neoliberals argue, but that it reduces science to an organized endeavor of pragmatic problem solving and implicitly denies that it may have anything to do with a search for truth.

Needless to say, the search for truth is a concept that must be handled carefully in what Habermas called a "postmetaphysical age," so let me clarify the limitation of Friedman's view. In focusing on prediction, Friedman seems to opt for a philosophy of science that makes the case for science to identify regularities (if x, then y), which enable predictions and, by the same token, successful interventions into reality. Such a philosophy of science can be labeled "conventionalist" and "instrumentalist," and it could be traced back to Hume and Nietzsche. The problem with such a view is that all it requires of science is that it tells us *that* something will happen, not *why* it will happen. To use a famous example, according to Friedman's view, the goal of science is accomplished as soon as we can reliably predict that two or three days after the appearance of red spots all over someone's body the person will have the measles. Obviously, though, the red spots do not *explain* the measles, although their presence enables us to make a prediction. If a view of science is adopted that expects it to yield not only predictions but also explanations, which is arguably the more enlightening aspect of science, instrumentalism is found wanting (see Caldwell 1990, 146; Sayer 2008, 94).[1]

The other controversial aspect in Friedman's approach can be interpreted as a further expression of his instrumentalism or a problem in itself, which also raises questions about what kind of falsificationism he ultimately subscribes to: his antirealism. Friedman goes to great lengths in defending "unrealistic" theories that are still successful in predicting certain phenomena, which is absolutely plausible up to a certain point. Theories and hypotheses have to abstract from the "white noise" of reality and attribute explanatory/causal power to certain factors at the neglect of others, and they may construct ideal types, the very point of which is that they do not correspond with reality. A theory that does not engage in such abstraction is as descriptively accurate as a map with a scale of 1:1—and just as useless. But Friedman is not content with this and pushes the issue further. Not only is it unproblematic to rely on unrealistic assumptions in a theory; the lack of realism is a veritable indicator of its "power": "in general, the more significant the theory, the more unrealistic the assumptions (in this sense)" (Friedman 1953, 14). Such a radical antirealism is somewhat difficult to bring in line with very basic intuitions about science and what constitutes good theories, because what Friedman contends is that a predictively accurate theory that relies on assumptions that are descriptively completely inaccurate is preferable to one that is accurate in both respects.[2] In my view, Friedman wants to make the case for parsimony as the prime scientific value aside from predictive power, but parsimonious assumptions are not necessarily the same as antirealistic ones. Furthermore, a metatheory that focuses entirely on the maximization of parsimony could be criticized for an overly narrow focus on one scientific value when there might be others, such as descriptive and predictive accuracy, to be considered; and the recipe for an elegant theory would be to optimize these and potential other values rather than maximize one. Although Friedman does not consider this, it stands to reason that there is a trade-off between descriptive parsimony and/or inaccuracy and predictive accuracy, which suggests that theory building is best understood as a balancing act. However, Friedman is not willing to yield to this idea, which is of great importance, not least because it indirectly concerns one of the most notorious concepts in neoliberal thought, *homo economicus*. Friedman does not mention it in the essay, but his example of the maximization of returns on investment as an assumption about the behavior of companies is close enough, and the arguments against it are ultimately the same. Friedman vigorously defends this "unrealistic" assumption, and by the same token he would defend the use of *homo economicus* against those who critically point out its empirical inaccuracy.

One last point may indicate an internal inconsistency that haunts Friedman's science of positive economics aside from the noted one-sidedness in various respects. Friedman agrees with Popper that the best way to avoid the problem of induction is falsificationism: An empirically testable hypothesis is generated, and if it is not borne out by reality, the theory must be considered falsified and its parameters at least modified. The most fundamental question here is how the commitment to falsificationism, which still understands itself as an endeavor to approximate truth ever more closely, although it remains ultimately unattainable, accords with the marginalization of any truth value of theories in instrumentalism, which Popper, in fact, rejected. Leaving aside this question, which would require a long detour, what remains unclear in Friedman's essay is to what extent the theory and its assumptions would have to be modified if it fails to account for certain phenomena. Consider an example from the world of monetary economics, the theory of rational expectations: The government spends money in public investment to stimulate the economy. However, *homo economicus* is aware that, ultimately, the money spent has to come from somewhere and the investment will have to be financed, however belatedly, through higher taxes. Anticipating this, she will cut back on spending because she already factors in the future loss of money, and thus the stimulus remains ineffective. But what if it turns out that there is no such effect to be observed? Needless to say, there are a number of factors that might be able to explain the noneffect, but at some point one would have to consider whether the assumptions underlying the theory might be wrong, such as the assumption about the extremely long time horizon of actors who already factor in potential events of the distant future. The question is would Friedman be willing to relax these assumptions in the sense of making them descriptively more accurate after all of his efforts to reject the call for such modifications? Or would those assumptions, in contrast to actual theories, not be subject to revision, turning Friedman's into a rather limited falsificationism that remains dogmatic with regard to its fundamental assumptions?[3]

Walter Eucken and Alexander Rüstow have a strong belief in the powers of science, but their thinking about science is completely opposite to Friedman's. While Eucken was employed in academia at the time and Rüstow was working in the research department of an industrial lobby organization, both were aligned in the attempt to rejuvenate the discipline of political economy in Germany that was in its Weimar days still torn between the two opposing poles of what Eucken called the "Great Antinomy" (1951a, 34). The debate had been going on for decades and pitted the "Historical School" against a much more theoretically oriented current that relied on deductive abstraction rather than historical ex post facto accounts that were rich in detail but lacked formal rigor. Eucken and Rüstow were clearly leaning toward the theorists in this debate, who had more ambitious hopes than the Historical School for what a methodologically rigorous science could achieve, so it is a widely shared mischaracterization to place ordoliberal political economy in the middle between the two rivaling paradigms.

It is, however, true that Eucken was not entirely satisfied with the direction of theoretical economics because he suspected its agenda to be too formalistic and its models too far removed from economic reality.[4] Eucken was adamant that science required methodological rigor and abstraction, but the starting point for all scientific endeavors had to be concrete experience, as he put it, thus betraying a phenomenological influence through Husserl and others but also Weber's notion of the social sciences as "experiential sciences" (*Erfahrungswissenschaften*). However, Eucken gave experiential sciences a methodological twist that put them on opposite ends of a spectrum. His two important methodological works (which he did not want to be referred to as methodological because that suggested a distancing from concrete economic problems, which he had criticized in the theoretical paradigm) are *Was leistet die nationalökonomische Theorie?* and *The Foundations of Economics* (Grundlagen der Nationalökonomie).

The key to bridge the gap between abstraction and experiential reality that Eucken introduces in the *Foundations* are ideal types of economic orders. The starting point is indeed the concrete economic problem, from which Eucken, through what he calls the "method of 'isolating' abstraction" (1951a, 107), distills two basic ideal types, the market economy and the centrally administered economy, and approximately one hundred subtypes. With these, Eucken claims, all of economic reality can be captured; thus, there is an almost dialectical understanding of theory as an abstraction from concrete reality that can and must subsequently be brought to bear on the analysis of this reality and, possibly, be refashioned through this encounter with the concrete and the particular. So in what ways does this view of economic science differ from Friedman's? To be sure, Eucken agrees with Friedman that science must be problem driven to some extent, lest it succumb to the ivory-tower-ism of the "general-theoretical approach." However, Eucken could not disagree more with the strictly instrumentalist conclusions that Friedman seemingly draws. In fact, science is very much concerned with the quest for *truth* in the most emphatic sense: "By reaching truths on the basis of the method described that are necessary, general, and simultaneously relevant to reality [*wirklichkeitsnah*] by expressing these in theory, political economy has found the Archimedean point, from which objective and exact knowledge of certain relationships in individual, concrete reality can be generated." This kind of theory aims at "objective, generally valid truth irrespective of any arbitrariness and subjectivity" (Eucken 1954, 29).[5] The emphatic claim to truth also has a political function, but for now let us simply note that the standards Eucken puts in place for scientific findings seem ambitious if not strictly out of reach in light of contemporary (positivist and post-positivist) understandings of science, given the almost metaphysical connotations of his concept of truth. Eucken

and Rüstow thus represent the complete opposite of Friedman in their understanding of science as providing valid, and thus useful, knowledge as well as
privileged access to the realm of truth, which is granted to only a few on the
basis of the correct methodology. This fundamental difference also extends to
the matter of assumptions and the respective (anti)realism. For Eucken, the
ideal types and assumptions underlying them have to be revisited cyclically
on the basis of the empirical studies they inform. In Eucken's view this must
lead to a steady refinement of the analytical instruments employed, a postulate
that places him, once more, in diametrical opposition to Friedman: What is
wrong about the notion of *homo economicus* is not "its hypothetical character,
but that it is much too far removed from concrete reality and thus amounts to
an arbitrary construct." He concludes: "Theoretical research has no need for
homo oeconomicus" (ibid., 22–23). While critics of the contentious notion
of *homo economicus* may appreciate Eucken's distancing from it as representing an approach to science that fails to address economic reality properly, his
particular way of constructing ideal types, including the assumptions built
into them, has also drawn criticism.

Eucken criticized Weber not only for his subjectivism but also for misunderstanding the link between ideal types and real types. Ironically, Rüstow, an
otherwise ardent supporter of Eucken's view of science, theory, and method,
was the first to point out that Eucken's distinction between the two types was
as least as confusing as Weber's, which is not surprising, because Eucken's
postulate of a "realistic refinement" of his concepts is bound to lead to a conflation of the two types. But Rüstow also pointed out that Eucken's types of
economic order lacked the multidimensionality of Weber's types and focused
only on the dimension of how many planners there are in an economy, thus
forming "partial concepts" (*Partialbegriffe*) rather than ideal types (see Rüstow
1940; Goldschmidt 2001, 51). Furthermore, Eucken is far from rigorous in
his construction of types based on this criterion (the relevance of which is
never discussed but simply assumed). Although he acknowledges that there
are subtypes of centrally administered economies with (partially) free choice
in consumption, he still fails to draw the conclusion that in such an economy
there is obviously more than one planner, which is the sole criterion for a
centrally administered economy; so consequently this form would have to be
subsumed under the exchange economy type (see Haselbach 1991, 103–105).

Some observers suspect that the notably cavalier way in which Eucken constructs and subsumes types may be related to the final conceptual difference
with Friedman that is at least as important as the other ones. While there is
a debate within ordoliberalism whether it is a necessary feature of Euckenian
Ordnungspolitik and whether it has to be spelled out in this particular way, there
can be no doubt that Eucken himself was not willing to accept Friedman's
distinction between normative economics and positive economics. In other
words, science is not confined to describing and analyzing empirical orders.
Its supreme task is to contribute to the search for the order that ought to be,
what he characterizes as an order "that is in accordance with the nature of
man and the matter at hand" (Eucken 1960, 372). And while science identifies it, *Ordnungspolitik* is charged with implementing this "free, natural and
God given" order (ibid., 175–176). The notion of a natural order comes with
a lot of normative metaphysical and/or religious baggage, and Eucken's fellow ordoliberals hold some corresponding views. I cannot pursue this issue
much further, but this normative naturalism pervading ordoliberal thought
is strongly at odds with Foucault's interpretation of ordo-/neoliberalism, who
argues that it is the artificiality of the competitive order and its rejection of
a deist naturalism à la Smith that constitute the major dividing line between
neoliberalism and its liberal precursors (2008, 120). True, the desired order
does not come about all by itself, but that does not mean that it is of artificial
design; this is actually a concern among those neoliberals, like Röpke, who
are skeptical of an excessive rationalism in and beyond science. But even
those who do not share this concern, first and foremost Eucken, describe the
"natural order" as a hybrid between a discovered and an invented order that
figures as the telos inherent in nature, which nevertheless has to be implemented by humans.[6] In short, Foucauldians had better taken a closer look
at the sources he interpreted while probably relying strongly on secondary
literature before they adopt his stance on what distinguishes the various liber-
alisms.[7] However, what matters in the present context is that this ordoliberal
naturalism is imported into science, albeit only by the enthusiasts of science,
while Röpke, who is arguably the most committed to the notion of a natural
order, characteristically ties it to religious ideas.[8] For Rüstow this is not an
option because despite his roots in religious socialism, his views become more
and more critical of religion in the Judeo-Christian tradition because of the

individualism it fosters.[9] But even Eucken, whose religiosity is undisputed,[10] is adamant that the natural order can no longer be grasped through some kind of "immediate experience" to be derived from natural law; it can be identified only through the efforts of the scientifically equipped and supported intellect (1960, 347). After all, in Eucken's view only science is capable of inquiring into social relations on the level of individual orders and their interdependence—the totality of the social. In light of this it becomes clear that Eucken's political economy faces truly Herculean tasks, as it has to transform itself into a virtually transdisciplinary science that not only overcomes the specializing tendencies within any single discipline, which is bemoaned by all ordoliberals as well as Hayek,[11] but must also reach beyond disciplinary boundaries and integrate the other social sciences.

In Rüstow's works the link between the normatively charged natural and science takes on a slightly different form. He envisages a novel "science of man," a "new anthropology that must and will work out what we were lacking so far, namely a scientific foundation of our idea, our view and the direction of our will" (Rüstow 1963, 166–167). The scientific inquiry into the nature of humankind is to yield the contours of the appropriate social order, which in this sense is also the natural order. While the postulate of abstention from value judgments in scientific inquiry must not be radicalized into the fetish of pure objectivity, it seems difficult to dispute that Eucken's and Rüstow's burdening of science with far-reaching normative aspirations has highly problematic implications, not the least of which are political ones. For now we turn from the enthusiasts of science, who want to enlist it in various ways for the neoliberal project, to those neoliberals who tirelessly warn of the dangers of scientism or even, more generally, of a misplaced faith in the powers of human intellect.

The *positive* convergence point between Hayek, Röpke, and Buchanan, who figure in this rubric, is, first of all, an understanding of economics/ political economy as a very particular science, the object of which is spontaneous orders generated on the basis of individual choices: "Economics is, or can be, scientific in a sense that is, I think, unique. The principle of spontaneous order is a scientific principle, in that it can be readily divorced from normative content" (Buchanan 1979a, 84). Spontaneous orders develop through choices between alternatives and—importantly—exchanges with others. Therefore, in Buchanan's and Röpke's version of the argument, political economy can be a "science" of choices/exchanges (see ibid., 39; Röpke 1963, 14) but not a quantitative one of maximization. This leads Röpke and especially Buchanan to a veritable vendetta against mainstream conventional economics that Röpke takes to task for its "quantitative mode of thought," incapable of taking into account qualities, structures, and forms (Röpke 1950b, 50), and is derided by Buchanan for its useless modeling mania: "I challenge any of you to take any issue of any economics journal and convince yourself, and me, that a randomly chosen paper will have a social productivity greater than zero (1979a, 90).[12]

Röpke and Buchanan tend toward a deflated account of science despite an occasional gesturing at the possibility of a "pure theory of politics or a genuinely scientific politics" (Buchanan 1979a, 159). The reason for this lies in an understanding of political economy as a social science that studies complex interaction patterns, not social utility functions, and Buchanan's searching discussion of the limitations of the *homo economicus* model (ibid., 207). To be sure, Buchanan relies heavily on the model, but that has not kept him from subjecting it to a scrutiny that is unrivaled among the neoliberals and that, as we will see later, leaves him in a highly precarious position.

The heart of the matter concerns assumptions about an agent's individual utility function: If prices drop, will the agent buy more? If they rise, will the agent cut back on consumption in line with assumptions about the elasticity of demand? The question here is how substantive the behavioral assumptions are that inform economic theories. If nothing is assumed about preferences and their ordering, the model can make sense of all choices, but by the same token it can generate no hypotheses and predictions (see Green and Shapiro 1994). In Buchanan's somewhat cryptic wording, this "logical theory is indeed general but empty; the scientific theory is non-general but operational" (1979a, 46). So what and how much do we assume about the utility function of the agent? This becomes a particular vexing question for Buchanan, because actors are not fully aware of their own utility function but have only an implicit knowledge of it (ibid., 87); even more important, utility functions change constantly and are thus unable to provide a stable foundation of a "science of choice."

But first let us take a closer look at how Buchanan defends the concept of "economic man." Along the lines of Friedman's argument, Buchanan

highlights the usefulness of *homo economicus* as a "uniquely appropriate cari-
cature of human behavior, not because it is empirically valid but because it is
analytically germane" (Brennan and Buchanan 1985, 53). Still, the question
is how thick or thin the rationality assumptions are that inform the model.
Here, Buchanan begins to maneuver himself into a corner that ultimately
turns out to be one of the major weaknesses of the entire approach.

Rational behavior is not limited to self-interested actions narrowly understood. Utility may also be derived from helping other people, but we should
not infer that the benevolence of actors could be commonly relied on (Brennan
and Buchanan 1985). So it would seem that there is little predictive power
to the concept, as any kind of behavior must be considered rational because
otherwise the actor would not have engaged in it. The thin assumptions about
what it means to make rational choices result in a general but empty theory,
in Buchanan's words quoted earlier. But not only is the utility function of economic man underdetermined; in his most philosophical moments Buchanan
goes even further: "We are, and will be, at least in part, that which we make
ourselves to be. We construct our own beings," and he refers to humans as
"artifactual animals" in this sense (1979a, 94). The consequence of this view
of the self-production of subjects within certain limits is a problematization
of cost-benefit analysis as the grammar of a utility function, because economic
man "cannot do otherwise than become different. And as he does so, he must
embody a different utility function" (ibid., 97). Buchanan employs this argument in a critique of Gary Becker's approach and contends that the potential
return on "investments" in human capital cannot be ascertained properly
by *homo economicus* because, in part, it is an investment in changing oneself,
or "spending on becoming" (ibid., 96). As tempting as it is to follow these
philosophical considerations further, we must stick to the methodological
implications of economic man as artifactual man. On the one hand, there
is a degree of sophistication in this way of conceptualizing the behavioral
model that makes it difficult for critics to dismiss it as nothing but the theoretical justification of egotism. On the other hand, it seems that Buchanan
would have to pay a price for ratcheting up the complexity of the model in
the form of the reduced ability to generate determinate hypotheses about
behavior in certain settings. But while his reference to political economy as
the science of spontaneous orders that should not pretend to know how to

manipulate macroeconomic aggregates, as the Keynesians supposedly do (see Buchanan 2009), is consistent with his pleas for science to be wary of providing expertise for the political system, he ultimately is unwilling to accept the full consequences of artifactual man and pay the price mentioned. However, as discussed later, this proves to be a stance that is not only theoretically inconsistent but also deleterious to Buchanan's political project.

This brings us to Hayek, who is the most pronounced skeptic among the neoliberals regarding the powers of science and derives this skepticism from a view of spontaneous orders that emphasizes the limits of individual reason. For Hayek, spontaneous orders emerge as the consequence of human action but not human design, to use a phrase he borrows from Adam Ferguson. No single actor or institution could ever do what the market as a spontaneous order does because of the aforementioned limits of reason, or what Hayek provocatively calls "our institutional ignorance" (2003, 1:13). While nobody can predict the outcome of markets because we lack the knowledge about far too many particulars involved in the process, the result is not chaos but "ordered anarchy," or what Hayek with his characteristic penchant for introducing novel vocabulary calls "catallaxy." Much has been written about Hayek's epistemological assumptions about markets and spontaneous orders more generally, but in the present context what interests me most is the characterization of catallaxy as a complex phenomenon, which is the crucial reason for Hayek's reservations about the knowledge claims of a science of economics.

In Hayek's view the processes taking place in a market or in contexts such as an ecosystem or the emergence of a language are too complex to yield the kind of knowledge science can generate by analyzing other object domains. This complexity allows for only a specific kind of knowledge about general patterns, and as often done, neoliberals invoke the metaphor of games for clarification. In Hayek's Nobel lecture, "The Pretence of Knowledge," he argues that if we know the rules of a game, specific plays are virtually impossible to predict, but this does not mean that nothing can be said about the game at all. "But our capacity to predict will be confined to such general characteristics of the events to be expected and not include the capacity of predicting particular individual events" (Hayek 1978c, 33; see also Hayek 1967b). Consequently, the "science" of spontaneous orders that economics should consider itself is more modest than the natural sciences—not because of the inferiority of its analytical framework but because of the inherent difficulties of its object domain. Scientism is the result of a failure to recognize this profound difference between economics and, for example, mechanical physics, and it creates the gravest dangers for society. Without dwelling on this issue, I at least note the ambivalence of Hayek's critique. To be sure, there are those who paint Hayek as an anti-Enlightenment thinker bent on subverting the authority of reason, but the project could arguably also be described as "not an abdication of reason but a rational examination" (Hayek 2009, 61), and he would not be the only one to reject criticisms of such an agenda as the "'blackmail' of the Enlightenment" (Foucault 1997, 312). That is, the self-critique of reason is not per se a reactionary project; it might be seen rather as an attempt to enlighten reason about its own limits, which, after all, was Kant's intention in his critiques of reason. It may seem overly provocative to place Hayek in intellectual proximity to Foucault and Kant; however, I have no intention of turning Hayek into a Kantian or a Foucauldian nor of turning Foucault into a Hayekian, as is currently in vogue in some quarters. It is simply a matter of pointing out the ambiguity of an approach that chooses as a starting point the limitations of individual reason and undertakes a critical examination of its properties. By the same token, there is no doubt that Hayek's railing against scientism is ultimately aimed at what he considers the hubristic assumption that socialist planning could be based on science. However, many scholars who continue to work in a broadly socialist tradition, as well as most of those working in what they consider "critical" fields and traditions, could probably subscribe to the general critique of scientism as a faulty application of the methods that worked in the natural sciences to the object domain of the social sciences. The natural sciences, we can conclude with Hayek, are an ill-suited model for the social sciences since they suggest the attainability of knowledge and respective control over social processes that is simply beyond social sciences' reach.

This limitation of a science of mere general pattern predictions places Hayek in obvious and direct opposition to Friedman's view, which is the reason that Hayek thought of the *Essay* as "in a way quite dangerous" (Hayek 1994, 271).[13] Friedman could be charged with the same kind of hubristic aspirations that Hayek, but also Buchanan and Röpke, attribute not only to the socialist would-be planners but also to the Keynesians intent on fine-tuning the economy. The skeptical camp around Hayek might have some concerns regarding the emphatic notion of truth underlying Eucken and Rüstow's version of science, but especially the political implications of such a science must be most worrisome. Eucken may believe that an incorruptible science can prove conclusively the superiority of an exchange economy along ordoliberal lines over a centrally administered economy, but what if the socialists claim the opposite and with reference to an incorruptible science? However, even the skeptics are not willing to give up entirely on mobilizing science as a resource to bolster political claims, but they do not invoke the almost metaphysical truths of ordoliberalism.

The skeptics are more, but not entirely, in agreement with Eucken and Rüstow, concerning a principally value-neutral science. Buchanan makes the most pronounced endorsement of a science undergirded and to some degree driven by values. He even contends that "we must become more normative in our efforts. . . . We must use the 'is' to implement the 'ought' which the 'is' suggests, regardless of the methodological impropriety of this relationship" (1979a, 179). It is not really clear how this far-reaching demand is compatible with Buchanan's qualifications of the powers of political economy, but it speaks to an overall inconsistency in this matter that we continue to highlight. Hayek, of course, candidly pointed out that everything he had to say in *The Road to Serfdom* was derived from ultimate values (see 2001, vii), but it may be disputable whether Hayek considered this book scientific even in his more modest sense of the term.[14] Something similar might be said about Röpke, who published scholarly work but whose more famous books are not easily characterized as science in his sense. He confronts the issue of value judgments directly and commits himself to the well-known Weberian position, according to which value judgments necessarily underlie any scientific endeavor. Furthermore, he warns of a politicized science drawn into the realm of interests but nevertheless wants to retain the right to speak about "highest values," as he arguably did himself before going into exile (see Röpke 1949, 154). But then Röpke characteristically suggests that these underlying value judgments are not discussed because they are not controversial, which prompts the question how this is ascertained. The more subjective they are, he contends, the more they are contested, and the obvious follow-up question leads him

back into the potentially conservative terrain of "natural normalcy," because
societies are characterized by certain norms that are ultimately derived from
"*anthropological* facts" that justify the highest values, such as "truth, justice,
peace, community" (ibid., 158).

An ambiguity concerning this particular point is characteristically pronounced in the case of the skeptical camp and concerns the question whether
neoliberal discourse itself considers itself to be a scientific discourse. In the
case of the enthusiasts, especially Eucken and Rüstow, there can be little
doubt about the scientific self-understanding, but already in Friedman one
could argue that *Capitalism and Freedom* is a very different genre from that
of *A Monetary History of the United States*, although Friedman himself would
probably have claimed that even his more popular books are strongly based
on economic science and its predictive power. Buchanan's voice at times
oscillates between the economist in his sense and the passionate supporter
of political reform, and we see the two continue to clash in the following
discussion. Hayek and Röpke wrote scholarly treatises that they probably
would consider scientific in their specific sense, but most of what they did as
neoliberals is better located in the realm of social philosophy than in a science
of pattern predictions. However, this philosophy does not exist in isolation
from their scientific work, and there are complex cross-references between
the two. We cannot disentangle these connections here but can, at least, point
to the ambiguous status of the discourse of neoliberal skeptics of science,
which nevertheless can claim some consistency with their overall position. If
science-turned-scientism is more dangerous than helpful in addressing the
neoliberal problematic, not only for substantive but also strategic reasons,
since the neoliberals' antagonists aggressively refer to the authority of their
scientific foundations, the general strategy of downplaying the positive powers
and political significance of science suggests that there is simply not as much
to be gained for this variety of neoliberalism in explicitly presenting itself as
science and insisting on this elevated status.

Let me conclude by situating the persistent concerns about scientism
in a more encompassing diagnosis about modernity that characterizes the
neoliberal point of view—to some degree even across the divide between
skeptics and enthusiasts of science. Recall that scientism's fallaciousness as
well as its fatal effects stem from a confounding of the realms of natural

and social sciences. The result of this import of natural science methods and philosophies of science is what might be called the hubris of feasibility: Social scientists assume that their exact and predictive quasi-natural sciences provide them with an arsenal of instruments that enable social engineering to whatever effect, thus wreaking havoc on social relations that are not malleable and controllable in the same way as the relatively closed systems in the physical world, where interventions stand a better chance at being successful.

For thinkers like Hayek and Röpke in particular, contemporary scientism is only a syndrome of a more far-reaching trend in modernity they label "rationalism" and criticize vehemently. Röpke weighs in against a "strictly scientific rationalism" (1950b, 158), and Hayek even refers to the "revolt against reason" through "rationalist constructivism" (2003, 1:31). Here the critique of scientism is integrated into an interpretation of intellectual history that distinguishes between an evolutionary rationalism and a constructivist one (Hayek), or a constrained one and an excessive one (Röpke). Both coincide in their intellectual historical narrative in blaming the French Enlightenment for the respective aberrations in the use of reason; and in Hayek's case the positive aspect of the rationalist tradition predictably belongs to the Scottish Enlightenment thinkers such as Adam Ferguson and David Hume, who show an awareness of reason's own limitations per se and in its application to the realm of the social.

In Röpke's narrative, rationalism represents the "violence of abstraction," which pays no heed to the concrete realities of life that in his framework are time and again hypostasized into basic anthropological constants, disregarded at any reformer's own peril. In seeming opposition to Röpke, Hayek views the rationalist revolt as "directed at the abstractness of thought" (2003, 32), but this is to be understood in the context of Hayek's defense of abstract rules/the rule of law. Generally, excessive conceptual abstraction is as much a fallacy of rationalism for Hayek as it is for Röpke, as illustrated by Hayek's critique of *homo economicus*: This "celebrated figment" belongs much more "to the rationalist than to the evolutionary tradition" (2009, 55), and, accordingly, Hayek sees it as a rather questionable concept. The charge of abstraction can even be traced to the other side of the neoliberal divide on science, where its echoes are heard, if only faintly, in Eucken's critique of the formalism of the general-theoretical approach and, much more audibly, in Rüstow's world-historical point of view of a fateful bifurcation of reason and emotion that leads to a continual struggle between the forces of irrationalism and rationalism. Rationalism, in Rüstow's narrative, manifests itself in the abstractions and blindspots of nineteenth-century laissez-faire, which was, simultaneously, of a "sub-theological" character, which is obviously a reference to the deism of Smith and others (Rüstow 1957, 160), but makes for a very curious kind of rationalism. Even though Rüstow is highly critical of rationalism, which he sees in line with a problematic belief in the progress of the natural sciences and technology, this does not preclude him from strongly supporting ambitious scientific endeavors that target not only political economy but nothing less than human nature itself, which, ultimately, puts him among the science enthusiasts.

The only ones immune to the *topos* of antirationalism are, unsurprisingly, Friedman on the enthusiasts' side and, somewhat more surprisingly but also more equivocally, Buchanan on the other. Despite Buchanan's harsh criticisms of scientism, he never extrapolates from this what in Röpke and Rüstow amounts to a tragic if not outright negative philosophy of history, that unbounded rationalism may spell doom for civilization. This is how fatal Röpke and Rüstow consider rationalism to be—as does Hayek, although with less baggage of a philosophy of history. Hayek draws a direct connection between the hubris of reason and the rise of modern totalitarianism that Röpke concurs with to a significant degree (see Hayek 2010a, 2010b), while Rüstow is more Solomonic in his diagnosis: Communism is the pinnacle of a one-sided rationalism, while National Socialism is the expression of an equally one-sided irrationalist revolt against it (see Rüstow 1957).

Neoliberal Science and Politics: Technocracy versus "Scientized Politics"

The final issue is one that throws the variety of neoliberal positions into sharp relief. It is the question of what role science, however understood, should play in relation to politics; whether its efforts should be directed at an audience beyond academia; and, most important, what the appropriate audience is. Here, Eucken and Buchanan represent two opposing positions. Needless to say, their perspective on the political role of science is closely related, though not entirely derivable, from their respective concepts of a science of political economy. So it is not surprising that Buchanan, as a representative of the skeptics of science, harbors some reservations about the political role of science.

Among the neoliberals, Buchanan is certainly the most outspoken about the role that science must *not* play in relation to politics: to offer its services in a form of scientific policy advice. Almost all others may have more or less grave concerns but are not principally opposed to such a role, even if they do not actively demand it, as in the case of Eucken. It is solely Buchanan who radically rejects the scientist in the role of policy adviser and thus represents one end of the range of neoliberal views on this matter. There are two main reasons underlying his view. The first is not related to his view on science but rather a consequence of his public-choice commitments. If Buchanan is correct in his analyses of politicians' and political parties' behavior, and both tend to do anything to gain or remain in power, then the political economist who approaches them with plans for constitutional reform that could be supported by the citizenry would have to appear naïve at best. Why would politicians adopt such a reform agenda when it is designed, among other reasons, to make it more difficult for them to play the rent-seeking game? At worst, sharing their insights about economic and politico-economic issues, the scientist may even provide political actors with a knowledge they can use for their own purposes and thus inadvertently play into the hands of incumbents who aim to consolidate their power at the expense of the citizenry as a whole: "'Economic science' is not to be conceived as offering assistance to selected agents who seek to use scientific knowledge to control others" (Buchanan 1986, 38). The reason is clearly that "the constitutional perspective is irreconcilably at odds with the benevolent despot model" (Brennan and Buchanan 1980, 4). In fact, Keynesianism, socialism, and welfare economics, with its "social utility function" that must be maximized, are to blame for their erroneous views on strictly economic matters as much as they are to blame for the mistaken belief that their scientific expertise would be welcomed and heeded in the corridors of power. Even if Keynes had been right about the political economy of crises and the state's ability to steer the economy through its cycles, disregarding the fact that politicians pay at least as much attention to *election* cycles betrays either a quixotic or a technocratic-elitist view of politics, or even both, in Buchanan's view.[15] Keynesianism is a program that relies on the government to act in the scientifically prescribed way but shows no acknowledgment of "the institutional world where decisions are and must be made" (Buchanan and Wagner 1977, 35). Buchanan thus offers a straightforward argument against the sheer possibility of political consultancy by science under democratic conditions.

But what if there were, hypothetically, benevolent despots? Would Buchanan refrain from advising them as well? This question points us in the direction of the other source of his reservations regarding scientific expert advice for decision makers. The most succinct formulation of the respective arguments can be found in the article "The Potential for Tyranny in Politics as Science." Buchanan's premises are that there is a categorical difference between the institutionalized practices of politics and those of science, which explains why conflation of both creates problems. In principle, there are two ways for this to happen, one of which is a completely politicized science, but it is the other possibility of a "scientized politics" (Buchanan 1986, 40)—or what we may call politics on a scientific basis, technocracy—that Buchanan is concerned with. Politics is a matter of values and interests, while science is concerned with points of view, in Buchanan's stylized juxtaposition: "Politics has the functional task of settling conflicts among individual interests and values" (ibid., 49). The peculiar nature of politics comes to the fore in one of its preferred instruments of keeping overt conflict at bay, compromise. It shows that diverging interests and evaluations can be "managed" and accommodated in degrees without any party to it being put in the wrong by a deal. This is a terrain that is profoundly different from that of science, which is concerned with the "truth" (Buchanan consistently puts the term in quotation marks) of the views we hold. Writing long before the onset of the "post-truth" era, Buchanan characterizes science as a practice that cannot tolerate alternative truths, where the rules of the practice stipulate that an accepted truth necessarily makes all alternative views false in what could be characterized as a zero-sum game. Consequently, there is no room for compromise and bargaining in regard to views and beliefs. Therefore, "science, as an activity, is much more analogous to religion than to trade" (ibid., 43)—not least in regard to the intolerance of dissenters: Someone who believes that the earth is round cannot simply accept that others profess it is flat, and the matter has to be settled—the truth has to be established one way or another to end the controversy. "The social function of 'science,' the activity of the specialists, is that of shutting off dialogue and discourse. . . . Agreement among the specialists in inquiry, along with the subsequent acceptance by nonspecialists, signals the end of scientific conflict" (ibid., 42–43). This is a slightly drastic formulation, but what Buchanan wants to emphasize is the "decontestatory" function of science that puts an *end* to conflicts rather than manages them. This binary structure radically distinguishes science from the graduality of interests and values.

Clearly, there is much to be questioned about this juxtaposition, and Buchanan himself concedes that there may be absolute values and that scientific truths are no longer considered either absolutely true or false. But let us accept it tentatively as a stylized contrast and see what conclusions he draws about science in politics. Politics is the realm of the relative, the parlaying, the provisional, and the partial. When scientific claims are brought to bear on this realm, its entire character changes. Once a truth has been established, all conflicts and negotiations end, and in this sense scientific politics is no longer politics as Buchanan defined them. Contesting truths is no longer seen as legitimate, and while conflicts of interests were tolerable, the epistemic ones can last only until a truth has been established; after that, disagreement turns into semidelusion. The authoritarian implications are obvious: "Those who do not 'see' must be 'shown the light,' perhaps preferably by persuasion but, if necessary, by coercion" (Buchanan 1986, 52). The scientifically vouched-for policy agenda crowds out all alternative considerations, especially in regard to the *maximization*, for example, of a social utility function; therefore, such technocratic rule must be rejected as inherently tyrannical, concludes Buchanan.

There are two points to be noted here, and both concern the question of what this implies for Buchanan's own scientific practice. It seems that he has no intention of offering his expertise to political decision makers (see Brennan and Munger 2014), but neither are his books written exclusively for academics. Recall that Buchanan places at least some of his hopes for a constitutional revolution in popular referenda, and consistent with this, his audience beyond the ivory tower is clearly the citizenry. "The subjects of our ultimate normative concern are taxpayers or citizens" (Brennan and

Buchanan 1980, 4), who are to be informed about the way they are suppos-edly exploited by their governments and what alternative rule options are available. This is a tenable position, but it also prompts the question of how advising the citizenry of political matters differs from advising politicians when the problem is science wherever it comes in too close contact with the realm of politics. In my view, there are two possibilities for Buchanan's response to the question: Either he does not claim the label of science for what he does, or he sticks to the label but provides knowledge that is of a dif-ferent nature than the zero-sum games he described as typical of science. For the latter option, consider the end of *The Power to Tax*, whose authors hope that they may be "shifting the grounds" in the debate over tax reform and do not "want to make the mistake of suggesting that a unique constitutional solution will necessarily emerge even from the most idealized modeling of constitutional choice" (ibid., 204). This suggests that it is still up to the people to decide what kinds of governmental constraints they favor; science does not present them with the kind of decontested certainty science sup-posedly provides. However, this kind of knowledge about alternative options seems far less tyrannical and might even be presented to benevolent despots, who then make the respective choices to the best of their abilities. To put it differently, when switching from the more general reflection on science and politics to the concrete work on constitutional reform, there seem to be less problematic ways of linking science and politics, as in the form of the dreaded "social engineer" of Keynesian or socialist colors. The second point is to note that Buchanan's work in many of its aspects goes beyond the hope that citizens opt for *some* kind of governmental constraint. After all, the balanced-budget amendment is not really portrayed as one among many options; if anything, its particular form might be negotiable. Even more im-portant, how consistent is it to problematize the decontestatory function of science when imported into politics while at the same time demanding pas-sage of a constitutional balanced-budget amendment that would have exactly such decontestatory effects? Just as science would, it would shut off dialogue and discourse on this issue and result in a lasting depoliticization. All these issues are thrown into even sharper relief once we include Buchanan's actual activities in our considerations. To be sure, one would assume that advice to politicians would be anathema to him because they are not benevolent dictators. Nevertheless, Buchanan and his colleagues at the Center of Public Choice did brief policy makers and businessmen about economic issues; and while this was confined to the Virginia political-economic elites at the time, once he joined forces with the Koch brothers, Buchanan's outreach through seminars and lectures gained significantly in scope (see MacLean 2017, 109).[16] One may wonder how advising extremely wealthy citizens differs from advising politicians, if the extremely wealthy citizens provide the donations to finance the exceedingly costly campaigns of these politicians. Finally, while it is difficult to ascertain Buchanan's role precisely, it is now established that Buchanan—just as Friedman and Hayek did—visited Chile and, as MacLean chronicles, provided advice on the specifics of what would officially be called Chile's "Constitution of Liberty." "Buchanan responded with detailed advice on how to bind democracy, delivered over the course of five formal lectures to top representatives of a governing elite that melded the military and the corporate world, to say nothing of counsel he conveyed in private, unrecorded conversations" (ibid., 158). Aside from the fact that how directly and deeply Buchanan was involved remains disputed, it is rather telling that he chose to keep this episode from May 1980 (followed by another trip for the MPS meeting in Santiago de Chile in 1981) entirely to himself—at least, it is never mentioned in any of his writings that I know of. Not only must he have been aware of the public backlash Friedman had faced; it must have also been clear to him that he had done what he had chided welfare economists and Keynesians for in the harshest words: providing expert advice for a governing elite whose sole intention is—and in this case it really was—to stay in power and exploit its population.

Moving toward the other end of the neoliberal spectrum in this matter, we see other neoliberals who show much less restraint in getting *openly* involved in politics: for example, Hayek met with Augusto Pinochet in Chile and sent letters to Margaret Thatcher when she was prime minister; and Friedman gave advice to Pinochet and served officially on the Economic Policy Advisory Board of the Reagan administration. In both cases we find few reflections on the proper relation between science and politics or, rather, the specific question of whether science can and should provide expert advice for political decision makers. In Friedman's case it is not far-fetched to assume that his predictive science should not only help decontest questions regarding normative economics in the public sphere, as mentioned in the *Essay*, but also inform policy makers on the effects to be reckoned with after passage of certain reforms. Even more important, scientific advice may instruct policy makers about the *futility* of certain reform efforts, such as Keynesian demand management, which according to Friedman's famous argument, does not create lasting growth but only inflation. So *negative* policy advice in this sense is arguably at least as important as its positive counterpart, in Friedman's view. Still, it is worth noting that politicians are well advised to take into consideration that negative and positive advice is based on assumptions that are self-consciously unrealistic. If a political reform fails and the public were to demand a justification, pointing to a science that prides itself on its antirealism may not provide the kind of "scientific legitimation" that, in fact, has decontestatory effects on the citizenry.

As we have seen, Hayek does have a lot to say about the impact of ideas on political macroprocesses, but only few considerations are devoted to the question of scientific policy advice. Some of the reasons can be found in Hayek's evolutionary view of cultural history, but it could also be related to Hayek's reservations regarding scientific politics. To be sure, the Friedmanite nexus between science and politics must appear deeply problematic to Hayek. However, what would a science of spontaneous orders have to offer to decision makers anyway? Is there any direct political use for pattern predictions? Not for the engineering mind, maybe, but possibly for the mind of the gardener. Hayek insists that "what helpful insight science can provide for the guidance of policy consists in an understanding of the general nature of the spontaneous order, and not in any knowledge of the particulars of a concrete situation" (2003, 1:64). And while this knowledge is useless for the control and manipulation of particulars, Hayek contends that it is still of political value, "not to shape the results as the craftsman shapes his handiwork, but rather to cultivate a growth by providing the appropriate environment, in the manner in which the gardener does this for his plants" (1967b, 34). While science thus has a more moderate and indirect impact on politics in the form of policy advice, Hayek obviously insists on its concrete political use.

However, the most systematic contemplation of science's role in politics coupled with the most far-reaching claim to direct political influence is found in the works of the ordoliberals, with the partial exception of Röpke, who retains a certain distance from politics, which is consistent with his concerns over scientism. While his view of science is undoubtedly elitist and he counts scientists among the *nobilitas naturalis*, which in many aspects resembles a Platonic guardian class,[17] he is still worried about the political appropriation of science and thus, in the last instance, is not entirely in agreement with Eucken and Rüstow.[18] However, this did not keep him from working on the Brauns Commission established by the Weimar government and acting as more or less official adviser to the first governments of the Federal Republic, for example, with reports on currency reforms (see Hennecke 2005).

Rüstow and especially Eucken represent a view of the link between politics and science that can be referred to only as technocratic. Accordingly, it is a matter of gaining access to political decision makers, and this is nowhere more clearly on display than in the "Ordo Manifesto," an editorial for a new book series, written jointly by the economist Eucken and the jurists Franz Böhm and Hans Großmann-Doerth in 1936: "We wish to bring scientific reasoning, as displayed in jurisprudence and political economy, into effect for the purpose of constructing and reorganizing the economic system" (Böhm, Eucken, and Großmann-Doerth 1989, 23). Let us reiterate that the scientific approach must be strictly interdisciplinary, overcoming disciplinary specialization (see ibid., 25), if it is to provide helpful knowledge about the totality of social relations and enable a coherent politics of the competitive order: "The treatment of all practical politico-legal and politico-economic questions must be keyed to the idea of the economic constitution" (ibid., 23). The economic constitution being the focal point of practically all public policy, science is portrayed as indispensable for its formulation since it is the sole available source of knowledge that can inform such an all-encompassing endeavor (Eucken 1951a, 37–38; Rüstow 1963, 15–16). The complexities of interdependent socioeconomic orders and possibly even the workings of a market-based economic system may simply lie beyond cognitive reach of the average layperson (see Rüstow 2009, 34). Therefore, while Eucken and Rüstow did think about ways to gain more influence in public discourse generally, from plans for a journal to writing op-ed pieces for newspapers, the main strategy was clearly to appeal to decision makers directly and offer them scientifically authorized policy advice.

At the top of every society are the "leading strata," Eucken writes in 1952, still echoing the Italian elite theorists (1960, 17). These elites have to be persuaded of the correct politics of a competitive order, Eucken states explicitly. This is especially consequential in light of the assumed irrationality of the masses, which remains a concern for all ordoliberals, who were traumatized by the disruptive politics and struggles of Weimar Germany. There is no doubt, then, as Gebhard Kirchgässner (1988) notes candidly, that the ordoliberals dreamed of economic policy, broadly speaking, as a domain of wise men who would base their decisions on nothing but science and the truths it supposedly generated. There are theoretical reasons for this, but there is also very concrete evidence for such a project in the form of the letters between Eucken and Rüstow in the late 1920s and early 1930s, which document that Eucken was hoping to gain access to political circles through Rüstow's connections. Rüstow, in turn, was eager to enlist Eucken's scientific authority in his own attempts to influence policy making on the eve of the National Socialist takeover (see Sala 2011, 46).

We will return to this mutually beneficial, if ultimately unsuccessful, cooperation between the two, but we must clarify why science is of such crucial importance for the politics of the competitive order and a ordoliberal project more generally speaking. It is not only the scope of scientific analysis that turns it into a necessary resource for such a project but, almost more important, because it is the only force that can cognitively neutralize the impact of pressure groups and their respective ideologies in pluralist democracies. Eucken could not be clearer in his dichotomous framing of the respective constellations. Scientists generate the truth—in the singular—but when they are cut out of the policy picture, "interested parties" and their *ideologies* take over. The link between interests and ideologies is important because it is not only the proper approach to political economy that enables the formulation of objective truths; it is also the fact that scientists are supposedly aloof from all self-serving considerations: "Men of science, by virtue of their profession and position being independent of economic interests, are the only objective, independent advisers capable of providing true insight into the intricate interrelationships of economic activity" (Böhm, Eucken, and Großmann-Doerth 1989, 15). Conversely, given the fact that societal groups are driven by a particular interest, they necessarily express ideological views, or at least this is what Eucken, Rüstow, and Röpke suggest. While science as a disinterested search for objective truth is thus aligned with the common good, the pluralist strife of groups that pursue particular interests is linked to distortive ideologies that can serve to justify just about any political project and are explicitly employed for the "economic struggle" (Eucken 1951a, 29, see also 30–33; Röpke 1950b, 134).

It is here that the decontestatory function of science is most clearly on display. The ordoliberals envisage a politics that is completely depoliticized; both Eucken and Rüstow subscribe to the idea that theory in its proper form yields one and only one (true) solution to any given political problem. If there are two opposing views on an issue, it is a matter of faulty science or outright ideology. Proper science can and must overcome these confusions and conflicts with an authoritative formulation of what is true and, accordingly, the right politics to pursue (see Sala 2011).

It is only at this point that Röpke parts ways with his fellow ordoliberals; despite the occasional elevation of the "men of science" and the pathos-laden talk of the "dignity of science" being "truth" (Röpke 1950b, 134), the skepticism with regard to the political dangers of science prevails when he polemicizes against what he calls "economocracy" (Röpke 1960, 149) and what amounts to the technocratic expert rule that Eucken and Rüstow espouse. And while Röpke never criticizes his fellow ordoliberals, he clearly rejects the authoritative if not absolutist claims they raise as "scientists": "the scholar would be foolish if he thought himself in the possession of objective truth" (ibid., 136).

Still, this ultimate and important divergence notwithstanding, for all three ordoliberals science provides the only beacon of stability and partiality for nothing but the general good in a world of politics that they experience as torn between fundamental antagonisms driven by particularistic actors that threaten to disintegrate the state and even society itself. It would seem almost redundant to criticize such a heroic and heavily anachronistic view of a completely disinterested science, were it not that the depoliticized technocracy it is supposed to inspire is clearly on display today, particularly in the European context, and that the mathematized formalism of today's mainstream economics may be less outspoken about it but clearly shares the view of a neutral science. So let us at least note that the view of scientists as constituting something

like a free-floating intelligentsia, to borrow a term from Karl Mannheim, is
not particularly self-reflective about its own position and simply declares itself
to be free from any distortive passions or interests.

While it is not even necessary to invoke this contrast to highlight the
blindspot of ordoliberal theory, the juxtaposition with the self-understanding
of *Critical* theory may sharpen that point even more. Somewhat surprisingly,
in his lectures on ordoliberalism Foucault speaks of the "curious closeness
and parallels between what we call the Freiburg School or ordoliberals, and
their neighbours, as it were, the Frankfurt School" (2008, 105), and there
is one broad analogy—ambition to grasp society in its totality and the corresponding commitment to interdisciplinarity—although the Frankfurt version of this took a turn toward philosophical disciplinarity later. However, all
other differences aside, the two could not be further apart in regard to self-
understanding and the requirement of a self-reflective science. While Eucken
posits the disinterested view of science from nowhere, or rather from a realm
that is aloof from societal pressures and political interests and must be shielded
against any such intrusions just as the strong state must be shielded from
pluralist demands, Critical theorists urge a constant reflection on science's
societal role and its position in the overall division of labor in a given social
formation. In other words, while both traditions insist on the need for theory
to counter the trend toward disciplinary specialization and the concomitant
effect of scientific inquiries being more and more designed to examine (micro)
phenomena in isolation from the overall context, only Critical theory (at least
on the programmatic level) stringently applies the respective scientific maxim
to itself. Ordoliberal theory may be adamant about the importance of an
"integrated theory" and the problems that loom if the mediation of a single
moment through the totality of social relations, to put it in Critical theory
terms, is disregarded. But they treat science itself as if it stood outside the
interdependence of orders and as if it—its practices and its "order"—could
be treated in isolation from this interdependence. Of course, other types
of criticism could be raised against ordoliberal theory and the depoliticized
politics it is to inform, but it is also and not the least inconsistent with its own
theoretical view of society as a totality of interdependent orders.

As in the case of Buchanan, I end with purely anecdotal evidence
that there is not just a theoretical but also a practical or performative

inconsistency in Rüstow's and especially Eucken's idea of a scientifically neutral policy consultancy that counters the interest-peddling lobbyists and pressure groups and in how both pursued the project. In 1928 Eucken and Rüstow had already been friends for a decade. Eucken was a professor in Tübingen, and Rüstow held a position in the research department of the VDMA (Verband Deutscher Machinen- und Anlagenbau), the association of German machine builders—a lobby group of German industry. At the end of 1927 Eucken had already begun to criticize the central bank's policy publicly and urged a change in its direction, assumedly speaking as an objective scientist offering rather harsh advice to decision makers who are simply following the wrong economic recipes or are possibly in the ideological grip of some particularistic lobby group. On January 10, 1928, he writes to Rüstow: "Thinking about this issue, it has become clear to me that the machine industry has to do something at once. Why don't you appeal to the national industrial association [Reichsverband der Deutschen Industrie]. The fact that Sch.[acht; the president of the central bank] severely damages the interests of the machine building industry is clear. On top of that, you have the chance of improving the position of the VDMA because it is always good to fight a false policy that must eventually collapse, early on" (cited in Sala 2011, 25). Eucken was clearly trying to instrumentalize Rüstow's position with the VDMA to gain influence for his own views on economic policy. In other words, instead of fighting against the distortive influence of lobby groups with the sword of impartial science, Eucken (and Rüstow) sought to mobilize the leverage and influence of such a group to further their own interests in influencing politics. This anecdote may not be of much theoretical significance, but it still paints a highly ironic picture and raises some doubt with regard to science as the realm of the disinterested search for truth that can outbalance and anchor the unruly particularism of pluralist democracy and its group ideologies. If necessary, it seems, science and scientists would have to become and thus turn out to be just another party to the "group anarchy" of pluralism (Eucken 1960, 171).

CHAPTER 5

Politics

The central claim of this book is that neoliberal thought contains a genuinely political theory or at least elements thereof. Still, does it have a theory of politics as well? This is the question we address in this chapter. I do not examine the neoliberal view of politics(s) in general, because to a certain extent, we already know a lot about this from the various crisis diagnoses discussed in relation to the state, democracy, and science. What interests me more specifically is how these views on politics can be reconciled with a possible *politics of neoliberal reform*. In other words, how do the neoliberals theorize a politics that would bring about the various solutions and remedies proposed for the ills of the Leviathan state, unlimited democracy and scientism? My overall thesis is that the politics of neoliberalism is probably the weakest link so far in the thought of the neoliberals, as it confronts them with a theoretical dilemma they appear to be unable to resolve. The basic pattern of the dilemma looks like this: The neoliberals paint a rather bleak picture of the status quo, to say the least, in which any number of pathologies related to state, science, and democracy unfold and manifest themselves. But what is worse, and what makes the diagnosis more compelling and the neoliberal warnings more pressing, is the suggestion that the "normal" politics that has supposedly led political communities to the brink of disaster is "locked in" for various reasons. This makes for a powerful critique, but what the overall approach gains from the very bleakness of the diagnosis it loses in regard to theorizing the politics of reform: sketching a plausible political pathway that would lead from A, the abyss of the present, to B or C, a society reformed in the spirit of the various ideals. While there is almost unanimous consensus regarding the "power of ideas"—the crucial long-term importance of developing ideas, discourses, or even utopias that present alternatives to the status quo as an indispensable precondition in order to prevail in the "great struggle of ideas that is under way" (Hayek 2009, 2)[1]—the possibility of implementing these ideas provides a real challenge for the neoliberals. This general dilemma takes on a variety of forms, ranging from a conspicuous silence on the possibility of reform (and lacunae abound whenever the question is raised) to major inconsistencies on display in the struggle between the neoliberal *critic* of the monotonous politics of the iron cage of the status quo and the neoliberal *reformer*, who must ultimately seek theoretical refuge in exceptionalist political strategies and/or an almost eschatological hope for a politics of the extraordinary to account for the possibility of real political change for the neoliberal better.

The Powerlessness of the Ordoliberal Ought

The title of this section alludes to Hegel's critique of Kant's moral philosophy, the precepts of which supposedly have such a weak obligating force that they amount to hardly more than exhortations. Rational beings should follow the maxims that accord with the categorical imperative, but if there is no *Sittlichkeit*, in Hegel's terminology, to back up the abstract ought of Kantian practical reason, its effects remain extremely limited, at least if we accept Hegel's argument. Arguably, the reform agenda of Eucken and Röpke is confronted with very similar problems. Remember the far-reaching transformations that Eucken and Röpke envisioned to overcome the dangers and pathologies of an overburdened state in the grip of vested interests. How should these transformations into monolithic and depluralized democracies be brought about? If one consults the passages on how the state ought to be restructured along Euckenian lines in order to become an "ordering potency" (Eucken 1960, 330), there is no recipe to be found for how the state could manage to disentangle itself from the interest groups that hold sway over it. At times, Eucken comes close to conceding that the paradox of overcoming pluralism and establishing the competitive order is irresolvable in his framework of thinking: "Without a competitive order no state capable of action can emerge and, conversely, without a state capable of action no competitive order can emerge" (ibid., 338). It seems, then, that the Euckenian agenda is caught in a paradox where actual transformations of the state already presuppose these very transformations. In this sense, the call for a strong and unified state remains as powerless as Hegel conceived of the Kantian ought. Just as Kant's rational beings lack any strong motivational resources to follow the precepts of morality, the masses, interest groups, and political parties that populate Eucken's crisis diagnoses are unlikely to develop any interests or motives to overcome the failing state of pluralism. There remain the men of science, who strictly speaking are defined by the very lack of any interest or particular economic motive and thus are destined to make the case for the objective superiority of the competitive order. It is therefore no surprise that Eucken also lists them as a potential "ordering potency" next to the state and the churches. However, while we have seen that science should provide expert policy advice for decision makers, this remains a desideratum equally as toothless as the call for a more robust state: "Overcoming the biases and prejudices, science must become an ordering potency" (ibid., 346), but it remains a mystery how and why this endeavor should succeed, when Eucken himself admits that it has failed so far.

However, while they are not explicitly mentioned, Eucken's writings might be implicitly addressed to another set of actors, who also have a prominent role in Hegel's thought. Who could be better equipped to realize the general interest and take the appropriate advice from scientists solely dedicated to the search for truth than what Hegel termed the "universal class," the state bureaucracy? Eucken might have rather been thinking of a strong decision maker committed to the common good than an army of administrators when it comes to realizing the competitive order,[2] since this was bound to be a matter of power and determination, but the orientation toward the common good and the ability to transcend the particular are the crucial characteristics of the actors needed to implement the Euckenian, and the Röpkean, agenda. What is needed is no less than an enlightened guardian class that will faithfully pursue the technocratic politics of the competitive order, as has been criticized especially from public-choice theorists who are otherwise rather sympathetic to ordoliberal ideas (see Kirchgässner 1988).

Röpke is more explicit in identifying the class of actors who are the appropriate addressees of his reform plans. At times, he simply follows Hegel and argues, "If the authority of the state is to be strengthened it is absolutely necessary that it should be headed by a qualified civil service small in numbers but equipped with the highest standard of professional ethics and a pronounced esprit de corps" (Röpke 1950b, 305); at other times he gestures more vaguely at the need for people "who feel responsibility for the whole" (ibid., 313). The most extensive characterizations are found in his reflections on the *nobilitas naturalis*, whose members he also describes as "aristocrats of the public spirit" (Röpke 1960, 131). But if Röpke's account has the advantage over Eucken's in that it explicitly identifies the actors that could be the transformative agents needed for a proper politics of neoliberal reform, it has the profound disadvantage of excelling in the proof of the utter improbability of such actors ever coming to exist or persist. Röpke calls for the "leadership of genuine *clercs*," who are nothing less than "secularized saints" (ibid., 130). But where should this rare species come from when the world has descended into collectivist tyranny? "Evidently, many and sometimes difficult conditions must be fulfilled if such a natural aristocracy is to develop. . . . It must grow and mature, and the slowness of its ripening is matched by the swiftness of its possible destruction" (ibid., 131). In other words, as soon as the cast of the ordoliberal reform orchestrations is introduced, they disappear again. It seems as if it would take an almost otherworldly breed of people to realize a neoliberal politics; at least the bar is set high enough to make almost all imaginable empirical actors fall short of the ambitious requirements of a *nobilitas naturalis*. The *nobilitas naturalis* thus acquires the status of what is commonly referred to as a deus ex machina, and the religious connotations of this phrase are far from misplaced in the context of the politics of neoliberalism.

Transitional Dictatorship

Among the ordoliberals, introducing benevolent custodians of the public good is not the only solution to the conundrum of reform politics under consideration. Rüstow, whose thought in many ways figures as the most

ambiguous among the neoliberal thinkers discussed here, explored another
avenue of reform early on that confirms the close proximity of some aspects
of his thought with motives found in the work of Carl Schmitt at the time.
In 1929 Rüstow gave a lecture at the Deutsche Hochschule für Politik in
Berlin that was also attended by Hermann Heller and Theodor Heuss, who
would become the first president of the Federal Republic of Germany. The
central question of Rüstow's lecture was how to overcome the deficiencies of
the Weimar political system, which even before the chaos of the early 1930s
had exhibited a unique combination of instability and paralysis. The title
of the lecture gives a clear indication of Rüstow's solution to the problem:
"Dictatorship within the Boundaries of Democracy" (Rüstow [1929] 1959).
Striking about the lecture is not only what Rüstow proposes but also the
extent to which he relies on Schmitt's analysis of the Weimar system and its
weaknesses. The main problem, according to Rüstow, is a pervasive "politics
of blame avoidance," to use a term coined by Kent Weaver (1986), albeit in
a very different context. The democratically elected political actors, both
individual and collective, seem to eschew responsibility whenever they can,
either by deferring controversial questions to the judiciary, thus leading to
what Schmitt had already chided as a juridification of politics, or by delegating such issues to an expert committee whose verdict still formally leaves
politicians in charge of the ultimate decision but substantially prejudges it.
Unsurprisingly, this systematic and collective irresponsibility is said to lead
to an "increasing political disintegration" (Rüstow [1929] 1959, 92), and,
admittedly, this is not *just* unfounded alarmism if viewed in the context of
the time, although the tone of Rüstow's admonitions to the political establishment is characteristically shrill.

So what exactly could be done to remedy the ills of an imploding democracy? Again, Rüstow bases his elaborations on Schmitt's anatomy of the Weimar Constitution that rests on four elements placed in a particular balance
with one another: president, cabinet, parliament, and chancellor. Rüstow
contemplates the chances of unlocking the political process for each of them
and arrives at a clear conclusion. While other intellectuals such as Schmitt
would have further strengthened the presidential element to overcome the
political stalemate, and other political forces at the time would have opted
for more power and less individual accountability for cabinet members, he

sees the most promising option in time-limited dictatorial powers for the chancellor: "This means the preservation of democracy because it is a time-limited dictatorship, not in the strict sense of the term, but, as it were, a dictatorship with a probational period" (Rüstow [1929] 1959, 99). After all, in Rüstow's analysis of the problems of the Weimar system, it is virtually impossible to pursue just about any kind of politics because it is far too easy for those who are affected negatively by any specific policy to forge veto alliances and oust the responsible cabinet members or the entire government. Therefore, if there is to be any chance at all for the kind of politics that the neoliberals envision, the powers of government, of the chancellor in particular, have to be augmented, if only temporarily. Concretely, this means that the head of government could introduce policies that would be enacted even if they were not backed by a parliamentary majority but only a qualified minority. These exceptional powers cease after a certain period of time, long enough for the government to prove its ability to govern and to assess whether the reforms introduced are beneficial.

This latter aspect is important for Rüstow because of the way the ordoliberals perceive proper neoliberal reforms and the ambivalent effects they are likely to have. Consider the example of the competitive order, the introduction of which Rüstow would also consider an appropriate goal for neoliberal politics. In the short term it will hurt various particular interests or the actors behind these interests, but in the medium and long terms it supposedly furthers the general interest and the common good. So Rüstow assumes that the reforms need some time for their beneficial effects to become manifest, and in this case, he assumes, the government will be confirmed. But why would all those representatives of particular interests such as political parties and lobbying groups suddenly support the politics that hurt them? Rüstow, it becomes clear, has a different base for this exceptionalist model of democracy in mind: "I believe that with this position the leader would have the opportunity to address the people directly, bypassing party organizations and irrespective of party constellations. I would think that such a position of leadership would command a strong plebiscitary force and it is this that I would find beneficial" ([1929] 1959, 99). Here we can see parallels to Buchanan's populist argument, that it is necessary to sideline established interests and actors to overcome political blockades.

But Rüstow's strategy of transforming the political system in a plebiscitary "dictatocracy" faces a serious obstacle that he himself is also painfully aware of. As long as this political system is to remain within the boundaries of constitutionalism, the necessary changes to the constitution have to be passed by the very actors that have no interest in passing them: "I am not enough of a utopian to assume that a proposition as I just sketched it would normally find a majority to change the constitution in the Reichstag today. This is obviously not the case. If we had a Reichstag where something like this was conceivable then the proposition would be unnecessary" (Rüstow [1929] 1959, 100). In other words, Rüstow encounters the very same paradox we have already seen in the case of Eucken. And while he vaguely gestures at the possibility of changing the constitution through a referendum (another similarity to Buchanan's tactics), he himself assesses the chances of success to be minimal. Still, Rüstow is adamant that something must be done to overcome the paralysis of the system, and it is not enough to wait for a "strong leader,"[3] as others suggest. He urges his audience "that we do our part in order to facilitate the coming of this leader," which implies that somehow the constitution must be changed because "our current constitutional conditions make the coming and prevailing of a leader exceedingly difficult" (ibid., 101). There is a chilling irony to this last assessment, considering that four years later the "strong leader" did arrive and needed only a few months to do away with the entire constitutional system of Weimar.

Rüstow may be the first but he is not the only neoliberal who entertains the notion of a transitional dictatorship as the institutional sword that would cut the Gordian knot of pluralist unlimited democracy.[4] Hayek has made the case for this exceptionalist option as a solution to the conundrum of a truly neoliberal politics most vehemently, but not exclusively, with reference to Chile. Needless to say, this is a highly contentious issue, and over the decades a lot of false or at least embellished claims have been made about Hayek, and also Friedman,[5] as apologists of the military dictatorship of Pinochet, so it is particularly important to be careful in our assessment here.

In his scholarly writings Hayek defended the notion of a liberal authoritarianism as preferable over an unlimited democracy. Still, Hayek faces the same issue that the ordoliberals confronted: If existing societies are already proto-totalitarian unlimited democracies, as Hayek suggests again and again, then how is it possible to turn them into liberal authoritarian regimes or the kind of depluralized democracies with a rule of law that figures as Hayek's ideal? Bridging this gap is the systematic function of transitional dictatorship in the overall architecture of Hayek's thought. The most extensive discussion of such an exceptionalist politics can be found in *Law, Legislation and Liberty*, although the terminology differs slightly. Here Hayek writes that the basic principles of the rule of law and a free society may "have to be temporarily suspended when the long-run preservation of that order is itself threatened" (2003, 3:124). Two years after the publication of Hayek's late magnum opus, he is much more concrete about the need for transitional dictatorships to overcome the threat to a free society. In an interview with the Chilean newspaper *El Mercurio* Hayek is asked about his opinion on dictatorships: "As long-term institutions, I am totally against dictatorships. But a dictatorship may be a necessary system for a transitional period. At times it is necessary for a country to have, for a time, some form or other of dictatorial power. As you will understand, it is possible for a dictator to govern in a liberal way. . . . My personal impression . . . is that in Chile . . . we will witness a transition from a dictatorial government to a liberal government. . . . During this transition it may be necessary to maintain certain dictatorial powers, not as something permanent, but as a temporary arrangement" (*El Mercurio* 1981, D9). It seems then that Hayek had persuaded himself that in the case of a totalitarian democracy (in the same interview he contended that the only totalitarian regime in South America was the Allende government) it was legitimate to resort to a transitory dictatorship. This stance becomes even more ominous if we take into account that the Hayek of the late 1970s was already convinced that just about every actually existing democracy was ultimately bent toward totalitarianism. Consequently, dictatorial politics would have to be considered a legitimate option in a large number of cases. Not only did Hayek send the Portuguese dictator António de Oliveira Salazar a copy of the *Constitution of Liberty* in the 1960s, arguing that this could be the blueprint for a renewal of Portuguese society, but he also famously wrote to Margaret Thatcher, who was already prime minister, supposedly urging her to follow the model of what Naomi Klein terms Chilean "shock doctrine" reforms. Equally famous is Thatcher's response, in which she reminded Hayek that such drastic reforms pushed through with (quasi-)

dictatorial means were absolutely incompatible with British traditions of constitutionalism.

There are obviously pressing normative concerns related to Hayek's defense of a transitory dictatorship, but instead of a potentially moralizing critique, I would rather problematize Hayek's account by highlighting the deep inconsistencies that are brought to the fore by this defense. After all, it was Hayek who had asserted in the *Road to Serfdom* that once a regime or a group is given unchecked power, it will do everything to consolidate its power, and even the most well-meaning liberal socialists will eventually turn a dictatorial system into a full-blown totalitarian system. Why could it ever be assumed that these mechanisms do not apply in the same way to the transitory dictatorships Hayek wants to defend? Either the latter are just as dangerous as the former,[6] or Hayek's slippery-slope argument in *The Road to Serfdom* loses a lot of its bite. So we see a familiar picture emerge: The gain in making the neoliberal critic's diagnosis more compelling comes at the expense of a plausible consistent vision of realizing the neoliberal reformer's agenda. Conversely, if there is to be the hint of such a vision at all, the critique would have to be scaled back considerably.

But Hayek's controversial defense of transitory dictatorship as virtually the only option of overcoming the ills of unlimited democracy and the inconsistency it introduces into Hayek's thought are only the top layer of a more fundamental rift related to politics that troubles his approach more than that of any other neoliberal. What he shares with Buchanan, Friedman, or the German ordoliberals is an ambitious reform agenda, the pinnacle of which is his model constitution discussed previously in relation to democracy. The activist streak of Hayek's approach is also clearly on display in the countless op-ed newspaper pieces, in which at times he calls for far-reaching reforms, and in the letters written to Thatcher and others. Aside from the fact that Hayek is forced into defending transitory dictatorships to make plausible that there is a way out of entrenched unlimited democracies, there is a more fundamental problem with the calls for radical reforms that becomes ever more virulent the more the mature Hayek grounds his thought in evolutionary theory (see particularly Hayek 1988, 11–28).

While this is not the place to discuss the overall merits and faults of his particular application of evolutionary theory and how it is linked to his epistemology and view on cognition elaborated on in *The Sensory Order*, we can ask how this stance complicates Hayek's reform agenda. The problem is that Hayek's idea of group selection and its connection to cultural evolution predisposes him to a rather functionalist view of social life. If cultural evolution manifests itself by some groups prevailing while others perish, there is a strong prima facie case for the institutions, traditions, and conventions of the prevailing group to be considered superior to those of other groups or societies. The longer such institutions and traditions, together with the respective societies, persist, the more reason to keep them and acknowledge them as achievements in the process of cultural evolution that are of unmeasurable value to the respective group. Hayek thinks of institutions and traditions as vessels of accumulated wisdom and knowledge; traditions are especially important because they can transmit the kind of tacit, implicit knowledge that Hayek deemed invaluable.[7] At this point, it is clear that Hayek has backed himself into a theoretical corner with his reliance on arguments from evolutionary theory, because it commits him to an almost Burkean conservatism that had chided the iconoclasts of the French Revolution for their foolish disregard for conventions that supposedly contained the wisdom of the ages.

Hayek famously laid out the reasons that he was not a conservative in the postscript to *The Constitution of Liberty* (see Hayek 2009, 343–355), but his critique of constructivist rationalism, the praise of traditions and conventions, and his thoughts on cultural evolution inevitably lead him to an assessment of the status quo that is effectively indistinguishable from that of a conservative like Burke, although the theoretical frameworks are obviously vastly different. But while it is not impossible, it is difficult to be a Burkean reformer; and a reformer Hayek clearly wants to be. If it is true that the persistence of groups and their institutions suggests the "efficiency" of the respective arrangements, then Hayek would have to make peace with a number these institutions, first and foremost, the welfare state, which would no longer figure as the first step on the *Road to Serfdom* but a tried-and-tested institution that has clearly prevailed for more than a hundred years. Furthermore, even Burkean or Oakeshottian conservatives can arrange themselves with reforms, if the reforms are clearly limited in scope and resemble the pattern of organic growth more than the disruptions caused by drastic and far-reaching innovations. However, Hayek's proposals are far from limited in scope,[8] and of course nothing distinguishes them from the abstract blueprints for social reforms he criticizes with a view to constructivist rationalism. He may argue that his model constitution does not manifest a radical break with the status quo because it seeks to restore a system of the rule of law as it once existed. But it was Hayek who called for the development of neoliberal "utopias" (see Hayek 1960), a choice of terminology that would suggest something far more ambitious than the simple restoration of the status quo ante—although it would still constitute a radical break with the status quo. Hayek must have been aware of this fundamental ambiguity, if not to say contradiction, pervading his late work, but there are only very few instances where he seeks to address the tension and show that it is apparently quite possible to suggest that the best politics is to do nothing but cultivate the growth of spontaneous orders and, simultaneously, submit page after page packed with any number of reform proposals that are a far cry from watching traditions grow and develop in slow motion.[9] Still, the overall impression remains that sketching out what a consistent neoliberal politics of reform would look like and what its (realistic) conditions of possibility are remains a challenge, because the assumptions underlying the various frameworks of neoliberal thought seem to preclude the very possibility of such a politics.

Change as the Politics of the Extraordinary

James Buchanan was deeply unconvinced by Hayek's turn to evolutionary theory and on several occasions made it clear that there was no more reason for a Hayekian evolutionary optimism than there was for a respective pessimism: "The institutions that survive and prosper need not be those that maximize man's potential. Evolution may produce social dilemma as readily as social paradise" (Buchanan 1975, 167). Obviously, Hayek's oscillation between evolutionary fatalism and reformist activism was foreign to Buchanan. While he viewed Hayek as having erred on the side of the former, which amounted to what he called "'extreme constitutionalism' because of its elevation of the status quo to sacredness" (Buchanan 1986, 56), Buchanan located himself firmly on the side of the latter:[10] Constitutions needed to be crafted and deliberate reform efforts were required for political communities to get closer to his own ideal of a free society. But if Buchanan holds some serious reservations concerning Hayek's approach to the politics of neoliberal reform as Buchanan interprets it, the same is true for his view of the ordoliberal option of trusting in the somewhat unpredictable appearance of benevolent aristocrats of the public spirit. The intraneoliberal antagonism in this case could not be more extreme, at least at first glance: Buchanan was the one who most vehemently insisted that the idea of benevolent rulers had to be rejected categorically to carry out any realistic analysis of politics. So it would seem that he can bypass the dilemma of ordoliberal politics of reform.

Nevertheless, Buchanan's approach exhibits its own oscillations and exemplifies the pattern identified at the beginning of the chapter as none of the other neoliberal varieties do. Buchanan is also the most instructive and possibly the most fascinating case of them all, because he does not attempt to gloss over the problems as most others tend to do. On the contrary, an inquiry into Buchanan's vision of a neoliberal politics of reform reveals the struggles between the fierce critic of actually existing democracy and its establishment and the reformer who must essentially break with the very assumptions that yielded the critical diagnoses lest the diagnoses remain without any possible therapy.[11]

Let us take a closer look at these tensions and recall what Buchanan has to say about *homo economicus* as a crucial ingredient of his approach. The innovative move in Buchanan's thinking was, among other things, to assume that politicians and bureaucrats behaved according to the model of *homo economicus*. This implied that under democratic conditions politicians would have an overriding interest in securing their reelection, first and foremost, through logrolling with other political actors and responding to rent-seeking demands from organizations or movements representing constituencies considered of vital importance to these efforts. The results are incoherent state policy, short-termism, inflation, and the accumulation of public debt. The solution is (constitutional) rules, the balanced-budget amendment in particular. The simple yet theoretically rather devastating question then directed at Buchanan is, Why would one assume and how could one expect that politicians as rational utility maximizers who benefit from the nonexistence of effective rules would ever pass such laws? In other words, who and where are the agents of neoliberal reform? Obviously, this dilemma resembles the ordoliberal conundrum, but in Buchanan's case the focal point is the conceptualization of *homo economicus*, which most ordo-liberals rejected. However, he ultimately does not end up too far from the views of Röpke and Rüstow. Buchanan clearly has a keen awareness of the challenge he is facing; despite the various attempts to address it, he seems unable to resolve the antinomy between a locked-in politics of debt and a politics of neoliberal reform. Let us take a closer look at the manifestations of Buchanan's struggles.

One first possible way out of the dilemma, in my interpretation, is the embrace of referenda to introduce a balanced-budget amendment. Embold-ened by the successful Proposition 13 adopted in California at the end of the 1970s, public-finance hawks across the United States were discussing this model of capping state expenditure (although Proposition 13 actually capped state revenue) and reining in the politics of the budget on both the state and national levels. The referendum option at first glance is very much in line with the more populist or antielitist aspects of Buchanan's thought, and if it is true that the current arrangements benefit the forces of the political establishment, from lobbying groups to individual politi-cians, at the expense of tax-paying citizens and their debt-laden offspring, then what would be more sensible than trying to bypass political elites and place the decision in the hands of the citizenry? Their representatives may have an incentive to resist the introduction of "debt brakes," but citizens, whose time horizon may not be confined to the next election, might be the appropriate addressees for Buchanan's reform proposals. However, soon after Proposition 13 had been passed, he already seemed skeptical about the extrapolation of the success of this specific initiative to the national realm (see Buchanan 1979b), and, speaking more theoretically, Buchanan barred this way out of the dilemma of neoliberal reform for himself when he made it clear that in his framework people, "whether as constituency members or as political agents, retain essentially the same behavioral characteristics that they exhibit in their nonpublic roles, as participants in ordinary private pursuits" (Buchanan and Musgrave 1999, 126). And in a certain sense, this is the only tenable position if Buchanan wants to defend the need for strict fis-cal rules, because if "ordinary people" had a less narrowly conceived calculus of utility that could also encompass future utility of others—for example, their children—without massive discounting, then the question would arise why there was any need for strict rules without the possibility of exceptions and exemptions in the first place. After all, even self-interested politicians and their parties could simply run on a ticket of fiscal responsibility or even budget surpluses and would be rewarded by citizens with electoral victories—or at least this would not be ruled out as a general possibility. Obviously, Buchanan cannot concede this possibility and insists that "while there is little political resistance to budget deficits, there is substantial resistance to budget surpluses" (1991, 95), as if electoral defeat was a foregone conclusion for such a political platform.

Yet Buchanan is not willing to entirely give up the chance of appealing to the citizenry with his constitutional reform project; thus, the view of the actors who populate Buchanan's world becomes more nuanced and enriched the more he is pressed on the possibility of reform.[12] In one instance he gestures at a dualist political anthropology, when he refers to "the struggle within each of us . . . between rent-seeker and the constitutionalists, and that almost all citizens will play, simultaneously, both of the roles (Buchanan 1991, 2, 10). The constitutionalist attitude can be inferred negatively from how the constitutionally "illiterate" are characterized: "It becomes impossible to ask such persons to think of their long-term interest, and certainly it remains folly to ask them to think of the interests of the more inclusive community" (Buchanan 1986, 56)—it is an attitude that would foster support for a balanced-budget amendment.

If we follow the thread of this argument further, the politics of Buchanan turn into a much more far-reaching undertaking, because if it is true that there are constitutionalists in each of us that neoliberal reform efforts could appeal to, this presupposes that *homo economicus* is not a monolith. Recall that Buchanan's descriptions of this behavioral model are not easily reduced to the cliché of "economic man" dedicated single-mindedly to seeking to maximize his narrowly understood utility. Not only has it already been confirmed that economic man is just one of the personas that make up the actual agent; it was far from clear what it meant to maximize one's utility when "artifactual man" turned out to be constantly in the making, including his changing utility function. In light of all this, what emerges is a view of the subject characterized by a certain degree of fluidity, which also implies a certain degree of malleability—at least, this is what Buchanan suggests by the way he describes his own project. Consider the following: "The reform that I seek lies first of all in attitudes" (Buchanan 1975, 176), and it seeks to "facilitate the genuine transformation in behavior patterns that must occur" (Buchanan and Musgrave 1999, 207). Buchanan may claim in other contexts that "this [his] approach starts with the empirical realities of persons as they exist" (Brennan and Buchanan 1985, x), but this is certainly not where it ends; rather, it aims to foster the constitutional attitude vis-à-vis the rent seeker's just as Rousseau thought the *citoyen* had to be strengthened vis-à-vis the bourgeois. It is, to put it differently, a struggle for the soul of man; and while this religious terminology may seem inappropriate at first, not least because Buchanan, self-professedly, was anything but a religious person,[13] we will come to see that it captures the thrust of his endeavors quite well.

In *The Soul of Classical Liberalism* Buchanan starts out with the provocative thesis that "we have, over more than a century, failed to 'save the soul' of classical liberalism" (2000, 111). Of course, his reference to the soul is not to be taken entirely seriously, but it is not just a jest, because his concern is that advocacy of liberalism may be based on two different motivations. One is the arguments of science and the appeal to self-interest; the other "stems from an understanding of the very soul of the integrated ideational identity" (ibid., 112). Liberalism will not prevail if its support is solely or predominantly based on the former: "Science and self-interest, especially as combined, do indeed lend force to any argument. But a vision of an ideal, over and beyond science and self-interest, is necessary, and those who profess membership in the club of classical liberals have failed singularly in their neglect of this requirement" (ibid.). Buchanan goes as far as to suggest "invoking the soul of classical liberalism, an aesthetic-ethical-ideological potential attractor, one that stands independent of ordinary science, both below the latter's rigor and above its antiseptic neutrality" (ibid., 114). These are remarkable statements because they are a clear testimony to Buchanan's conviction that profound social transformations along broadly liberal lines required a campaign that could not rely only on the better "scientific" arguments, but neither would it be able to rely on appeals to the self-interest of the rent-seeker persona in ourselves.[14] It would have to be a campaign that addresses individuals on a different level and appeals to them as the constitutionalists they partly are, with a vision or an ideal that is not attractive to them because it resonates with any short-term preferences but because it aims to change attitudes, behaviors, preferences, and an entire worldview. In other words, Buchanan hopes to convert people to liberalism, and again, this evangelical vocabulary may sound far-fetched, but he writes that "it is not surprising that those who seem to express the elements of the soul of classical liberalism best are those who have experienced genuine conversion from the socialist vision" (ibid., 117) and famously, if half-jokingly, described himself as a "born-again economist" (Buchanan 2007, 68). The neoliberal vision cannot be implemented if it is based solely on rational self-interest of political actors and/or citizens (see Brennan and Munger 2014, 339); a genuine conversion is needed to break the hold of rent seekers over constitutionalists, and thus genuine neoliberal change turns effectively into a politics of the quasi-religious extraordinary. The impetus for reform takes on the air of an almost eschatological yearning for a profound rupture (a "constitutional revolution") of the monotony of the ever-same.[15] Similar characterizations in Friedman and Rüstow confirm this interpretation in their dream of truly "great politics; the politics that is the art of the impossible, that which wrongly was considered to be impossible" (Rüstow 1960, 117). They characterize the moment of rupture as the time when "what seemed impossible suddenly becomes possible" (Friedman and Friedman 1990, xiv).

We are left with a noteworthy conclusion: The politics of neoliberal reform is fraught with lacunae and tensions, whether the ordoliberals Röpke and Eucken's hope for benevolent guardians, Rüstow and Hayek's defense of transitory dictatorships, or Hayek's commitment to evolutionary thought that leaves his own agenda of deliberate reforms with a questionable status. Buchanan's approach is a final and perfect case in point. Based on the assumptions of his own approach, he is unable to explain how the neoliberal reforms he is striving for would ever come to be realized. As he candidly noted, "To hold out hope for reform in the basic rules describing the sociopolitical game, we must introduce elements that violate the self-interest postulate" (Brennan and Buchanan 1985, 146). As a result, he has to resort to the hope for conversion and revolutions: in short, an eschatological politics of the extraordinary.

There is a final point to be made as we transition from a sole focus on neoliberal theory to integrate considerations of neoliberal practice in the context of the European Union. It takes us back to the beginning of this book and the comment about the greatest trick that the devil ever pulled, which was not invented by the scriptwriter for *The Usual Suspects* but by Charles Baudelaire in his short story "The Generous Gambler." Remember that in the controversies over neoliberalism one of the starkest contrasts is between those critics who speak of neoliberal hegemony and those sympathetic to neoliberalism who still profess that it has never really existed—at least in actual practice. In light of the discussion we have to conclude that there is another twist to this somewhat bizarre constellation because it seems as if the neoliberals themselves are also virtually a part of this debate, as their inability to theorize a proper politics of neoliberal reform offers inadvertent proof that the devil, indeed, *cannot* exist.

But what additional conclusions are to be drawn if there is empirical proof that neoliberal reforms *are* in fact passed and, for example, balanced-budget amendments are introduced despite Buchanan's difficulties in theorizing the possibility? Of course, it is possible to argue that this has no implications because the politics of austerity and the debt brakes adopted in the EU could be simply an instantiation of those rare windows of opportunity for a politics of the extraordinary. However, in my view, even those who strongly oppose the talk of a "neoliberal age" as too sweeping and mostly politically motivated would concede that neoliberal practices and their respective reforms may not be hegemonic but are far from a rare anomaly in an otherwise solidly entrenched *non*-neoliberal status quo. So I think the rather simple conclusion to be drawn for the moment is along the lines of old-fashioned Popperian falsificationism: If the theory is not borne out in practice and empirical observation contradicts it, there must be something wrong with the theory and its assumptions. Buchanan's own attempt to account for the fact that, empirically, politicians have at times closed certain constitutional loopholes concedes as much: "The political economist who tries to remain with a rent-seeking model of democratic politics cannot explain these events" (1991, 11). Concretely, this means that the neoliberal critiques of state and democracy especially become questionable in at least some of their aspects because they rely on assumptions and analytical frameworks that yield results that are—if only in certain respects—simply incongruent with observed reality.

PART II

Disciplining Europe

We now broaden the scope of the analysis to ascertain how political theory relates to the world of actually existing neoliberalism in the context of the EU as it has been reshaped over the course of the financial crisis, particularly in response to the Eurozone crisis.

We focus on this spatiotemporal context for two reasons. First, I am interested in an analysis of "our neoliberal present," using Foucault's expression, what it looks like after one of the gravest crises since the Great Depression and what marks, if any, the crisis has left on its current shape and form. Second, I focus on Europe because the EU and EMU easily represent the most advanced laboratory for the development of neoliberal political forms. Here we find neoliberal ideas encapsulated not just in nation-states and international (trade) regimes but in a supranational federation (with a common currency). Furthermore, while many of the alleged causes of the financial crisis have not been addressed on either side of the Atlantic, the Eurozone has seen a flurry of far-ranging institutional reforms in response to the so-called sovereign debt crisis over the last decade. The implications are so far ranging that it is no overstatement to suggest that Europe today constitutes one of the most important sites for the development and contestation of neoliberalism.

My main thesis is that we witness a transformation of the EU, which amounts to its increasing ordoliberalization in many important aspects. In other words, its structural setup has come to resemble ever more closely the vision(s) put forward especially—but not exclusively—by those thinkers who belong to the ordoliberal current within neoliberalism, and within this current, particularly Walter Eucken. Building this case requires several preliminary steps in the argument. First, we briefly look at the financial crisis and compare the European and US responses. Initially the political approaches to deal with the socioeconomic fallout of the crisis did not differ dramatically, but there was a marked divergence with the onset of the Eurozone crisis in late 2009. In the following years, the gap between the economic development of the United States, which had a relatively speedy or at least continuous recovery from the crisis, and that of the Eurozone, which had a prolonged economic slump, widened significantly, which prompts a question concerning the merits and defects of the European crisis management. To scrutinize this, I briefly introduce the various major reforms in economic governance structures and policy measures and their effects. However, to gain a full understanding of the reforms, we must also briefly scrutinize the structure, workings, and effects of the EMU. This also gives us the opportunity to explore to what extent the EMU had already conformed to neoliberal tenets regarding economic federations even before its most recent reconfiguration.

It is indisputable that while members of the EU through their respective institutions officially decided on the reform process—and less officially in the Euro Group in matters that pertain only to the Eurozone—Germany has commanded the most influence since 2010. Germany was already one of the most powerful EU members due to its economic weight, and the economic crises propelled it into a leading position in orchestrating the rescue of the Eurozone from its looming breakup. Therefore, we review varying attempts to explain Germany's reform strategy. We must also tangentially address a complex issue and an equally complex and perennial debate, which concerns the explanatory framework and the underlying ontological assumptions used in accounting for actors' behavior. In principle, there are three main factors to consider in such explanatory endeavors: interests, institutions, and ideas, possibly in varying combinations. Needless to say, much has been written about these issues, so I confine this discussion to making the case that neither exclusively interest-based approaches, those based on rational choice, nor their purely institutionalist counterparts offer an adequate account. In my view, this position is generalizable, but it is particularly convincing in the case at hand because ideas matter even more than usual under certain conditions that can be described as fundamental uncertainty. Under such conditions, which the European crisis produced in its several iterations, actors are not even sure what their interests are and must consequently rely—more or less consciously—on ideas and heuristics to chart their course of action. Therefore, in times of crisis ideas must be taken particularly seriously; and it is ordoliberal ideas that provided German policy makers with the basic frameworks and road maps to interpret the crisis and conceive of the appropriate remedies to overcome it. The result is the increasing ordoliberalization of Europe.

CHAPTER 6

European Crises: Causes and Consequences

At this point there exist numerous accounts of the global financial crisis of 2008 and what led to it, from the erudite analyses of political economists like Joseph Stiglitz or Nouriel Roubini to investigative journalistic narratives such as Michael Lewis's *The Big Short*, which was even turned into a movie. Given the abundance of literature on the topic and the fact that it is of no immediate relevance to my purposes, there is no need to once more recapitulate at length how cheap money provided by the Federal Reserve, surplus international capital in search of investment opportunities, sophisticated but ultimately fatal financial instruments such as mortgage-backed securities developed by Wall Street, and a real estate market bubble in the United States eventually led to the collapse of Lehman Brothers in 2008. This triggered the crisis through the shockwaves it sent into the political economies on both sides of the Atlantic and even beyond (see, e.g., Roubini and Mihm 2010; Stiglitz 2010) and which many on the political left considered a crisis of neoliberalism at the time (see Stiglitz 2008; Birch and Mykhnenko 2010; Duménil and Lévy 2011).

Actors in financial markets responded to the unwillingness to save the rather small bank with panic, and a fire sale of all those assets suddenly turned toxic in the balance sheets of much larger financial institutions. This threatened to trigger a financial meltdown of truly epic proportions. To prevent this from happening, in the United States a Republican administration under George W. Bush decided to bail out the financial sector through the $700 billion Troubled Asset Relief Program and turned the Federal Reserve Bank into a "bad bank," into which those toxic assets could be transferred and thus disappear from the balance sheets of the private sector. The administration also de facto nationalized some of the major US financial institutions, and this would not be the last of the policy surprises.

Despite the bailouts the financial sector was paralyzed and interbank lending was anemic, which translated into restrictions on economic activity on the supply side, resulting in lower investment. Furthermore, the burst of the real estate bubble, house foreclosures, the erasure of pension funds, and the overall sense of insecurity added less-than-favorable conditions on the demand side as (debt-financed) private domestic consumption threatened to collapse as well, and with it one of the former pillars of the American accumulation regime.[1] So the newly elected Obama administration continued the course of unconventional policies begun by its predecessor with a multifaceted attempt to stimulate the "real" economy that had begun to slide into a recession. Funds were appropriated for public infrastructure projects through the American Recovery and Reinvestment Act, a Cash for Clunkers program was initiated to subsidize the ailing American car industry (only to eventually nationalize parts of it as well), and the government essentially sent out checks in the form of tax rebates to approximately 130 million households so their members would spend money. The fiscal stimulus was flanked by a monetary one by the Federal Reserve Bank, which lowered its interest rates dramatically and kept them this low until early 2017. Furthermore, under Chairman Ben Bernanke the Federal Reserve also ventured into new territory with multiple rounds of "quantitative easing," which amounts to the creation of new money and injecting it into the economy—the privilege and, some would say, one of the major advantages of a central bank. One of those who saw this capacity as a major advantage was John Maynard Keynes, and it stands to reason that he would have approved of the US strategy in countering the strong recessionary tendencies in the economy, because Keynesianism it was by all accounts. To be sure, for some commentators, such as Paul Krugman, the magnitude of these measures was still insufficient given the massive scale of economic contraction the country underwent, but it is still noteworthy that *thirty* years after the "Volcker Shock" had officially buried Keynesianism and ushered in monetarism in the United States,[2] the portfolio of Keynesian stimuli measures was suddenly back in demand. Moreover, it was almost *forty* years ago, when Richard Nixon found himself declaring, "We are all Keynesians now!" This seemed to be true again, because not only the United States rediscovered the instruments of demand management, which brings us to the (immediate) European response to the crisis.

In the early months of the financial crisis the European attempts to rein in its fallout hardly differed from the American strategies. Banks that were particularly exposed, because of their activities in the US real estate market and because financial sectors on both sides were simply too deeply interwoven for the European ones to be unaffected by the events in the United States, had to be bailed out to the tune of billions of euros, especially in Ireland, the United Kingdom, and Germany. And as in the United States, the banking crisis and the ensuing credit freeze promptly triggered a downturn in the economy more generally speaking, which the Europeans also sought to contain with fiscal stimuli; the German Abwrackprämie actually served as the model for the American Cash for Clunkers version. But while it seemed that in 2009 we were all Keynesians again—even the Chinese introduced a massive stimulus to shield their mainly export-driven economy from the repercussions of a global contraction—the Keynesian revival, at least in Europe, was short-lived, and what followed was a dramatic course reversal (see Woodruff 2016, 82). The retreat from Keynesianism and the beginning of the divergence between European and US economic strategies and outcomes can be dated fairly precisely to October 2009, when the incoming government of Greece publicly announced that the public deficit was not a little more than 6 percent of GDP but a little less than double that. It was the beginning of the Eurozone crisis,[3] as rating agencies refocused their attention on public debt and deficits and Greece's bond rating was eventually downgraded from A to BBB-. This put the country immediately on the brink of default because its bonds were reduced to junk status and their yields spiked, which meant that the burden of debt including interest would increase even more. Not only Greece caught the eye of rating agencies but also other countries such as Spain and Ireland, who had been fiscal poster children up until the crisis, but they had to absorb the fallout of their own real estate bubbles bursting in 2009, which led to dramatically increased levels of public debt. In the changed context of a global recession, the possibility of a Greek default,[4] fears of ensuing "contagion effects," and the obvious but crucial fact that Eurozone countries could not issue debt in a currency they controlled (see De Grauwe 2011, 2), Italy and Portugal, whose debt levels did not see a rise comparable to those of Ireland or Spain, suddenly also found themselves on the list of countries whose debt levels were considered potentially unsustainable and whose bonds were downgraded as well. With them the group of countries that would come to be referred to as GIPS was complete (Greece, Ireland, Portugal, and Spain, with Iceland later adding another "I"), and just as the acronym wrongly suggested that they all suffered from the same financial problems for a common reason, fiscal profligacy, a common solution was rolled out, and not only for them: the politics of austerity.

Austerity, in the words of Mark Blyth, who has written its authoritative critical intellectual and natural history, "is a form of voluntary deflation in which the economy adjusts through the reduction of wages, prices, and public spending to restore competitiveness, which is (supposedly) best achieved by cutting the state's budget, debts, and deficits" (2013, 2). Thus, fiscal consolidation, tax rises, expenditure cuts (especially with regard to the welfare state), and labor-market reforms to overcome "rigidities" and increase flexibility became the order of the day. At the G20 summit in Toronto in 2010 the declaration signed by the finance ministers of participating countries gave a clear indication the tide was beginning to turn, as it emphasized "the importance of sustainable public finances," which, despite the avowal to "follow through on delivering existing stimulus plans" marked a notable shift from only a few months before when the position had still been to ensure the recovery through a continuation of public spending ("G-20 Toronto Summit Declaration" 2010).[5] Among the G20 countries, particularly the Europeans, especially the Germans alongside the British, opted for a change in course. German finance minister Wolfgang Schäuble had an op-ed piece published in the *Handelsblatt* in June 2010, in which he stressed that the risks of an abrupt end to these policies notwithstanding, "a stimulus of aggregate demand financed through credit must not become a drug-like state of permanence," and therefore they needed an "exit strategy." Addressing the criticism from the United States, he added that "for the German population sound public finances are of considerable importance; public debt levels considered too high, conversely, prompt anxieties—even if this is difficult to comprehend on the other side of the Atlantic" (Schäuble 2010). Schäuble's most vocal supporters were the incoming chancellor of the exchequer in Great Britain, George Osborne, and European Central Bank (ECB) director Jean-Claude Trichet. Addressing the British parliament in 2010, Osborne presented his first budget, which combined expenditure cuts (80 percent) with tax increases (20 percent) of an overall volume of 40 billion pounds with the words: "This Budget is needed to deal with our country's debts. This Budget is needed to give confidence to our economy. This is the unavoidable Budget. . . . The country has overspent; it has not been under-taxed," thus ushering in the era of austerity in Britain. Trichet (2010b) wrote that "we expect governments to confirm their determination to consolidate their public finances" and provided specific recommendations for the methods as well: "Adjustment on the spending side, accompanied by structural reforms to promote long-term growth, has typically been the best strategy, especially when combined with a credible long-term commitment to fiscal consolidation." In an interview with *La Repubblica* a month earlier he had already dismissed the mounting criticisms of the German course summarily: "I am pleased that the German government is concentrating on discipline. And what I think about Germany also applies to the others" (Trichet 2010a).

And so the stage was set for an approach to the Eurozone crisis that would seek to keep the EMU together, at least for the time being; rescue packages were created to bail out the respective countries and protect—once again—the banks that had stockpiled the countries' bonds and were too big to be saved by individual governments. However, the availability of these funds was strictly conditional on the implementation of the notorious "structural reforms" in the respective countries that would have effects in line with those of the politics of austerity.[6] Furthermore, even for those European countries not on the verge of bankruptcy, fiscal discipline became the order of the day—or rather a state of permanence—crowding out most other considerations and recipes regarding a viable road to economic recovery. But before we take a closer look at these measures, two points are worth highlighting: First, the European approach differed strongly from that pursued by the US government, which is illustrated by the American position when the transatlantic rift began to open at the G20 summit in Toronto. In a letter to the G20, Secretary of the Treasury Tim Geithner pointed out that "concerns about growth as Europe makes needed policy adjustment threaten to undercut the momentum of the recovery" (cited in Giles and Oliver 2010). To be sure, the United States experienced its own fair share of austerity over time, from the "fiscal cliff" to the "sequestration" of the budget, which led to significant retrenchment, especially on the substate levels that are legally required to balance their budgets (see Krugman 2012, 213–214; Peck 2014). However, the rigidity of the European course in the face of no signs of recovery led to increasing puzzlement that was not confined to the expected outrage by committed Keynesians such as Paul Krugman. Others such as Joseph Stiglitz, Martin Wolf, and Erik Jones regularly wrote columns in the *New York Times* and *Financial Times* chiding the European Union, especially Germany, for a misguided and counterproductive attempt to save their way toward recovery. Even the US government, which routinely takes a more market-oriented position than most of its European counterparts, strongly recommended a review of the current course, citing concerns over the economic health of one of its most important trading partners and urging the Europeans not to "free-ride" on the expansionary politics elsewhere—prompting the German response along the lines of Schäuble's, quoted previously. More important, while the divergence between the respective approaches may be initially accounted for by the Eurozone crisis, which simply was not a factor in the context of US crisis management, this will not suffice as an explanation. While the austerity strategy may seem intuitively plausible as the only possible response to debts and deficits, it really is not, and neither was there no alternative, because the often-cited financial markets had supposedly demanded it (see Woodruff 2016, 104).

A curious expression that Schäuble used in the *Handelsblatt* op-ed reveals the inherent contradictions of the austerity path toward fiscal sustainability. What was needed now, wrote Schäuble, was "expansionary fiscal consolidation"—but it is far from clear how this might be achieved. After all, if a country is burdened by debts and deficits and embarks on a course of retrenchment, the immediate effect to be expected is a contraction of the economy, which leads to additional expenditure in the form of "automatic stabilizers," such as unemployment support and massively reduced tax revenue. It is unclear where exactly the expansionary aspect in fiscal consolidation can be found.[7] The counterargument is to cite the need to restore confidence in the fiscal sustainability of a country, which may lead to a reduction in yields on sovereign bonds.[8] However, the "confidence fairy," as Krugman came to call it mockingly in his columns (2012, 195), is a fickle creature because one would assume that in the short run confidence in fiscal sustainability is best restored through economic growth. Therefore, markets were at best ambiguous with regard to the viability of the austerity strategy and for years did not show much sign that their confidence was restored—to the contrary. This brings us to the second point, which, from a practical political point of view, is arguably the more important one and concerns the socioeconomic development of the United States and the Eurozone over the following years.

The recession in the United States technically lasted from December 2007 to June 2009. In the Eurozone the initial recession lasted from January 2008 to April 2009. However, beginning in the third quarter of 2011 it relapsed into a prolonged recession that lasted another two years. Since 2014 there were only two quarters in which economic growth across the nineteen countries was higher than 0.5 percent. In terms of GDP per capita, the Eurozone shows a picture of steady decline until the first quarter of 2017. If we compare the Eurozone and the United States with regard to this indicator from 2007 to 2015, the former's poor performance is thrown into sharp relief. While Eurozone GDP per capita declined by 1.8 percent, in the United States there was an increase of 3 percent.

These diverging economic trends are also reflected in what is arguably the most fateful socioeconomic indicator, unemployment. As of 2014, American unemployment was at 6.7 percent; in the Eurozone it was almost twice that, with Spain and Greece having to endure levels of 26.7 and 27.8 percent, respectively, with a punishing 57.4 and 59.2 percent level of youth unemployment. In 2015 unemployment slowly began to decline in the Eurozone, but at the end of the year it was still as high as 10.4 percent. And while 2016 has seen the strongest recovery—the overall rate in December fell to single digits (9.4 percent) for the first time since spring 2009—this figure compares unfavorably with the 4.7 percent in the United States in the same month. Furthermore, what the average hides is the continuing high levels in the countries hardest hit by the crisis. In early February 2017 Greece was still confronting a staggering overall unemployment rate of 23.1 percent; and Spain, 18 percent.[9]

In Greece and other Southern European countries epidemiologists can literally measure the reduction of average life expectancy and increased levels in (mental) illnesses due to the crisis. It seems that Europeans have paid a heavy toll over the course of "expansionary fiscal consolidation" in what has been described by commentators as a lost decade. This assessment seems hardly exaggerated even though the Eurozone is finally showing signs of a sustained recovery driven not only by the German economy. But after almost a decade of recession, an eventual upswing is surely to be expected. So the question that we will come back to is this: If even the traditionally fiscally hawkish Americans advised against it, if the markets were ambiguous at best, and if it subjects entire populations to at times unbearably harsh sacrifices, why was the politics of austerity pursued in such a single-minded manner in Europe?

Restructuring the EU/EMU: An Overview of the Major Reforms

The first major reform triggered by the Eurozone crisis was an immediate response to the situation in Greece that was designed to keep the country solvent—just enough so it could be held in debt bondage forever, more critical voices would say—and prevent it from having to leave the EMU as a consequence.[10] The European Financial Stability Facility (EFSF) was established in 2010. It did not provide funds but only guarantees and was specifically introduced as an emergency measure limited to three years to make sure it would not conflict with the now (in)famous no-bail-out clause of Article 125 of the Treaty for the Functioning of the European Union (TFEU), which prohibits member states or European institutions from financing national budgets. However, it soon became clear that the EFSF could not placate investors' concerns and that Greece would not, contrary to early predictions by the European Commission and the proponents of austerity, return to economic growth anytime soon, not to mention countries like Spain, Portugal, and Ireland, which were also in need of financial assistance. So in July 2011, after the TFEU had been amended accordingly, the European Stability Mechanism (ESM) was created to replace EFSF and to provide Eurozone member states that applied for financial support with both guarantees and actual money: 80 billion euros were available in paid-in funds by member states and another 620 billion of callable capital. However, this money was made available only with strict conditions.[11] Recipients, which include at the time of writing Greece, Spain, Portugal, Ireland, and Cyprus, had to agree to sign a memorandum of understanding, in which they committed themselves to implement structural reforms in the spirit of austerity. The typical measures demanded applicants for ESM funds to carry out tax increases; cuts in state expenditures, especially related to social policies, such as reduction of pensions, health-care coverage, and unemployment benefits; privatization of public assets; and deregulation of labor markets. Given that these measures resemble very closely the typical contents of the Structural Adjustment Programs the International Monetary Fund (IMF) would prescribe to countries in need of financial assistance as condition for its support, it may not be a surprise that the IMF also became involved in the ESM rescue packages as part of the infamous Troika, which is now officially referred to as "the institutions." Still, it is noteworthy that an international organization was brought in to complement the European Commission and the ECB in their task of monitoring the progress made by the recipients of funds in implementing the required reforms. It stands to reason that the assumption was that the regime would be even stricter if an external organization with a reputation for insisting on the implementation of its often harsh adjustment programs was brought in and that the threat to withhold the next tranche of financial aid in the absence of significant progress would be more credible. It is highly ironic, therefore, that of the three institutions the IMF has emerged as the least hawkish and even threatened to leave the arrangement if there were not significant debt restructuring in Greece. In any case, with the Troika a strong and strict enforcement agent has been created, and it does not seem exaggerated to say that the governments of EFSF/ESM recipient countries have little room to maneuver in regard to accepting and implementing the various memoranda—even against the expressed will of their own citizenry.[12]

The ESM-cum-Troika arrangement is the part of the euro rescue operation that is most easily and rightfully scandalized; commentators in the respective countries sometimes refer to the Troika as an "occupation regime" (the Troika officials actually visited the countries in question to make a firsthand assessment of their progress, implicitly suggesting that the reports filed by the local administrations and government were not trustworthy) and the memorandum as an "economic dictate." However, for my thesis the other three major reforms are arguably even more important because they do not concern emergency rescue operations of countries on the verge of bankruptcy but constitute a structural transformation of the economic governance of the EU/EMU.

The so-called Six-Pack, deliberations over which began in March 2010 in the middle of the initial debates over a Greek bailout, was officially adopted in November 2011; it is a far less prominent subject of public debate than the Troika, but it has far-reaching implications for the restructuring of the EU/EMU. Its rather masculinist name derives from the fact that it consists of five regulations and one directive—it is part of secondary EU law—and its main effect can be described as tightening and complementing the existing Stability and Growth Pact (SGP) from 1996–1997 passed in the run-up to the introduction of the euro and designed to placate particularly German concerns over the stability of the future European currency. The signatories essentially committed themselves to adopt what is often referred to as a quintessentially German "culture of stability," which translated into the measurable parameter of a rule of a maximum of 3 percent deficits and 60 percent public debt. However, the efficacy of the SGP had always been a matter of debate among Europeanists (see Heipertz and Verdun 2010; Savage 2007). The respective questions regarding the SGP's efficacy loomed even larger when in the early 2000s France and Germany repeatedly violated the deficit rule. Even though the commission wanted to initiate the pact's excessive deficit procedure, because procedural rules were unclear and, more important, because a sufficiently large number of the Economic and Financial Affairs Council (ECOFIN) members resisted, neither country was sanctioned. Consequently, the SGP was reformed, but in the eyes of many observers the regime of fiscal discipline was considered so toothless that it was practically irrelevant—at least in regard to powerful nations such as Germany and France (see Leblond 2006).

So the Six-Pack was to build on and restore the SGP in three ways. First, it tightened the already existing excessive deficit procedure by explicitly including debt levels in it. This means that a procedure can be initiated against a country even if it does not fail the deficit criterion but has a debt level above 60 percent of GDP. Second, the lesson from the standoff between Germany, France, and the commission in the early 2000s incorporated in the Six-Pack is the introduction of the "reverse qualified majority" as a decision-making rule in the council. Before its introduction, the commission's recommendation to initiate a procedure had to be backed by a qualified majority in the council in order to go forward, obviously opening up the possibility of forming blocking alliances with others for the countries in question. Now the recommendation to initiate the procedure and whether to fine member states continuously in violation is adopted if there is no qualified majority *against* it. Presumably, this makes it much more difficult to block the procedure and thus comes close to a quasi-automatic rule that is supposed to minimize political influencing, logrolling, and so on. The reverse-qualified-majority rule also applies to the final novelty included in the Six-Pack, which may be seen as an immediate response to the Eurozone crisis but, in its implications, is also that part of the reform package with the most far-reaching implications: the Macroeconomic Imbalance Procedure (MIP).

The MIP can be considered a lesson from the debt crisis to the extent that "for most euro periphery member states, the crisis was mainly a balance of payment crisis, due to the building up of persistent macroeconomic imbalances from the launch of the single currency in 1999" (Howarth and Quaglia 2015, 466). In other words, it was now assumed that not only excessive deficits and debt constituted a problem individually for the country in question and collectively for the EMU, but excessive imbalances would also have to be monitored through the preventive arm or rectified through the corrective arm of the procedure, which in this respect was designed after the model of its excessive deficit counterpart. Although deficits and debts are much less unambiguously and objectively certified by some third party such as the commission than one may think, because accounting systems vary and sometimes are intentionally made to vary,[13] this is even more the case with regard to a macroeconomic imbalance and the question of when it becomes "excessive." Macroeconomic imbalances can be related to relative competitiveness, which obviously does not make matters easier, because the question then concerns the measurement of competitiveness. Accordingly, the political economists of the commission have designed an economic scoreboard consisting of eleven indicators that together are supposed to give a quantifiable expression of this relative competitiveness. I cannot dwell long on this scoreboard and the questions it raises,[14] but briefly the indicators in some cases measure flows and relative changes over time; in others, static conditions; and with regard to all of them the scoreboard identifies certain thresholds that delimit the range of acceptable variation. If one or more indicators move outside this range, the commission can initiate the preventive arm of the MIP and, typically, conducts an in-depth country review; based on the review, the commission either sees no further cause for action or, more likely, makes recommendations about how to address the imbalance through the appropriate reform measures. If excessive imbalances that require actions are not remedied in due time, the commission can eventually initiate the corrective arm of the procedure and, as in the case of excessive deficits, sanction the country with financial fines. What is noteworthy about the indicators for a macroeconomic imbalance is what makes the effects of the procedure so far reaching: effects include balance of payments, real effective exchange rates, public and private debt levels, and real estate prices and unit-labor costs. Some of these effects are subject to rather limited direct governmental influence; to the extent that they actually can be influenced by governmental policy, the measures putatively required can pertain to policy areas that are explicitly outside EU competencies, such as social and labor-market policy. Accordingly, the MIP broadens the scope of European influence through the commission on national policy far beyond the formal domain of the EU, and it presupposes a much more in-depth knowledge of domestic politics and arrangements, as an official from the secretariat general of the commission confirms: "The excessive deficit targets are relatively straightforward, but advising member states what to do about the development of real estate prices, their pension systems, or their unemployment benefits requires a completely different kind of knowledge" (cited in Savage and Verdun 2015, 110). One can argue that the MIP constitutes a step away from the exclusive focus on debts and deficits and is therefore to be welcomed, but it nevertheless broadens the scope of the commission's scrutiny and influence dramatically, which is not only questionable from a democratic but also from an EU law point of view.

The next reform package is the Two-Pack, consisting of two regulations adopted in 2013. Its main purpose is to standardize the national budgeting processes of the Eurozone members in the framework of the so-called European Semester introduced in 2011 and to increase the commission's supervisory powers over national budgeting. In the intricate schedule introduced by the reform package, national governments have to submit their draft budgets at a particular time to the commission for review to assess whether it is in line with medium-term budgetary objectives based on forecasts regarding the economic development of the country in question. Importantly, the budget has to be submitted to the commission, which expects a response to its assessment regarding its feasibility *before* the national parliaments can view and debate the budget. To be sure, national parliaments ultimately decide officially on the budget, and over the course of the European Semester the European Parliament and the council are also consulted and can give opinions, but the overall effect of the reform is a significant shift in influence from the legislative to the executive branches, which is noteworthy given that budgetary power of the purse is historically considered the core competency of parliaments. But it also involves a shift from the national to the supranational scale, as the commission acquires unprecedented monitoring and at least indirect influencing capacities over national budget processes. Finally, these new rules, just as monitoring done with regard to the preventive arms of excessive deficit and macroeconomic imbalance procedures, apply not only to exceptional cases of countries facing bankruptcy, as in the case of the ESM-cum-Troika regime, but to all member states of the EU, or the Eurozone in the case of the European Semester.

The final and most recent reform we consider is the Treaty on Stability, Coordination and Governance that was signed in 2012 and came into effect in 2013. Originally, it was not part of EU law but an international treaty signed by all EU members except the United Kingdom and the Czech Republic. However, in December 2017, it was adopted as part of EU law. While it includes other elements that consist mostly of calls for increased cooperation and coordination, its most important part is the Fiscal Compact. The

Fiscal Compact once more targets deficits and debts because it requires the signees to pass balanced or surplus budgets; the maximum deficits allowed in accordance with the pact are –0.5 percent or –1 percent if a country's debt is significantly below 60 percent of GDP. If a country is above the 60 percent threshold, it is required to work toward reducing its debt by 5 percent annually. Again, it is first and foremost the commission that is in charge of monitoring adherence to the Fiscal Compact, and it presents the countries in violation with restructuring programs designed to bring their fiscal status in line with treaty requirements. In addition, it can install stability councils in the respective countries. If a country fails to deliver on the requirements, the commission and individual signatory states can take the matter to court and sue in the European Court of Justice (ECJ), which may fine the country. Last, and by far not least, the Fiscal Compact stipulates that all signees should introduce a "debt brake" or balanced-budget amendment along the lines of what Germany passed in 2009 through national legislation, preferably on the level of constitutional law. The balanced-budget amendment seemingly is informed by practical experience and scholarship on the efficacy of supranational fiscal rules, which suggests that such rules tend to have a much more tangible effect if they are part of national legislation rather than international or EU law (see Marneffe et al. 2011). With these major reforms clarified in their basic contours and respective thrust, we now explore how they fit into the larger context of the EU/EMU.[15]

The Evolution of the EU

It goes without saying that it is impossible to provide a comprehensive account of the EU and its transformation from its nucleus, the European Coal and Steel Community to the European Community established sixty years ago in the Treaty of Rome to the set of overlapping unions—the EU proper, the EMU, and the Schengen Area—which are not in complete congruence. It is also beyond the scope of this chapter to provide an exhaustive analysis of the various institutions of the EU from the European Parliament, to the European Commission, the Council of the European Union / the European Council, and the ECJ, although I will reference them on occasion. The twofold task of this section is more limited. First we need a basic grasp of the structure and dynamics of the EMU to comprehend how they contributed to the specific characteristics of the Eurozone crisis and to allow us to assess the logic of the various reforms described previously. We can then pursue the question of whether and to what extent the EMU—even before the most recent restructuring—conformed to neoliberal visions of a federation as they are found in the works of Hayek, Buchanan, and Röpke, analyzed in Chapter 2.

After the Single European Act of 1986 revived the aspirations first expressed in the Treaty of Rome, the European Community was committed to form a "common market" based on what is usually referred to as the "four freedoms": free movement of goods, capital, services, and people across borders. The aim was to form a market on which there would be no restrictions for "insiders" to move and allocate. In the legal language used by the ECJ, the market was to be based on a rigorous application of the principle of nondiscrimination of EU citizens, companies, and other organizations. One of the essential preconditions for markets and effective competition is to increase mobility of factors and reduce restrictions on their allocation as far as possible. Companies should be able to invest their capital and even relocate wherever the law of value suggests without having to face bureaucratic hurdles or other protective measures like tariffs from the jurisdiction in question, even if domestic competitors might be negatively affected. People also should be able to take a job and simply decide to live in whatever jurisdiction they choose without any restriction, although the assumption among the creators of the common market always was that people would exhibit the least mobility compared to that of goods, capital, and services; consequently, the aim was to create efficient "local factor markets" rather than count on people migrating between countries in massive numbers (see Jones 2013, 149). In the eyes of many observers the EU has a rather disappointing record regarding integration and development of common positions, such as in the area of foreign and defense policy, but the common market has always been regarded as an area where "integration through law" had proceeded most forcefully. The commission emerged as a determined actor in enabling and fighting any restrictions of competition; competition policy is probably the most Europeanized policy area in the EU. The ECJ, similarly, established itself as a strict guardian and enforcer of the principle of nondiscrimination, granting all legal or natural persons who considered themselves restricted in their market access and their right to compete on equal footing the right to take the case to court; and the large majority of cases were decided in their favor.

With the Common Market spearheading European integration, the next logical next step would seem to be to enable even more efficient factor allocation and trade by introducing a common currency. However, behind the Euro and EMU were not only economic but also political considerations. Even before German reunification the former Federal Republic of Germany was an economic heavyweight with regard to output and a currency, the Deutschmark, which represented stability to the extent that several other European countries had their currencies more or less officially pegged to it. The idea of a common currency was born in the negotiations over a potential German reunification in 1989–1990. Among the former Allies, especially the United Kingdom, there was considerable concern over the prospect of a reunified Germany, which possibly would put the "German question" back on the agenda: how a Germany located at the geographical center of the continent, too small for a hegemon but much bigger, especially economically speaking, than all of its neighbors, could be peacefully accommodated in a European framework. The answer to the German question, albeit provisional, was the euro. To simplify, the deal struck particularly between France and Germany was that the Germans would give up their highly valued—both in real and symbolic terms—Deutschmark in return for French support of reunification and the pledge to ensure institutionally that the future euro would be as stable as the Deutschmark had been. The ECB was to be fashioned after the model of the German Bundesbank with complete independence from political influence and a mandate that was, arguably, to be even narrower than the Bundesbank's in its sole focus on and limitation to ensuring price stability. Furthermore, the Germans insisted not only on strict convergence criteria, especially regarding deficits/debt and currency stability, for countries to be eligible to join the EMU; they also wanted assurance that countries, once they had joined, would not slide back into possibly running deficits and accumulating debt. Rather, countries were expected to live up to the requirements of a "culture of stability," as it is typically referred to, and thus the SGP was conceived. Finally, and also

most fatefully, in Article 125 of the TFEU the no-bail-out clause was codified, making it illegal for any member state or the ECB to directly finance
the budget of another member state, thus supposedly ensuring no country
could ever be held liable for another's debt and signaling clearly to each
member state that it could not rely on anyone's support if it found itself in
dire financial straits.

It is quite obvious from this clearly selective and simplified recapitula-
tion of the events leading to the formation of EMU that the initial political
case for the euro was arguably strong among all concerned parties. The new
arrangement gave France, the Netherlands, and Belgium, who joined EMU
right away, at least a seat at the table of monetary policy, since the national
central bank directors formed the board of the ECB; previously these countries
were affected by the monetary course of the Bundesbank without having any
say in it. The Germans, however, were granted the approval to reunify and
received the institutional guarantees they wanted from the ECB's mandate
to the no-bail-out clause. Furthermore, the EMU became especially attractive for countries that had not been known for their culture of stability and
therefore had had to pay high yields on their sovereign bonds. Once they
had met the convergence criteria and joined the euro, the yields dropped
to almost German levels, with investors obviously operating under the assumption that Italian or Spanish debt was ultimately guaranteed by German
economic power. In this sense there were obviously good economic reasons
for these countries to join the euro because their access to capital increased
tremendously. However, although Spain did indeed benefit from its debt being
effectively treated like German debt, the Germans, in turn, benefited from
their currency not only being treated like the Spanish one but it in fact being
the same. As a consequence the value of the euro was much lower, relatively
speaking, than the Deutschmark would have been, thus providing exchange-
rate levels that were highly favorable for a country that had come to rely
strongly on an export-led accumulation regime and, with the euro, would
come to depend on it even more.

While there were strong economic reasons to join the euro, economic
reason did not necessarily look favorably on the EMU, because as soon as
the idea of the common currency was codified in the Maastricht Treaty in
1992, there was no shortage of economists who pointed out the vagaries of

such an undertaking. The future Eurozone, they pointed out, was not an "optimum currency area" (Mundell 1961), essentially meaning that there was not sufficient ability to absorb asymmetric shocks, such as an economic crisis, through labor-force mobility and interregional transfers; and the disparities between widely differing varieties of capitalism or accumulation regimes would ultimately drive the currency union apart (see, e.g., Feldstein 1997). If at all, the euro should be introduced at the end of a long process of economic convergence, the argument went; but in combination with the political rationale of an ever-closer union with a common currency the opposite view was victorious in the debate. The existence of disparities between the EMU members was not disputed, but the sequence of the "coronation theory" that saw the euro as the crowning achievement at the end of economic convergence was reversed: Now the Euro was to provide the common monetary framework that, once adopted, would slowly but steadily push the various economies toward convergence.

However, the years following the introduction of the euro in 1999 instead showed a pattern of persisting, if not widening, gaps between the various political economies. One of the major reasons for this development was what many consider to be the fatal flaw of the EMU and among the root causes of the debt crisis, a common monetary policy that had to operate according to one size fits all without a common fiscal policy. What happened in the early 2000s can be exemplified by Germany and Spain. For a number of reasons in the early years of this century, Germany was not the economic powerhouse it is seen as today. In fact, it was considered the "sick man of Europe," with sluggish growth, high unemployment, an aging population, and what commentators at the time chided as an oversized welfare state and rigid labor market. Before the EMU was established, the value of the Deutschmark might have decreased to the benefit of the export sector in this situation. Furthermore, given the very low levels of inflation, the Bundesbank could have provided some monetary impulses to spur economic growth. However, the value of the common currency did not decrease, and the ECB had to consider not only Germany's economic fate and its position closer to the bottom of the business cycle but also that of Spain, which experienced a massive influx of capital; the resulting economic activity, especially in the real estate sector, heated up the economy, resulting ultimately in rising wages and prices. The dilemma the ECB was in and continues to be faced with is obvious. An expansionary German monetary policy with lowered interest rates would have been well within its mandate, given the low real inflation levels, and recommendable, given the slow economic growth; but Spain, which experienced the opposite conditions, would have required a much more contractive course in monetary policy. Aside from some minor instruments of regionally fine-tuning its policy, the ECB simply had to strike a balance between the two and all other EMU member states. In the reality of a nonoptimum currency zone the one-size-fits-all policy of the ECB turned out to be closer to one size fits none. Given the obvious dilemma and the resulting deficiencies of ECB policy, one cannot help asking why the EMU was introduced without a common fiscal policy that could, for example, provide funds for interregional transfers and in other ways provide the instruments to counterbalance the uniform monetary policy according to national/regional needs and conditions. It is a question we return to later but can only speculate about at this point. It is well known that especially in the early years, European integration took place not necessarily behind the backs of the European citizenry but in the face of its benevolent indifference to the technical details of coal and steel market integration or competition law. The theory that captures this pattern best is neofunctionalism; according to its key concept the prime engine of ever-deeper integration was spillover effects of a mostly but not exclusively functional nature. If a particular policy area had been integrated, it simply made technical sense to integrate those affected by this integration accordingly, and there may have been the hope that the spillover effect from a common monetary policy could be a common fiscal policy in the framework of a real political union. However, for manifold reasons, the cunning of neofunctionalist reason failed this time and left the EMU to stand on just one leg of monetary policy.

To return to the situation in the early 2000s, the German government made a decision with far-reaching implications to overcome the economic difficulties through Agenda 2010, which primarily aimed at a labor-market deregulation resulting in an increased commodification of labor power, which, in combination with union wage restraint, drove down production costs in the German economy and enhanced its relative competitiveness. At the same time, Spain enjoyed the influx of capital because of its booming economy but also because banks were happy to buy government bonds, either assuming that Spanish debt would be as good as German debt or wagering that if they only bought enough bonds, the banks would have to be bailed out in the worst-case scenario. The result was, first, a decrease in Spanish competitiveness for reasons already mentioned and, second, an ever-closer but fateful union, not between European countries but states and banks, in what is often referred to as the "sovereign-bank nexus," which proved to be one of the problems in the Eurozone crisis.[16]

But what happened to all of the capital that flowed into countries such as Spain, Ireland, and Greece up to the onset of the financial crisis? Was it all spent on "women and drink," as the president of the Euro Group, Jeroen Dijsselbloem, quipped inflammatorily in a 2017 interview? Whatever it was, a lot of it came from Germany: While the hegemonic crisis narrative is that of profligately spending states and individuals in Southern Europe, suggesting that the only plausible and moral response is to tighten belts, resort to the politics of austerity, and become more competitive like the Germans already had done, this narrative omits, once more, the other side of the equation of the German recovery and fails to appreciate the conditions of economic interdependence. Cost-cutting your way to economic growth is difficult in a closed economy, because those producers—employees who now earn less—also buy less as consumers, and therefore the strategy can work only if someone else buys all the goods that are now produced more cost-competitively. To exaggerate a little, it is not least due to the willingness of Spaniards and Greeks to use the cheap money available to them to buy products made in Germany that Germany was able to return to economic growth. If their fellow Europeans really were to follow the German example in a more determined manner, a lot more products would be produced at cheaper prices, but in Europe no one would buy them (see Sandbu 2015, 18).

So here we have the deeper roots of the Eurozone crisis, which has, of course, something to do with macroeconomic imbalances, relative competitiveness, and debt, all of which are supposedly addressed by the reformed economic governance structures. But they are not necessarily the responsibility of any individual country and its alleged profligacy, but they are at least coproduced through a systemic context of overleveraged banks in a deadly embrace with indebted states, a nonoptimum currency zone, and an economic policy for the Eurozone that has to act solely with its one monetary arm, the fiscal one being tied behind its back.

Neoliberal Thought and European Integration

Before we return to the institutional responses to the Eurozone crisis, how they can be accounted for, and to what extent they correspond to the tenets of the political theory of ordoliberalism in particular in the next chapter, we must first assess in which respects the European Union already conformed to neoliberal precepts long before the recent restructurings and even before it became a monetary union and was only the European Economic Community (EEC) founded through the Treaty of Rome in 1957. Obviously, Eucken's untimely death prevented him from an assessment of early European integration, and Rüstow rarely discussed the issue in a detailed manner. However, the few times he addresses the EEC in his published works, his views are surprisingly skeptical. He contends, for example, that "the common market in reality . . . has further divided Europe" (1963, 111, see also 22).[17] Röpke (1955) is by far the most prolific commentator on early European integration, and despite his strong support of federalism in the abstract we already know that his criticisms of the concrete European integration project, from its earliest manifestation of the European Coal and Steel Community onward, are harsh. Röpke's position is centered around three core arguments:[18] First, if the overall goal of economic policy is to free market interaction from undue constraints beyond the rules of an economic order, this goal can be achieved through both a common market and a free-trade zone (which would still leave decisions on trade policy with nation-states, to name but one important difference). This would simply mean that each nation-state liberalizes its trade regime and opens up its market for foreign capital, goods, and so on, and in this sense true economic integration "starts at home," as he puts it (Röpke 1954, 311). The advantage of such a free-trade zone is that it comes without the risk Röpke highlights with regard to the common market and a customs union: an inside-outside dialectic, in which internal liberalization corresponds with external protectionism. Such regional economic blocks could pose an obstacle to what he still has

in mind as an ultimate telos of international integration, a universalist, mul-
tilateral world market along the lines of those of the late nineteenth and
early twentieth centuries (see Röpke 1958, 171; 1953a, 21; Slobodian 2018).
Specifically, he warns of the potentially exclusionary thrust of a post-Rome
core Europe that would seal itself off economically from both the remaining
European states and the United States. Instead, Röpke promotes the idea of
an *openly* integrating common market, which not only offers access to other
European countries but would also, in due time, include the United States
in a transatlantic union, a vision undoubtedly fueled by Cold War anxieties
as well (see Wegmann 2002, 325–328).

Second, Röpke is concerned about the mode of the integration process,
which in the early years and decades of European integration in many respects
followed the pattern of sectoral microlevel integration that would produce its
own spillover dynamic and thus lead to ever-more-encompassing integration.
Arguably, the crucial recipe for success of this mode of functional integration was
to strategically favor economic over political integration, and as we can infer
from Röpke's views of federalism more generally, he strongly objected to
economic integration *preceding* political integration (see 1954, 313).

Third, and most important, Röpke was well aware that while there is
an undeniable "ordoliberal imprint" on the EEC (Joerges 2015, 74), there
were other rivaling projects pursued within the framework of the common
market, hoping to apply to it the techniques of Keynesian macroeconomic
management. After all, Italy and especially France, as founding members
of the EEC, had a long history of a more statist understanding of economic
governance, which in the 1950s and 1960s merged with Keynesianism and
thus provided the European antipode to predominantly German ordoliberal
views of the single market. For Röpke, there is a real danger that Europeanization of certain competencies in economic and especially competition
policy, which is the requisite of building the single market, will be seized on
by the forces of Keynesianism and dirigisme in their attempt to reconfigure
the EEC into the dystopia of a centralized "collectivist European state"
(1953a, 26). And concomitant with such a "superstate," Röpke suspects a
sweeping "harmonization" of regulations and social standards, if not even a
"race to the bottom" with regard to monetary discipline that will leave the
EEC with ever-rising inflation rates (ibid.).

This last line of argument is a curious one because rhetorically it often figures as the core of Röpke's position, as he continually raises the specter of large-scale collectivism. But at the same time, the urgency of Röpke's warnings is significantly diminished when he ensures his readers that a centralized European state can never become reality, thus echoing Hayek's prewar argument regarding the supranational scale in federations. Both are adamant that it is inconceivable for European nations to delegate to "such an international Leviathan power competencies that the majority of them would not even grant their own national government" (Röpke 1953a, 26). So while there seems to be no real danger of a collectivist Europe, Röpke's rhetorical strategy relies as much on what he views as the benefits of free trade as on his premonitions of European integration gone awry in a centralist fashion. What we have then is an initially surprising finding: While many commentators point to the neoliberal and ordoliberal elements in the EEC (see Dardot and Laval 2017, 194), the one ordoliberal thinker who has extensively written on early European integration is, on balance, more of a critic than a supporter. In my reading, Röpke's reluctance to endorse European economic integration because of concerns over an excessively centralist supranationalism is also related to the lingering tensions in neoliberal thought regarding the prima facie contradictory strategies of decentralizing and recentralizing state structures, discussed in chapter 2. Remember that while one variety of neoliberal thought opted for the decentralization of statehood, including Hayek, Röpke, and Buchanan, the other emphasized the need to recenter the nation-state with Hayek and—to some extent—Röpke arguing this case as well. Röpke's overall critical stance with regard to European integration can be read as an expression of his theoretical undecidedness in these matters. Ultimately, Röpke's abstract embrace of federalism as the crucial step in overcoming national sovereignty stands in stark contrast to the overall line of argumentation in the context of European integration, where he vehemently points to the continued importance of nation-states within federations, which is consistent with his notion of federalism. Beyond that he suggests that the real desideratum of international economic order, free trade, can be achieved best in a classic Westphalian system of nation-states in which each signs bilateral agreements with the others.[19] So it is not even entirely clear whether in the concrete European context, Röpke is no more than a federalist in name only. His last text on Europe from 1964 is symptomatic in this regard, as he spends the better part of it pointing out the ills of harmonizing policies and delegating powers to the supranational scale up to the misconceived plan of a "common European government" (1964, 235). He then adds in the very last sentence the reminder that "everything should be done to promote the political and cultural integration of Europe" (ibid., 243). It remains a mystery what political integration refers to, if not exactly to those processes of Europeanization Röpke opposes.

Before looking at the neoliberal views on the EMU, we should inquire what neoliberal logic—now in the sense of Hayek and Buchanan—prevails in the single market, all of Röpke's concerns notwithstanding. The most consistent and systematic arguments I highlight in this regard come from what I am tempted to call the Cologne School of scholars in political economy/sociology based at the Max Planck Institute, such as Fritz Scharpf, Wolfgang Streeck, and Martin Höpner. For them, the crucial effect of the single market is the loss of boundary control of the various nation-states. This leads to a bigger market, more efficient factor allocation, and increased competition between private market actors, as well as to a *competitive federalism* not dissimilar to Hayek's and Buchanan's visions. Scharpf analyzes the inner workings and dynamics of this arrangement (1999, 2010).

By most accounts, building the single market based on political negotiations in the council (under the unanimity rule) and the principle of harmonization of technical standards and other production and product-related regulations stalled in the years after the Treaty of Rome was signed. The achievements of integration through politics thus remained rather limited, but in this situation a new actor, the ECJ, emerged who would come to shape the single market and the EU in general in a lasting way (see Höpner 2014). The first landmark ruling of the court pertained to the trade of goods and established principles that would later be applied to the other freedoms as well. In the famous *Dassonville* case from 1974 the court ruled that all trading rules that hinder trade, whether directly or indirectly, actually or potentially, were inadmissible (see ECJ C-8/74, *Dassonville*). The preconditions for this ruling had been provided by the court itself in two earlier cases from the 1960s, when it had effectively established the doctrine that European law trumps national law and ruled that the Treaty of Rome rules granted individual rights so that natural and legal persons could sue against alleged violations of the four freedoms. The court had thus empowered itself in a rather remarkable manner and, with the *Dassonville* case, set the tone for a much more aggressive stance on what may be considered undue constraints on cross-border economic activities. *Dassonville* was soon followed by the equally famous *Cassis* ruling that introduced certain exceptions to the principle of *Dassonville* to increase its flexibility, but this also meant that the court acquired much more discretionary power in deciding whether national rules could be justifiably upheld or would have to be struck down. Furthermore, the ruling introduced the doctrine of "mutual recognition," the recognized equivalence of national rules and regulations. This doctrine eventually served as the cornerstone of a new strategy of integration that would prove far more effective than harmonization, when the ruling held that there was no valid reason that products produced and marketed in one member state could not be introduced into another member state (see ECJ C-120/78, *Cassis de Dijon*). These rulings in particular reinvigorated the project of the single market as integration through politics was increasingly replaced by integration through law. However, in political negotiations integration in principle could be achieved through removal of market-constraining rules and passage of new, possibly market-embedding rules, but integration through law is mostly limited to negative integration in the form of removal of portions of national legislation and regulations. This gives the integration of the single market its particular thrust. Although in the wake of the Single European Act the council adopted the qualified majority rule in decisions pertaining to the single market, there is still a marked asymmetry between the two modes of integration. In the language of Karl Polanyi, the disembedding judicial activism of the court strongly outweighs attempts of compensating for the loss of national rules through market-reembedding legislation on the European scale. The result is a market that may have impressive positive effects for consumers but in which, for example, the rights of labor based on national law are struck down if they seem to conflict with the economic freedom of companies, as ruled in *Laval*, *Viking*, and other cases; it is a market in which companies can pursue a strategy of regime shopping and elect to choose the least-regulated business environment (see ECJ C-438/05, *Viking*; ECJ C-341/05, *Laval*). While some commentators contend that the ECJ must not be exclusively viewed as an agent of liberalization and labor-market deregulation (see Caporaso and Tarrow 2009), Scharpf and others in the Cologne School make a strong case that despite some pro-labor rulings, the overall effect remains a *negative* form of integration through law (see Höpner and Schäfer 2010). They conclude, first, that the very structure of what might be tentatively called the economic constitution of the single market established through actual legislation and further developed through the doctrines developed in ECJ rulings is biased against certain forms of capitalism. Scharpf, in particular, argues that the setup of the single market systematically puts the socioeconomic arrangement of what the varieties of capitalism literature knows as coordinated market economies at a disadvantage and, conversely, favors liberal market economies. In this sense, the single market can never be what in the German context (but also in some European documents) is referred to as a social market economy, with its particular historical compromise between capital and labor relying, for example, on exactly those labor rights that the court deemed inimical to economic freedom (see Scharpf 2010, 238). Furthermore, there is reason to assume that the preponderance of negative integration may lead to a growing politicization of the single market and its effects, as workers in particular may feel disenfranchised by the court rulings. The likely response is a growing resentment against the EU and the strengthening of national-protectionist orientations, which seems to conform squarely with the recent surge of right-wing nationalist populism not only, but particularly, in the EU (see Höpner and Schäfer 2010, 25).

It seems, then, that Buchanan's and Hayek's designs of a competitive federalism we encountered in chapter 2 are realized to a remarkable degree in the single market: As Buchanan favorably notes with reference to the EU, the "ordinary citizen may be affected much more by the constraints, or limits, that the Europeanization of the economic will place on the powers and authority of the politicians, within his or her own country or region, to interfere with his or her life, both economic and otherwise" (Buchanan and Lee 1994, 221). And while Hayek did not anticipate the central role a court would play in dismantling national regulatory regimes, his overall assessment of the skewed nature of the integration process proved to be fairly accurate: "In a federation, certain economic powers, which are now generally wielded by the national states, could be exercised neither by the federation nor by the individual states" (1980, 266). In other words, the ability to influence socioeconomic arrangements broadly speaking that are lost on the national scale is, if at all, only insufficiently compensated for through supranational competencies. The result is a market of jurisdictions, which have to compete over highly mobile capital, in particular, with the supranational scale, which has relatively few competencies in other areas but considerable powers for enforcing the rules of this single market. This matches precisely Buchanan's demands for the split of competencies between the various governmental levels: "Reform requires the establishment of a strong but limited central authority, empowered to enforce the openness of the economy, along with the other minimal state functions. In this way, and only in this way, can the vulnerability of the individual European to exploitation by national political units be reduced" (1995a, 266).[20]

The reasons for this disparity in European powers are also related to a theoretically trivial but rather crucial point: Competition policy comes at a rather low "price," while those policies that could ameliorate the hazardous effects of increased competition in the single market would mostly involve more or less voluminous financial transfers; and aside from some social, structural, and cohesion funds, the EU simply lacks the monetary means for such policies. It may be that Hayek and Röpke were right to assume that citizens and nation-states would be unwilling to cede far-reaching and costly competencies to the supranational level, but the more tangible reason is the EU's ineligibility to independently levy taxes.[21] In this sense it also conforms to a considerable degree to Buchanan's key idea with regard to the fiscal constitution of federations, which called for a model of reverse revenue sharing, ensuring that the revenue base at the supranational level would be strictly dependent on revenue sharing at lower levels.[22] Despite some minor aberrations from his precepts (see Buchanan and Lee 1994, 225), the overall result must have been to Buchanan's liking. The community budget is primarily financed by member states' dues and, unsurprisingly, is much too small to serve as a financial resource for policies that would counter the logic of the single market; in 2017 it will be around 150 billion euros and thus not even half the German budget of 329 billion euros for the same year. The coming months will show whether this will change, given that French president Emmanuel Macron has put forward a proposal for a Eurozone budget, which was met with unsurprising wariness by the German government at the time.

Finally, we look at the neoliberals' views on a monetary union, the EMU in particular. Needless to say, the ordoliberals had no firsthand experience of EMU, and while Rüstow and particularly Eucken had much to say about monetary orders, to my knowledge they never discussed the possibility of a transnational monetary union. Recall that Röpke was a supporter of the gold standard but by the 1930s had given up hope that it could be reestablished. Beyond this, he was obviously adamant about the necessity of a stable currency, but it is only in his postwar writings that he addresses the question of a European monetary order. Now he distinguishes between an *economic* monetary union based on, for example, a currency system like the gold standard and a *political* monetary union based on agreements between nation-states and contends that the latter has little chance of success (see Feld 2012, 8). Röpke clearly welcomes the potentially disciplinary effects of an international/European monetary union, as the gold standard proved while it lasted, but in the absence of this option, he is hesitant to support any alternative on the supranational scale. In 1964 he strongly opposes a European monetary union, including a European central bank, pointing out, somewhat presciently, that "such a system [a common monetary union] supposes a common economic, financial, and social policy" (Röpke 1964, 235–236), which he believed would never come to pass.

The remaining three neoliberals speak more directly to the advantages and disadvantages of a common currency in a federation. In the run-up to the introduction of the euro Buchanan is still strongly opposed to it and offhandedly dismisses "the premature project for a single currency and a monolithic central bank" that is certain to "fail" (1996, 255). However, the pragmatist/realist in Buchanan takes over when the euro is actually introduced and the ECB is charged with exclusive control of monetary policy. Buchanan always emphasized the importance of contextualizing analyses and diagnoses and starting with the status quo of the here and now when considering the desirability and feasibility of alternative arrangements and

respective reforms. Accordingly, in an article written in 2004 on the now
fully operational ECB, Buchanan distinguishes between two steps in his
inquiry: First, there is the question whether the EMU was the best possible
"constitutional choice" at the time, which Buchanan still denies, and he
actually points to the late Hayek's idea of a competitive currency regime as
a viable and even more desirable alternative (see Buchanan 2004, 14). More
important, though, in the second step the question is whether there is a
more desirable alternative to the institutional status quo, and Buchanan is
not of two minds in this regard: "That is to say, the ECB does pass muster
as being 'constitutionally efficient' in this sense" (ibid.). Elaborating on
this diagnosis, he addresses the core problem many, especially the rather
monetarist-minded observers, see in the powers of a central bank, which is its
potential discretion in decision making, whereas the ideal would be "actions
to be automatically triggered by shifts in objectively agreed upon economic
parameters" (ibid., 15). Nevertheless, Buchanan commends the bank for at
least having found a feasible second-best alternative with the target of price
stability, which is assessable somewhat objectively; accordingly, the public
can hold the bank accountable if it fails in this task. Furthermore, Buchanan
highlights the political independence of the ECB and thus concludes that
"a 'runaway' ECB, one that exploits its range of discretionary authority in
allowing gross departures from monetary stability to be generated, seems
much less likely to emerge than in the case of any single-country central
bank" (ibid., 16)—an assessment that many of today's critics of the ECB
would undoubtedly find premature. This is a matter we will revisit later.
Now we turn to Milton Friedman's perspective, which is almost diametrically
opposed to Buchanan's and Hayek's.

It goes without saying that Friedman also harbors concerns regarding the
ECB's discretionary powers; after all, he advised that monetary policy was
too important to be left to central bankers and instead raised the signature
demand of monetarist neoliberalism, a legislated rule of a steady expansion
of the money supply (see 2002, 54; 1960). Friedman is quite clear that rules
for central bankers may not achieve a maximum constraint with regard to
their discretionary powers, but it is the optimum in his view.[23] The alternative that would constrain central bank power even further, to the point of
almost irrelevance in terms of making independent decisions on monetary

policy, would be an arguably fully automated commodity-backed currency like the gold standard. But in contrast to others like Röpke, Friedman, who built his scholarly reputation not least on a detailed study of US monetary history, has a thoroughly unnostalgic view of the gold standard, which is not only no longer feasible, as Röpke would agree, but was never desirable in the first place. "It is not desirable because it would involve a large cost in the form of resources used to produce the monetary commodity. It is not feasible because the mythology and beliefs required to make it effective do not exist" (Friedman 2002, 42).

But what does that mean with regard to the EMU? Friedman has never addressed the core concern of the discretionary power of the ECB, and he passed away before a solid empirical assessment of the ECB's policies was possible, but he may have been placated by Buchanan's arguments regarding the rather clear and narrow mandate of the bank.[24] However, Friedman addressed other aspects of the EMU in a succinct but outspoken fashion. In a short article written around the time the SGP was passed in 1997, Friedman examines the merits of the euro's introduction and offers a skeptical, if not outright damning verdict. He points out the limited ability to absorb (asymmetrical) economic shocks due to the greater rigidity in prices and wages and lower intra-European mobility compared to that of the United States, as well as the lack of federal/supranational funds to offset adverse effects in the wake of (regional/national) economic crises. Friedman notes furthermore that a core group of countries has already pegged their currency to the Deutschmark, so it is a de facto monetary union, which anybody else could in principle join as well—but everyone would retain the option of simply unpegging their currency if need be, for example, through a depreciation in case of a crisis or other shocks. A monetary union without either political unity or exit option would create a scenario that sounds strikingly familiar in light of the developments since 2010: "It [the adoption of the euro] would exacerbate political tension by converting divergent shocks that could have been readily accommodated by exchange rate changes into divisive political issues" (Friedman 1997).

The scene is now set for a virtual intraneoliberal disagreement concerning not so much the strictly economic effects of EMU but rather, I argue, a diverging assessment of the possibilities and risks involved. Despite his occasional theoretical brinkmanship, Friedman is actually the more conservative voice in this virtual debate, as he highlights the risks of an EMU that deprives nation-states of their monetary policy, leaves them no formalized exit option, and remains "incomplete," that is, without a fiscal complement worth mentioning, let alone a full-fledged political union. However, what if this situation is exactly the goal of the federal arrangements? Remember that Hayek's federation was imagined to have a common currency, and, accordingly, "the states within the Union will not be able to pursue an independent monetary policy" (1980, 259). Hayek does not rule out a common fiscal policy (ibid., 256), which could then do what the federal government in the United States does in case of regional crises, but the crucial assumption in Hayek's federative arrangement is that peoples and nation-states will refrain from granting the central authority highly interventionist and/or highly distributive policy competencies (including the power to tax), because there is not enough social capital available to routinely engage in institutionally mediated solidarity among strangers. So a fiscal policy will not complement the monetary arm of the federation in due course, and this appears to be far from a construction mistake but rather the intended effect because, after all, Hayek's overall rationale for a federation was to eliminate certain policy options on the national scale without the chance of gaining an equivalent on the supranational scale. Obviously, while there is a supranational monetary policy, it clearly does not offer the equivalent of possibilities of a national monetary policy. In this sense one could conclude that while there may have been observers that had placed hope in the EMU being completed through the cunning of neofunctional reason, which would in due course and in light of the technical necessities add a fiscal arm to the EMU, the more sober reading of the situation is that the locked-in incomplete EMU actually already manifests the cunning of reason—not neofunctionalist but neoliberal reason. Buchanan drives this point home. While his assessment of the trajectory of the ECB may be considered slightly off target, he clear-sightedly analyzes the opportunities for (neoliberal) reforms in the setting of an "incomplete" EMU: "The EMU has been criticized because it is alleged to take away one dimension of adjustment to shifting economic circumstances in particular countries and to force internal institutional adjustments in place of exchange rate shifts. It may be argued, however, that because exchange rate adjustments cannot take place that serve to cover up the requirement for internal reforms . . . the institutional structures will be moved to further reforms" (Buchanan 2004, 16; see also Feld 2012, 12). Thus, the EMU as it exists may be viewed as a potentially disastrous arrangement that some neoliberals such as Friedman do not consider to be worth taking the risk and actually warn of its consequences. Others, such as Hayek and Buchanan, in my reading, are willing to accept the risk in light of the transformative potential involved with regard to long-established and seemingly entrenched politico-economic structures and policies within the member countries. The EMU thus turns into a gigantic lever that may effect changes even in status quo–biased democracies, which, otherwise, Hayek and Buchanan could imagine to be possible only under the conditions of (transitional) dictatorships and the politics of the extraordinary of a genuine constitutional revolution.

CHAPTER 7

Ideas, Uncertainty, and the Ordoliberalization of Europe

I now address the thorny issue mentioned earlier pertaining to the link between (neoliberal) theory and practice. My main point to prove in this far-reaching debate is the indispensability of ideas for any comprehensive approach to understanding political developments, because these developments cannot be reduced to institutional path dependence or the pursuit of agents' interests. I begin by showing that, despite the apparent parsimony of purely interest- or institution-based accounts, they run into problems that necessitate the introduction of ideas as an additional variable. However, ideas are mostly treated as "auxiliary variables" in these approaches, brought in only when there is an anomaly that cannot be accounted for in standard ways through institutions and/or interests. I argue instead for an approach along the lines of what is now called discursive or constructivist institutionalism, which systematically integrates ideas and considers them to be of explanatory importance, not only during times of turmoil and crisis but whenever we seek to explain and understand phenomena of the social world.

Ideas, Crises, and Uncertainty

Discursive institutionalism is the youngest of the "new institutionalisms." To a certain extent it is a response to the complementary deficiencies of

those three new institutionalisms: rational choice institutionalism, historical institutionalism, and sociological institutionalism (see Hall and Taylor
1996; Schmidt 2008). The problem lies in the institutionalisms' poor ability
to account for the dynamics of institutions. Here we have to differentiate
between rational choice institutionalism and the other two because their
respective difficulties are mirror images of each other. Rational choice institutionalism views institutions as the result of interested-based rational behavior of agents. Institutions help individuals realize gains from cooperation
and/or coordination by reducing free-rider problems—that is, they enable
collective and binding decisions and, more generally, decrease uncertainty
(see, e.g., North 1990). However, rational choice institutionalists find it difficult to account for the stability of institutions despite strong incentives to
defect, and they also find it difficult to explain why a particular institutional
settlement has been "rationally" chosen by individuals when others would
have been equally possible (see Gofas and Hay 2008, 16). While in this
case it is mostly actors that shape institutions, which will in turn provide a
set of constraints on actors, historical and sociological institutionalists assume a more profound influence of institutions on the behavior of agents.
Institutions are even considered capable of shaping the very preferences of
actors through their impact on their self-understanding. Consequently, it
is fair to say that in the case of historical and sociological institutionalism,
institutions shape behavior—unless it is behavior that shapes institutions,
and this qualifier concisely contains the other two new institutionalists'
main problem. Their biggest challenge concerns the question of how it is
possible that there are time windows in which things seem to operate the
other way round: Actors shape and reshape institutions. The view of history
that emerges from these perspectives is one of "punctuated equilibriums"
in which, for the most part, institutions are stable; however, in periods
of unrest, external shocks, and so forth this equilibrium is interrupted at
intervals and its place taken by a situation of largely unpredictable flux that
ultimately gives way to a new institutional equilibrium. Ideas are brought
in, then, as the decisive factor that constitutes the difference between a
"normal" situation of institutional stickiness that shapes actors' behavior
and the opposite, in which institutions become the object of reform and
actors reshape them.

The problem with both versions of bringing ideas into an explanatory institutionalist framework is that they are mostly only afforded the status of auxiliary variables. This means that both rational choice and historical institutionalists tend to turn toward ideas only when their conventionally used approach fails to provide satisfactory explanations. But as long as it is not deemed necessary, both research traditions opt not to take ideas into consideration and instead rely on the supposedly more parsimonious explanations based on interests or institutions. The basic contention of discursive or *constructivist* institutionalism (see Hay 2010, 66), which is the preferable term in my view, is to argue, in contrast, for the systematic integration of ideas into explanatory frameworks, not just as an auxiliary add-on.

I share the view that ideas (or discourse for that matter) must be an integral element in any comprehensive explanatory approach simply because the alternative of relying solely on institutions or interest is an unviable strategy in most contexts. Let me briefly spell out the problems with regard to interest-based accounts.[1] The appeal of interests as the fundamental explanatory variable is clearly the alleged parsimony of such an account, which is typically based on the assumptions that actors have certain interests that translate into preferences that are rationally pursued, as in the case of the conventionally understood *homo economicus*. But what exactly is in the interest of an actor in a given situation? Rational choice scholars face the challenge of going beyond a tautological definition of interests as "revealed preferences" through the actions of the agent because in this case whatever these actions are and however misguided they seem, they would by definition have to be in the interest of the agent; otherwise, she would have acted differently. Instead, the assumption is that the interests of an actor can be derived from the particular strategic context in which the actor is situated, and, as a consequence, behavior becomes predictable. But what if the actor fails to behave in the way the researcher had predicted? This points us in the direction of the complexity of a seemingly simple concept such as (real) interests. After all, what the identification of actual interests presupposes is a considerable amount of knowledge on the part of the researcher and the agent: Clarifying which course of action is in the best interest of an actor in a given situation, strictly speaking, presupposes knowledge of every possible option and, even more dauntingly, also requires knowledge of the various intended and unintended consequences that a particular course of action yields. It is "a combination of omniscience about the present and perfect foresight" (Hay 2010, 76). If this is an accurate assessment, then interest-based accounts are far less parsimonious in their assumptions than they appear to be, because in any but the most stylized model scenarios the real interests of actors are far from self-evident. A further complication stems from the fact that interests become actionable only to the extent that they are interpreted through cognitive and normative ideas—ideas regarding how the world hangs together and ideas regarding what I should do as a (moral) actor who is also trying to realize his idea of a good life. Concretely, whether it is in my best interest to light up a cigarette right now is, strictly speaking, undecidable as long as my normative design for life (somewhere between "live long and prosper" and "live fast, die young"), as well as my views, for example, on the reliability of the findings in medical research, are not taken into consideration. The consequence of both arguments is that what matters for explanations are not real interests but *interests as they are perceived and interpreted by agents in light of ideas*. This complicates things considerably, at least for those who hold aspirations for social science to turn itself into a quasi-natural science with predictive capabilities. After all, in a purely interest-based account it mattered relatively little who the agents in question were, because any given agent would act in the same way in a given situation if provided with the same information. If interests are always ideationally impregnated and mediated, it *does* matter who the agents are, what beliefs they hold, and through which discourses these beliefs were formed. While this is a sobering prospect for a predictive social science, on the bright side there is the potential for more comprehensive explanations based on this broadly constructivist view of things. Furthermore, in restoring agency in the proper sense to actors instead of modeling them as agents that are capable only of "behaving" in the Arendtian sense, such an approach also addresses the problem we have encountered in differing degrees and forms in both neoliberal and some variants of institutionalist thought: how to theorize change in a theoretical framework that suggests that the status quo is more or less "locked-in." We must be careful not to overstate the significance of ideas and note at once that they are only *one* factor that may drive change, but they may also further cement the status quo, not least through widely shared conventions. Incorporating this dimension and the variance it introduces in how interests are perceived and rendered actionable stands a much better chance of providing a theorization of change than its purely interest- or institution-based alternatives.

There is one other line of argumentation that must be considered in regard to the significance of ideas and discourse for political practice. In many ways this is the smallest common denominator in what is sometimes called the "ideas debate," since both constructivists and rational choice scholars could probably agree that it is in times of *crisis* that ideas matter most and have the greatest potential impact on political practices and institutional reshaping. There are two main reasons for this: First, crises are not objectively given. Strictly speaking, a crisis comes into existence only once it has been called a crisis and this signification resonates sufficiently with the relevant audience (see Blyth 2002; Hay 1996). The sheer fact that there is an economic slowdown even for a prolonged time does necessarily turn the situation into a crisis. What constitutes a crisis is thus not just a matter of (economic) data but also a matter of interpretation, construction, and narration.[2] Arguably even more important is the question of what kind of crisis it is. Again, this is a question that cannot be addressed by simply looking at the facts, because there will be more than one explanation that fits a particular set of facts, and, moreover, what constitutes a relevant fact is to some degree a function of the explanatory hypothesis itself. Crises thus need to be interpreted, and which interpretation prevails is obviously of the utmost importance, because with the diagnoses of what the nature of the crisis is, the therapies prescribed and the measures of crisis management undertaken vary. Considering the example we have discussed in the preceding chapters, it matters significantly whether what ails the EU and the Eurozone is considered a banking crisis, a sovereign debt crisis, a euro crisis, or a combination of all three, because in each case the responses would have to differ to a certain degree. Needless to say, given the underdetermined nature of crises, which of the various crisis narratives prevails is emphatically not just a matter of more or less accuracy or correspondence to facts but one of discursive power and contestation.[3] Interpretation and narration as two crucial elements in the construction and definition of a crisis are ineradicably idea laden, and their import thus indirectly shapes both crisis management and, possibly, institutional transformations.

Finally, crises not only enhance the influence of ideas generally; they may also serve as an opening for new ideas, particularly if the crisis also extends to the established frameworks of interpretation. Hence, it makes a significant difference whether the dominant narrative is that of a crisis *in* Keynesianism or a crisis *of* Keynesianism, to again refer to the context of the 1970s: The prevailing narrative then suggested that the Western world was confronted not only with an economic crisis but also an epistemological one, as the dominant framework of socioeconomic interpretation was arguably incapable of explaining one of the most prominent manifestations of the economic crisis, stagflation. As a result of this "invalidation" and fading support, erstwhile marginalized alternatives like monetarism could challenge Keynesianism and ultimately replace it as hegemonic paradigm. However, we must note at once that the crisis of a paradigm, even if plausibly narrated, must not necessarily result in its replacement by an alternative, as the example of the recent crises show. While there were commentators who proclaimed that neoliberalism was experiencing its own "stagflationary moment," there is literally no one who would argue that we have witnessed a departure from neoliberalism tout court as a dominant but far-from-uncontested framework of interpretation or the respective practices. The reasons are related to the second source of ideational influence in times of crisis, which is uncertainty. Even among rational choice institutionalists uncertainty is considered one of the main reasons that ideas can matter under certain circumstances. In situations characterized by complexity, when it becomes exceedingly difficult to compute all relevant information and accordingly calculate actions and consequences, actors turn to ideas as "heuristics" to bridge the informational gap and provide them with "road maps" for a terrain that is difficult to survey (Goldstein and Keohane 1993, 8). While I agree that ideas can serve as heuristics and road maps among other things, in my view the informational problem pertains to crises as well as most other situations. Furthermore, the question is what exactly we understand by uncertainty. Mark Blyth has argued persuasively that uncertainty is more than complexity in the sense it was just described. Drawing on a distinction made famous by a member of the "first" Chicago School, Frank Knight, who was a teacher of both Friedman and Buchanan, he argues that crises produce situations that are not characterized by risk but genuine uncertainty (see Blyth 2002, 31–34). In situations of risk it is possible, albeit at times difficult, to assign a certain probability to event x based on past experience and the frequency of events like x over a period of time. Uncertainty in the Knightian sense differs from this constellation because the situation in question is so unique that there are no empirical data from the past available to assign probabilities. When agents thus have to make decisions without being able to calculate effects and outcomes, they are acting under uncertainty in the strict sense of the term. Furthermore, in contrast to accounts that view uncertainty as sheer complexity, Knightian uncertainty is of a more fundamental nature; the problem for agents is not confined to choosing the right strategy to realize their interests as far as possible, but "agents are unsure as to what their interests actually are, let alone how to realize them" (ibid., 9). Under such circumstances of Knightian uncertainty, there is little else than ideas to turn to (not necessarily consciously) to develop a certain interpretation of the situation and a corresponding course of action. With a view to the Eurozone crisis and the response to it, my point is that the various crises produced multiple moments of genuine Knightian uncertainty in which actors were particularly unsure about what was in their best interests, and with decisions still having to be made under time constraints, ideas figure prominently as one important explanatory factor for the overall outcomes. Even those who are skeptical about the entire project of "bringing ideas back in" to empirical social science could probably concur with this view of a rare but decisive impact ideas may have in moments of crisis-induced Knightian uncertainty. In principle, I could have simply resorted to this argument to make my case regarding the significance of an ordo-/neoliberal interpretive framework for the European crisis management over the last half decade. However, what I am arguing is that the stark juxtaposition of normal times when ideas do not matter and the few moments of crisis and uncertainty when they do is difficult to maintain given the general ideational impregnation of interests; it also remains too close to a view of political change resulting from exogenous shocks and rare moments of the extraordinary, as seen in some neoliberal accounts. Ideas may matter in particular in those moments of crisis, but this does not mean, conversely, that they do not whenever such circumstances do not prevail[4]—ideas matter in general, but they particularly do so in times of Knightian uncertainty.

Furthermore, the view of our (political) environment as one that presents us with risk and the respective task of risk management most of the time, while uncertainty is an exceedingly rare occurrence, may also be inaccurate, because we simply mistake for risk management what is actually acting under uncertainty. After all, how do we know that we have sampled the past sufficiently to assign probabilities when it is not clear whether we know the actual generators of a phenomenon such as a financial crisis? As Blyth argues, the appearance of normalcy and stability may indeed itself be a matter of constructions based on ideas that provide the foundations of institutions. Despite this stabilizing work, ontologically speaking, the world is still one of uncertainty; and despite the efforts of turning it into a world of risk, "unfortunately, we actually have succeeded only in constructing a world of fat tails, where risk and uncertainty live side-by-side. We therefore think and model the world as a world of risk while living in a world of uncertainty; where contingency reigns, we see necessity; and where stability is constantly reconstructed and renegotiated by agents, researchers look for equilibria as the norm" (Blyth 2010, 96). During crises uncertainty may be extreme, but its pervasiveness suggests both that the status quo is never quite as locked in as neoliberal accounts suggest and that the power of ideas may be enhanced during crises but is not confined to these episodes, because they always matter.

The Ordoliberalization of Europe

As we approach the end of this inquiry into the political theory of neoliberalism, the European Union, and the current crises haunting it, it is time to draw the various argumentative threads together for a final diagnosis of "what our present is" (Foucault 1989) and what the distinct characteristics of actually existing neoliberalism in Europe after almost a decade of crises and crisis management are.[5]

What does it mean to refer to an *ordoliberalization* of Europe? The core of my argument is that the economic governance structures of the EU and the EMU in their current configuration can be interpreted as a competitive order or economic constitution along the lines of what particularly Walter Eucken (2017b) proposed as a framework for markets. However, the

economic constitution of postcrisis Europe is not just designed to organize the competition between private-market actors; more important, it is
a competitive order in which the actors are nation-states and their political
economies with the EU increasingly performing the functions that the ordoliberals and Eucken in particular had envisioned for the state in relation
to companies, trade unions, and so forth: an impartial enforcer of the, ideally, quasi-automatic rules of the competition game; an umpire that relies
on the powers of science in designing the rules and is unassailable by the
players in its decision making. Thus, I will show that the ordoliberalization
of Europe pertains not only to the level of policies and the goals pursued
through these policies—to increase competition and competitiveness as the
quintessential ordoliberal values—but also to the structural prerequisites for
implementing these policies, a technocratic regime of rules and sanctions
that codify the specifics of how competition is to take place. In short, as the
dust has settled after the most dramatic periods of the Eurozone crisis—and
such periods may well return, as the underlying problems have not been
solved altogether—the reforms have turned the economic constitution of
Europe into a competitive order that in many respects comes quite close
to what ordoliberals, especially Eucken, had in mind when they spoke of a
framework for a truly competitive market.

The first step in making this argument is to take a closer look at the
European crisis management and the actor(s) that shaped it decisively. Dealing with crises is typically the domain of executives, so when identifying
the institutional centers that shaped the overall thrust of European crisis
management, it is not the European Parliament or the ECJ that we must
look to, first and foremost, but the European Council as the forum where
members of national executives meet and make official decisions. Furthermore, the Eurozone finance ministers meet in the Euro Group and make
no official decisions, as it is not an official institution, but they still exert
considerable influence on the course of events, as the Greek delegation
around Finance Minister Yanis Varoufakis came to realize in the meetings
in the summer of 2015 (see Galbraith 2016). These two fora were not the
only institutional sites on the level of the EU that were of importance for
the crisis management; the ECB emerged as, arguably, the crucial European
actor in dealing with the crisis soon after the beginning of Mario Draghi's

tenure in late 2011. After all, it was Draghi's pledge to do whatever it takes to save the euro in July 2012 that finally placated markets and investors sufficiently to bring down the bond yields of the various crisis countries in the Eurozone. For now I focus on the other two fora and will return to the issue of ECB policies.

If the council and the Euro Group are the sites where the decisions on the reforms in response to the crisis were prepared and made, then the next question is obviously whether it is possible to provide assessments of the power structures within these (quasi-)institutions. Obviously, a detailed answer cannot be offered here, but it is also not necessary for my purposes, since I am mostly interested in the role that Germany plays and here the analyses found in the literature are practically unanimous. Over the course of the crisis Germany emerged as the indispensable nation for the EU. Another way of describing the status of Germany is to say that its resistance against a particular reform measure, for example, eurobonds, usually means that the reform will not happen.[6] And yet another way to describe the status, at least during the crucial periods of crisis management when reform decisions were made, is to refer to Germany as the quasi-, albeit reluctant, hegemon of Europe (see Bulmer 2013). Whatever the exact terminology may be, the fact remains that in the latest restructuring of the EU in response to the crisis, "Germany has played an outsized role," the various Merkel governments having acquired an "unprecedented amount of leverage in redesigning the institutional underpinnings of monetary union" (Art 2015, 183). So while Germany certainly did not act alone and unilaterally in reshaping the EU (ibid., 199), there can be little doubt about the crucial influence it had on the outcomes.

So if we have to focus on Berlin and Frankfurt when explaining the trajectory and substance of European crisis management, the next question is whether there is any plausibility to the claim that ordoliberal ideas figured at all in the perspectives of German political elites. Obviously, I cannot claim to provide an exhaustive empirical study of the attitudes and interpretive frameworks held and shared among those in charge of formulating and implementing strategies of crisis management, but there is a considerable amount of circumstantial and anecdotal evidence that suggests that it is at least far from *implausible* that ordoliberal ideas played a role in the process.

Despite its relative marginalization within economics departments, for anyone studying the subject it is quite likely that the individual will at some point be exposed and introduced to ordoliberal views, especially regarding the more practical issue of economic policy making (see Dullien and Guérot 2012).[7] Aside from the dissemination through academic socialization, ordoliberal ideas are transmitted indirectly through institutional heritages. The German Ministries of Economic Affairs and Finance, as well as the Bundesbank in particular, have long been considered strongholds of ordoliberalism, which is seen to provide the institutional DNA thus shaping the outlook of the actors within them as well.[8] It is well known that ordoliberal thinkers such as Böhm and Röpke had close ties to the Ministry of Economic Affairs in its early days, and according to the admittedly unrepresentative empirical study by Peter Nedergaard and Holly Snaith, the ordoliberal spirit has not vanished entirely in the Ministries of Finance and Foreign Affairs. "Yes, there is a very strong ordoliberal tradition within the administration, which is irrespective of left-right patterns," confided one official, and another added that there is a "deep ingrained preference for a kind of German ordoliberal crisis management" (cited in Nedergaard and Snaith 2015, 1097).[9]

But the Bundesbank also cultivates a basic outlook, which is at least highly attuned to ordoliberal views, and several of its more prominent representatives have also been outspoken about the importance of the ordoliberal tradition for their own approach to monetary policy. Consider Jürgen Stark, who held positions in the Ministries of Economic Affairs and Finance as well as the Bundesbank before he became a member of the ECB's executive board and its chief economist in 2006. In November 2008, at the height of the financial crisis, Stark gave a speech in Frankfurt in which he offered an ordoliberal interpretation of the financial crisis and appropriate remedies. The intellectual foundation of Stark's analysis is Eucken's *Principles of Economic Policy* and the six constitutive principles we encountered in chapter 2; he highlighted in particular the principle of unlimited liability: States mainly contributed to the financial crisis by, first, "neglecting their rule-setting role" in regard to (financial) markets and the resulting failure to establish the principle of liability in a determined manner. Second, "expansionary monetary policies around the globe" fed real estate and other bubbles, and thus the principle of monetary stability was violated, which would eventually have to lead to necessary but painful adjustments. What follows from this crisis narrative with regard to its management? In the short and medium terms, financial-market regulation should be improved, but aside from that there is no reason to resort to "activist" fiscal or monetary policy. Stark opposes fiscal stimuli and with regard to the role of the ECB he acknowledges its provision of liquidity to maintain the interbank market, but whatever it does, it must remain within the boundaries of its mandate, which is "to maintain price stability over the medium term. This mandate must be adhered to both in normal times and in times of crisis. The monetary policy stance appropriate to fulfil our mandate depends exclusively on our assessment of the balance of risks to price stability and nothing else."[10] Finally, Stark considers what can be done to prevent future crises beyond the immediate crisis management. The general answer is as simple as it is expected: "The commitment to price stability and sound public finances is the best contribution monetary and fiscal policies in the euro area can make to financial stability." More specifically, crisis prevention should aim to strengthen the forces of competition in markets, abstain from discretionary measures and instead devise general rules for markets (and states), and assert the principle of individual liability. We can conclude that the political-economic world would be in better shape, according to Stark, if it again adhered to Eucken's principles.

Stark may be an outlier in his outspoken enthusiasm for the *Principles of Economic Policy*, and while Lars Feld, the current director of the Walter Eucken Institute, who is also a member of the German Council of Economic Experts, once suggested (presumably in jest) that all politicians should sleep with the book under their pillow (Feld 2011), it is not my assumption that they heeded this advice. Still, while few were consciously consulting seminal ordoliberal texts in their assessment of the crisis and their considerations on the appropriate response, in light of what has been argued so far, it does not seem far-fetched to assume that ordoliberal ideas provided a basic interpretive framework for German political elites, which they more or less consciously resorted to, not just but especially during periods of Knightian uncertainty produced repeatedly over the course of the Eurozone crisis. Ordoliberalism provided the acting elites with ideas on the level of *problem definitions*, to make use of a common distinction (see Mehta 2011), and by the same token a crisis narrative; it also offered them concrete prescriptions in the sense of *policy solutions* aimed at tackling the problem as it was defined on the basis of ordoliberal reason (see Van Esch 2014).

However, before we spell out the specifics beyond Stark's comments, there is a final step to build the argument for the importance of ordoliberal ideas in understanding the response to the crisis. A skeptic of constructivist institutionalism may argue that it is unnecessary to resort to an idea-based account and thus complicate explanations when the German government simply pursued a course of action according to its national interests. I have presented some general points contradicting such a view of "objective" or "material" interests, but for the sake of the argument, let us consider what an interest-based account would look like. Frank Schimmelfennig (2015) has provided an explanation for the outcomes of the Eurozone crisis from the perspective of liberal intergovernmentalism, which can be considered representative of an interest- or preference-based approach. In his view, the debates over rescue operations and institutional reforms can be modeled as mixed-motive games where, for the most part, the common interest of the players was to maintain an intact Eurozone, while the divergent preferences concerned the questions of how to achieve this and how to distribute the costs. According to Schimmelfennig the outcomes reflect very closely the preferences of Germany as the most powerful actor in the respective negotiations, and, supposedly, this proves the ability of liberal intergovernmentalism to offer convincing explanations of the Eurozone constellation. This is a sophisticated account that goes beyond asserting some monolithic national interest, as it is found in some realist writings, but it is still worth taking a closer look at how it conceives of national preferences. For Schimmelfennig preferences are formed on the basis of conditions of interdependence and the "fiscal position of the state" (ibid., 191), but is it really convincing to derive the various preferences solely from the relative solvency of a state? In fact, it is Schimmelfennig himself who draws attention to an explanatory problem in his account, and the way it is solved is rather telling in light of what has been argued previously. France's position with regard to eurobonds is not entirely consistent with its fiscal position, but Schimmelfennig suggests that this anomaly is probably attributable to the relative influence of Keynesianism in France in contrast to the ordoliberal influence in Germany:

"The stark difference to German preferences, however, is difficult to explain by material conditions only, but points to the relevance of ordoliberal vs Keynesian economic ideas" (ibid., 183). It is a classic case of bringing in ideas as auxiliary variables whenever interests fail to explain behavior; thus, once again, interest-based explanations turn out to be more complicated than they initially appear. And again, my point is not that we should pit interest-based accounts against ideas-based ones, and I am not disputing the merits of analyses like Schimmelfennig's in a wholesale fashion, but while I agree that Germany mostly got what it wanted with regard to the crisis management, it got what it *considered* to be in its best interest in a highly volatile situation of Knightian uncertainty.

This means that we do not have to go as far as to suggest that the interpretive framework of ordoliberalism led German decision makers to act *against* their interests because, again, they do not exist in any other form than perceived interests. Matthias Matthijs shares this view generally, but in his assessment of the German-led crisis management there are a few formulations that come close to suggesting that they do: "Germany's ordoliberal policies would actually lead it down a road of *hurting its own national interests* by triggering contagion in the short run, while giving up further control over fiscal and financial powers in the long run, by delegating those powers to the EU level. Germany's ideas did not just lead to suboptimal outcomes from Berlin's interest point of view; they *actually caused the crisis by making it a systemic one*" (2016, 378).[11] Matthijs's point is that the reluctant and indecisive crisis management we have already addressed, together with the politics of "expansionary contraction," made the crisis worse and could be even said to have started it in the first place. If Germany had agreed to orchestrate a Greek bailout right after the news about the deficits and debt became public, the Eurozone crisis as a systemic crisis might never have happened. It would have cost German money but much less than it ended up costing, and the same logic goes for various other instances when Germany's insistence on ordoliberal principles ended up increasing the overall price tag of the crisis. There are accounts suggesting that it was Merkel's deliberate strategy throughout the crisis never to do more than just enough to keep the Eurozone barely afloat. This meant that she could present the reforms she wanted to see passed as being without alternative to stave off the imminent demise of the euro; furthermore, framing the rescue of ailing Eurozone members as necessary to protect the sheer existence of the euro ensured that the German Constitutional Court would not rule against the introduction of the ESM (see Art 2015). Still, this seems to overestimate the strategic foresight of actors—even if it is Angela Merkel—and in my view it is more plausible to argue along the lines of Matthijs and a constructivist institutionalist approach more generally: German decision makers were acting under uncertainty about what exactly would be the effects of their decisions, and what exactly lay in their interest, and thus went with the quintessential ordoliberal maxim that the rules must be upheld, as their *perceived* best interest. As Merkel put it in a speech before the Bundestag in December 2011, "The lessons are very simple: Rules must be adhered to, adherence must be monitored, non-adherence must have consequences."

Let us conclude for now that there are sufficient grounds to argue that ordoliberal ideas may have had a certain degree of influence on the crisis management led by the Germans and thus on the latest institutional reconfiguration of the EU.

So in which respects does the EU in its current form correspond to ordoliberal tenets, particularly those associated with the work of Walter Eucken? As mentioned previously, the crucial point is to strike an analogy between what Eucken described as the competitive order with its various principles and the role that the state, democracy, and science ought (not) to play in the politics of this order, on the one hand, and the economic constitution of the EMU as a competitive order for nation-states and national economies, on the other. My claim is that in many respects this latter supranational competitive order in its original form, but especially in its reformed form, comes close to Eucken's ideals.

Let us recapitulate the core assumptions in Eucken's view of desirable competition. The indispensable preconditions are first and foremost a functioning price system, because distortions in it send wrong signals to producers and consumers concerning scarcity, risks, and so forth. This means that inflationary tendencies and deliberate expansionary monetary policy have to be avoided because the latter distorts the "price" of money. Monetary stability is thus the most fundamental of the various constitutive principles of the competitive order.[12] But it is followed closely in importance by the principle of unlimited individual liability because it also ensures that there is no distortion of risk. It must be enforced, as competition is designed to produce winners and losers, and losing must entail bearing the full burden of the loss up to the point of market exit, just as much as winning means reaping all rewards individually (see Eucken 1960, 279). Obviously, this last principle not only is of functional importance but also has some significant moral import (e.g., not being held liable creates situations of "moral hazard"), since market competition in the Euckenian version is not just an evolutionary advantage, as the later Hayek at times seemed to suggest, but also a matter of ethics and norms. After all, it was not just any kind of competition that Eucken wanted to stimulate through the market framework but what he called *Leistungswettbewerb* (ibid., 247), which translates somewhat awkwardly into "performance competition." The notion of performance competition stipulates that gaining market advantage, making a profit, must be achievable only through a superior performance, which partly explains why Eucken is so vehemently opposed to cartels and monopolies, because they could gain market advantage through *Behinderungswettbewerb* (ibid., 43), or "competition through obstruction." Again, the normative aspect of this notion is clearly detectable. Profits must be earned properly (in contrast to "rents" incurred through monopolies) and are justifiable since they are reaped in exchange for some kind of real service at cheaper prices or better quality for consumers—whose interests are the only universalizable ones, as more contemporary ordo- and neoliberals would add.

So how do all of these elements figure into the European constellation? It almost goes without saying that the fundamental structural principle of ordoliberal thought—the legal framework of an economic constitution—already figured heavily in the basic setup of the EMU through the Maastricht Treaty and the SGP; with the recent reforms this rule-based regime has been extended further, specified, and tightened. Whether through the various procedures or the Fiscal Compact, the rules of jurisdictional competition have been further codified through the latest reforms, and while some argue that the economic constitution of the EMU has been undermined through the plethora of emergency measures in response to the crisis, I contend that the institutional and constitutional reforms passed do confirm the Maastricht Order and increase the chances of enforcing the various requisites.

It is true that almost every aspect of the crisis management, including the new rules introduced, are challenged by legal experts, but up to this point none of it, including the ESM, has been struck down in any court of law (see Joerges 2014), so it may be slightly too alarmist to raise the specter of an "emergency constitution," despite the occasional Schmittian inclinations found in some ordoliberal thought. The point remains that ordoliberalism can be seen as the ideational resource behind these reforms, not just with regard to substantive contents and goals but also in the sense of a definition of the problem and how to solve it technically. The ordoliberal mind-set suggests that rules need to be adhered to and the problem of the Eurozone crisis was that the rules were broken. Accordingly, the solution is to have more and better rules. In this sense, the crisis was the opposite of an opening for new ideas and approaches to political economy, as the presumed solution to the crisis is based on the same modal recipe as the supposedly flawed status quo ante.

If it is the function of the economic constitution of Europe, consisting of primary and secondary EU law, to establish a framework for desirable competition, as just recapitulated, the principles of liability and monetary stability must be realized. Jens Weidmann agrees with these assumptions, which is of some significance, because he is currently the president of the Bundesbank and may even become the next president of the ECB after Mario Draghi. Especially for those who are concerned about the ECB's course, and there are many among German policy makers, Weidmann would be the perfect choice, as he provides us with the ordoliberal theory of a competitive order for European jurisdictions and does so, aptly, in the Walter Eucken lecture in 2013.

Weidmann also highlights the principle of individual liability, which provides the main element of the ordoliberal crisis narrative, which also happened to become the dominant one in public discourse: The origin of the crisis lies in the behavior of individual countries that lost their "competitiveness" and accumulated debts that were unsustainable (Weidmann 2013). Consequently, the crisis is not a systemic one of a questionable architecture of the Eurozone, and neither is it a banking crisis that has morphed into something different; it is a *crisis of individual sovereigns incurring too much debt* and living beyond their means. According to the principle of liability, those responsible for entrepreneurial failure have to suffer the full consequences of their action; therefore, there ought to be no debt reduction because it would produce moral hazard. Furthermore, it was the failure to provide a credible commitment to the principle that contributed to the buildup of the crisis in the first place, according to Weidmann, because bond buyers did not believe that the no-bail-out clause would be adhered to when push came to shove, which explains why countries such as Greece had bond yields close to German ones. In other words, the pricing system of the bond market was distorted because individual liability was not established firmly enough, and the ensuing misleading signals about risks led to countries like Greece getting much more credit than they should have. And if more individual liability could have helped prevent the crisis, it is no surprise that Weidmann is at the least very skeptical, with regard not only to bailouts but also to debt mutualization. Individual market actors, whether companies or nation-states, have to be held fully liable if competition is to work. Since emergency bailouts of countries, as they happened during the crisis in several varieties, would undermine this principle, it is only stringent of Weidmann to consider rules for a sovereign default as an alternative. After all, from an ordoliberal perspective, the European market of jurisdictions remains flawed as long as the "lash of competition" (Eucken 2017a, 52) remains constrained by the impossibility of market exits. In my view, therefore, the introduction of a "sovereign insolvency order" along the lines of what already exists on the level of municipalities in the United States, for example, would consequently be the next step in the ordoliberalization of Europe.[13]

Let us take a look at the fundamental principle of monetary stability for functioning competition. As mentioned previously, the problem with monetary instability is that it also distorts the functioning of the price mechanism, so the question from an ordoliberal perspective is how to ensure that the ECB adheres to the Euckenian principle. From Weidmann's point of view, the monetary constitution of the EMU has two key elements to ensure stability. First, the ECB is probably the most independent central bank, which means that it is not easily harnessed for political purposes, particularly printing money, by any EMU member; and second, it has a decidedly narrow mandate that assigns it the sole task of ensuring price stability. Is this a structural setup of the monetary order that conforms to and realizes the ordoliberal principle?

This is a question that is, somewhat surprisingly, debated heatedly. Röpke and Eucken were proponents of the gold standard or some kind of commodity reserve currency because of the automatic adjustments of the system through the flows of gold, which had no need for any discretionary decision making by central bankers. However, it seems far-fetched in my view to infer from this that central bank independence (CBI) "is not at all compatible with Ordoliberalism" (Bibow 2004, 19). It is correct that Eucken was as skeptical as Friedman of central bankers' discretionary setting of interest rates and, in a typical fashion, sought to design a monetary system in which, ideally, there would be an "automatically working monetary stabilizer" (Eucken 1949, 91). Nevertheless, can we infer that from an ordoliberal perspective the combination of an independent central bank with a mandate to ensure price stability is a considerable problem? At least, this seems to come close to providing a rule for monetary policy: to aim at an inflation rate of just below 2 percent. However, what is interesting about Eucken's skepticism regarding CBI is how much it confirms his view of a strong and unified state and the persistent specter of "pluralism." The concern he has is that "an all too independent . . . central bank is difficult to fit into the structure of the state. It will be tempted to position itself in opposition to the general economic policy of the state. A 'pluralism' will easily develop that would jeopardize the unity of state policy" (cited in ibid., 16).

In their attempt at a direct refutation of the ordoliberalization thesis, Lars Feld, Ekkehard Köhler, and Daniel Nientiedt also go to great lengths to show that the institutional structures and mandates of neither the Bundesbank nor the ECB conform to ordoliberal precepts:[14] CBI may have been granted, but with that came also far too much discretionary power in monetary policy for the ordoliberal taste. But over the course of their working paper the argument takes a curious turn. The authors also bring up the principle of liability and conclude correctly that "the traditional rule-based perspective of Ordnungspolitik can explain the German stance against bailouts and further fiscal integration" (Feld, Köhler, and Nientiedt 2015, 15). But this led to unintended consequences because the unwillingness to mutualize debt contributed to a prolongation of the crisis and eventually caused Mario Draghi to interfere with his (in)famous statement that the ECB would do "whatever it takes" to save the euro. This is a problem for Feld and his colleagues not least because it politicized the monetary constitution of the euro and the resistance to debt mutualization; thus, further fiscal integration on behalf of Germany was essentially bought at the expense of CBI. The authors conclude that it would have been better to make concessions on partial debt mutualization than to jeopardize CBI (ibid. 2015, 18). This turns out to be even more important than the principle of liability after the director and two other members of the Walter Eucken Institute spent so much time proving that ordoliberals, Eucken in particular, were never in favor of CBI. At least they leave no doubt about why the general setup of the EMU must still be appreciated from an ordoliberal perspective. The answer, in brief, is that no Eurozone country has control over its currency, and therefore it becomes impossible to manipulate it through inflation or money creation for political purposes. In the ability to curb these possibilities EMU is only comparable to the gold standard—a similarity that thinkers as diverse as Wolfgang Streeck and Milton Friedman recognized and considered problematic for different reasons;[15] and for the gold standard supporters Eucken and Röpke, this may have been one more reason to appreciate EMU.

After this brief excursion into the issue of CBI we return to Weidmann and the principle of monetary stability. If countries cannot manipulate the unit of value and the central bank has the sole responsibility of ensuring price stability, then the only possible source of inflationary pressures that remains is excessive government debt: "Putting an effective limit on government borrowing is thus a primary pillar of any policy of stable money. Monetary union, as a union of stability, therefore required sound public finances" (Weidmann 2013). The SGP constituted the initial attempt to address this issue; the Fiscal Compact, Six-Pack, and the European Semester are intended to put it to rest at the price of constitutionalized austerity. So the picture of the normative ideal of jurisdictional competition within the Eurozone emerging from this is straightforward: There is a certain form of competition that is desirable, and its flames are stoked, but this presupposes that other forms of competition or strategies of gaining competitiveness are prohibited—and in this case simply as a matter of fact. After all, one possible way of gaining competitiveness in relation to another political economy is devaluation of the currency, because exports become cheaper and imports become more expensive. But just as "competition through obstruction" is not considered competition in the proper sense, competition through de-valuations is not considered desirable from an ordoliberal point of view because "they generally do not lead to any lasting gains in competitiveness. Often, renewed depreciations are necessary" (ibid.), which may result in "competitive devaluation" among various countries. But if this is an undesir-able, possibly even amoral, way of competing that does not involve any superior performance, then what is the proper way to become competitive?[16] The answer is clear because if adjustment processes cannot take place via exchange rates, which is impossible in a Eurozone of fixed exchange rates, then adjustment has to take place through internal devaluation, or the poli-tics of austerity: "a form of voluntary deflation in which the economy adjusts through the reduction of wages, prices, and public spending to restore com-petitiveness, which is (supposedly) best achieved by cutting the state's budget, debts, and deficits" (Blyth 2013, 2). The redesigned SGP in combination with the Fiscal Compact ensures that the state does not run excessive deficits and thus is constrained in trying to boost the economy through fiscal stimuli or public investment. But that is just the state dimension of austerity. Adjust-ment processes that lead to a gain in competitiveness crucially take place in labor markets. And if we take the Euckenian conviction seriously that the most important precondition for competitive markets is the undistorted functioning of the price mechanism, then this must also hold for the prices on labor markets. In other words, a lack of competitiveness might be ad-dressed through a downward flexibility of prices and wages; accordingly, the structural reforms required in the memoranda of understanding with ESM-recipient countries and implemented in many others always include measures aimed at liberalizing labor markets to tackle wage "rigidities" based on union power and/or labor-market regulation. Price and wage flexibility is the key to overcoming crises, as Eucken noted in a discussion of German crisis management during the Great Depression. While mass unemployment is considered a grave moral problem, the politics of full employment, Keynesianism, does not provide a real solution to it, according to Eucken, because it leads to "instability" in other markets and an ever-stronger trend toward centralization (1951b, 16). The real problem is thus not addressed, and the same is true for an expansionary monetary policy that provides cheap money and thus creates only a temporary stimulus and—even worse—pays the price of a distortion of the price system, because with cheap money any supply can find its demand.[17] The real problem, as we might have guessed, is economic power, or what Eucken refers to as the "corporative structure of the labor market" (ibid., 60), which prevents an adjustment of prices and wages. "In the crisis year of 1930, Berlin builders, for instance, had to reckon with relatively firm prices of materials, such as iron and cement, which were fixed by syndicates, and also with relatively fixed wages, where housing prices were dropping rapidly" (ibid., 78). According to Eucken, the consequence of the "stickiness" of prices was the deflationary depression that hit Germany in the early 1930s. So the only proper way of competing is through productivity increases, as the MIP scoreboard confirms: One of the eleven indicators is unit labor costs, and in a market of homogeneous goods these costs may fall in the medium term through investment in technology and human resources; but in the short run and in a context of an economic downturn the only realistic but still difficult option to achieve a reduction is wage suppression, including payroll taxes and employer contributions to insurance schemes. This prescription is backed by ordoliberal thought, as both Eucken and Rüstow considered it a bitter but necessary medicine (see Rüstow 1930),[18] as well as, supposedly, by the successful recovery of Europe's erstwhile sick man, Germany, at the beginning of the twenty-first century. After all, was it not the prudent and disciplined wage restraint of German labor unions, in addition to the liberalization of the German labor market and the increase of the retirement entry age (under a coalition of Social Democrats and Greens), that paved the way for this recovery? To be sure, it was bought at the price of real wage decreases for many, a more punitive approach to unemployment and increased social inequality, but German competitiveness on the eve of the financial crisis was restored—for whatever reasons, as the narrative that attributes the successful recovery to the Agenda 2010 is questionable in many regards—and in light of this ideational and empirical background, it is far from surprising that German elites established this recipe for all current sick men of Europe. Needless to say, this recipe comes with some serious side effects and can work only in certain conditions. This means that, strictly speaking, it would also have to affect Germany since it could only recover during the 2000s because other countries provided the required demand (often on credit). Additionally, competitiveness is a relative term: If there is to be at least a halt in the further divergence of relative competitiveness between Eurozone countries and Greece, Italy, and Spain are to gain in it, by definition, Germany must accept a decrease. So even if we assume for the sake of the argument that the ordoliberal analysis is correct, as long as Germany jealously defends its title of "export world champion" and shrugs off criticism of exorbitant current account surpluses, and as long as the German finance minister clings to the "Black Zero," which stands for a close to balanced budget, and refrains from increasing public investment significantly, the therapy that has caused so much misfortune, grievance, and outrage throughout Europe is bound to fail, because *"we cannot all be austere at once"* (Blyth 2013, 9).[19] The constellation is almost bizarre. While Finance Minister Schäuble professed that "we Germans don't want a German Europe" (2013), the German-led crisis management has given the Eurozone/EU an economic constitution that distinguishes between different kinds of competition, between jurisdictions and outlaws; or it otherwise makes impossible certain kinds of competition considered undesirable, so the only possible kind of competition happens to be the kind that conforms to ordoliberal tenets, which Germany specializes in: a textbook case of interests perceived through the interpretive framework of ideas. The EU has forced a certain model of competition on itself that gives a competitive advantage to certain varieties of democratic capitalism—that is, socioeconomic and political settlements. The result is increasing pressure on all those countries that differ more or less profoundly from the German settlement and its accumulation regime to adapt to this accumulation regime through structural reforms from social to labor-market policies—irrespective of the widely varying institutional preconditions and "cultures of capitalism."[20] We witness a "forced structural convergence in the Eurozone" (Scharpf 2016), and the point is not to defend this variety for its own sake, as Jürgen Habermas has critically noted in an exchange with Scharpf, but to draw attention, first, to the costs that are incurred in many currencies, including that of human life chances; and second, to the almost paradoxical nature of the endeavor, because Europe can become more German only if Germany itself becomes less German.

As we know from the discussions in part 1, the ordoliberals, particularly Walter Eucken, believed that a consistent politics of the competitive order was pursuable only under certain institutional conditions, which amounted to a technocratic form of rule that included a strong state relatively insulated from societal influence. With regard to Europe, both the content of the politics of the competitive order and these institutional preconditions suggest an increasing ordoliberalization of the EU.

This may seem like a stretch initially, but let us take a closer look at the various aspects of Euckenian rule. A strong state suggests that it is at least possible to switch to an authoritarian mode of politics to implement certain policies, even against the resistance of those subject to it.[21] The first thing that comes to mind is the Troika, its memoranda of understanding, and the supervision of correct implementation of structural reforms. It seems difficult not to describe this as a form of authoritarian rule, as it suspended the sovereignty of those under its rule and enforced policies against the expressed will of the citizenry, if it was even allowed to express its will officially. When Greek Prime Minister George Papandreou announced a referendum on the conditions of further European support, he was forced into resignation, and an interim government of unelected technocrats took over, similar to the interim government under Mario Monti that stepped in after Silvio Berlusconi's ouster in Italy. A skeptic may argue that this does not say much about a structural transformation of the EU, since the draconian Troika rule concerns only extreme cases of countries on the verge of bankruptcy. However, the Troika is also likely to serve as a model for how to govern an "ordered" sovereign default, analogous to a liquidator in a private insolvency, and what is already being tried in insolvency procedures in US municipalities: strict austerity, outsourcing, and privatization in exchange for partial debt forgiveness. Still, I agree that if it were the Troika alone, it would not be sufficient to redeem my claim, but it is not. The commission has been invested with far-reaching powers of surveillance, monitoring, and, if need be, sanctioning of member states that strike at the heart of a core competency of national parliaments, the power of the purse. It may seem ludicrous to bring up the commission as the equivalent of a strong state on the European level, but before we dismiss the point, let us not forget that the commission had indeed turned out to be the "unexpected winner of the crisis" (Bauer and Becker 2014). Intergovernmentalists are bound to respond that power is still centered in the council and even refer to a "new intergovernmentalism" that allegedly developed over the course of the crisis (see Bickerton, Hodson, and Puetter 2015). But this fails to acknowledge that the influence of the council has been explicitly and significantly reduced through the introduction of the reverse majority principle, which makes it much more unlikely that the council will stop a certain procedure once it has been initiated by the commission. But does the commission function as an effective watchdog over the new rules, making use of the new instruments? As James Savage and Amy Verdun (2015) show, the commission has responded to its new and expanded agenda with considerable internal restructuring, for example, including more directorates-general and the commission president in assessing the budgetary and overall economic situation of a member state and proposing reform measures. A member of the Secretariat-General characterized the changed role of the commission and especially the Directorate-General for Economic and Financial Affairs (ECFIN) in the following way: "What has fundamentally changed is that ECFIN has traditionally had more of an advisory and analytical role. With the crisis and a more comprehensive policy co-ordination [responsibility], they have become much more of a policy development DG . . . and rule implementation organization" (cited in ibid., 113). So it is not a stretch to conclude that the commission is at least moving closer to the ideal enforcing umpire that ordoliberalism wanted the strong state to be. Nevertheless, from an ordoliberal perspective, it still falls short of this ideal. The reasons are reliably laid out by Jens Weidmann, who acknowledges the attempt to tighten the rules and make them "quasi-automatic," but this is exactly the problem: They are only *quasi*-automatic. While the procedures themselves are shielded as much as possible from political influence, the decision about initiating them still gives too much discretion to the commission: "Torn in two directions in its dual role as a political institution and guardian of the treaties, the Commission is frequently inclined to compromise at the expense of budgetary discipline" (Weidmann 2017). Weidmann's concern is not unfounded, as the commission has been rather lenient in dealing with France's deficits and Italy's debt, citing overall positive prospects as reasons. But the commission's argument obviously offers no consolation for ordoliberals concerned about the oft-cited culture of stability in the EMU. For them the commission is still too political in its decisions instead of simply executing the rules. Consequently, Weidmann suggests what would be another next step in the ordoliberalization of Europe: "A more rigorous interpretation of the rules could be achieved by giving responsibility for fiscal surveillance to an independent authority instead of the Commission. At the very least that would clearly show where unbiased analysis ends and political concessions begin" (ibid.). The impartial and unassailable umpire stoically enforcing the rules unperturbed by political influence thus remains the overall ideal of the ordo-/neoliberal state executive or its equivalent on the supranational level.

But while to the dismay of ordoliberals, the commission remains at least a rudimentarily political institution, another precondition for a proper politics of the competitive order has almost been realized with its empowerment: Aside from the ECJ and the ECB the commission is easily the EU institution that is best shielded against the influence of democratic majorities, although the same cannot be said for the influence of lobbyists more generally, which makes matters only more problematic. Investing the commission with enhanced powers of budgetary surveillance and correction has been interpreted as "the relocation of political-economic decisions from the national to a new, specifically constructed international level . . . , an institutional context, in other words, that unlike the nation-state was consciously designed not to be suitable for democratization" (Streeck 2015b, 365). While I do not share Streeck's skepticism with regard to the general possibility of democratizing the EU, for the time being we have to note that he is correct when he writes: "Where there are still democratic institutions in Europe, there is no economic governance any more, lest the management of the economy is invaded by market-correcting non-capitalist interests. And where there *is* economic governance, democracy is elsewhere" (ibid., 366). Again, this is not even taking into consideration the blatantly undemocratic Troika rule but refers to the general budgetary regime in the EU/Eurozone that every member state is subjected to and that takes away fiscal decision-making powers from elected parliaments and places it in the hands of the commission. The commission may have a slightly more substantive democratic legitimation today than a decade ago, but it remains a rather thin one and, some would argue, deliberately so. This brings us back to Majone (1994) and his concept of the regulatory state. Majone argued in regard to the EU and its earlier incarnations that delegating certain powers to counter-majoritarian institutions such as the commission or the ECB could actually enhance their overall democratic legitimacy, as long as these powers concerned only Pareto-optimal, nonredistributive policies such as watching over product standards on the single market. This argument may have had its merits before the last round of reforms, although it was highly contested even then (see Follesdal and Hix 2006), but there is no question that the new powers of the commission cannot be justified with resort to it. Majone assumed that tasks for such regulatory institutions were narrowly defined, and the various new instruments and the MIP in particular expand the scope of surveillance and monitoring agendas significantly. Moreover, the various recommendations for reforms are the opposite of nonredistributive politics because they are bound to produce winners and losers in the process. Therefore, even Majone (2014) has voiced doubts about the continued legitimacy of the commission's agenda, and that does not even take into consideration that the new competencies expand the commission's influence to policy areas that are explicitly the domain of national policy making (see Höpner and Rödl 2011). Overall, we have to conclude that the latest restructuring of the EU has even enhanced its already significant democratic deficit. It is not my position that this implies that powers have to migrate back to the nation-state, but in the current multilevel institutional architecture it is striking how much power is invested in exactly those institutions, such as the commission and the ECB, that are farthest removed from electoral influence and parliamentary oversight. If one of the prime ordoliberal concerns was that there may be undue influence on economic policy making through the democratic masses—or just elected parliaments—this concern must be considered addressed in the distribution of competencies in the Eurozone of today.

Now we look at the third major ingredient of a political theory of ordoliberalism, science and the role it ought to play in politics. Eucken in particular invested considerable hope in the powers of science if it was practiced in the proper way and, consequently, postulated an obligation for scientists to become involved in the policy-formation process as experts, not only to contribute to the design of the competitive order but also to crowd out the influence of interested parties and, if need be, that of a misguided demos. Does the EU of today exhibit an equivalent of these technocratic notions? To be sure, the charge of technocratic rule is not exactly a novelty in the discussions of the EU, especially the work done by the commission. I have no intention of criticizing the commission for regulating the use of vacuum cleaners and light bulbs; however, there is a more disconcerting kind of technocratic element to the new governance structures of the Eurozone in particular, which have even prompted commentators like Habermas (2015) to warn of the "lure of technocracy." Through the European Semester and the preventive arms of the EDP, especially the MIP, the commission gains considerable influence on member state's policy making and not just with regard to fiscal policy in the narrow sense. Recall that the MIP scoreboard includes indicators that range from the trend in real estate prices to private debt ratios and labor-unit costs. So whenever the values of these indicators move beyond the acceptable threshold, the commission makes recommendations and monitors implementation in its in-depth country reviews.[22] "The remarkable point about many of these indicators is that their correction by all accounts would require measures in policy fields that are the domain of nation-states and that it is difficult for states to influence the prices of real estate markets or labor-unit costs if they happen to have a decentralized wage-bargaining system. However, what is most striking in the present context is that the question about the proper measures to address imbalances is often quite controversial. Furthermore, whatever the recommended course of action for a national government to implement, it will not be an example of regulatory politics in the sense of Majone. And these latter two points are the heart of the matter in regard to the lure of technocracy in Europe today. Eucken, Rüstow, and Friedman believed that science could be the anchor of stability, especially in times of socioeconomic upheaval, by depoliticizing questions of policy making by invoking the decontestatory authority of science. But if following scientific advice leads to a redistribution of burdens and there is not even a solid consensus on the policies in question, there is no other option than to call this technocratic rule, consisting in a failure to treat eminently and inherently political questions as such and instead treating them as if they were technical ones that could be addressed in a rational depoliticized way with resort to some established politico-economic wisdom. The politics of austerity, to choose but the most obvious example, neither were and are emphatically uncontroversial among "the men of science" referenced in the ordoliberal manifesto, nor were they nonredistributive. Therefore, putting the power to decide over this and other recipes into the hands of the undoubtedly exceptionally well-trained but poorly legitimated hands of the economists and lawyers in the commission and the ECB may have provided satisfaction at long last to those who lamented their dethronement in 1936, but it just adds to the legitimation gap of ordoliberal Europe. To be sure, other neoliberals like Hayek and possibly Röpke would have voiced concerns over what Hayek may have criticized as the "pretence of knowledge," but those on the other side of the debate on the powers and political significance of science, including Eucken, may have looked more favorably on these arrangements, which put scientists in charge at the expense of both politicians and the electorate. To quote Jens Weidmann (2016) in his musings on an independent fiscal authority, which will undoubtedly be one of the subjects of the upcoming debates between Germany and France, "That body should be staffed by experts, not politicians."

Final questions need to be addressed: To what extent are the commission's "personalized" recommendations still to be considered a rule-based politics (see Scharpf 2011)? And to what extent does the ECB's course constitute the *opposite* of a quintessentially ordoliberal rule-based politics as it acts as a "bond buyer of last resort" (Sandbu 2015, 158) and, arguably, disregards maybe not the letter but the spirit of the no-bail-out clause? The latter in particular is often portrayed as prime evidence for the decline of an economic constitution and thus of an ordoliberal kind of governing. In my view neither of these points serves as a refutation of the diagnosis of the ordoliberalization of Europe. First, it may well be worth questioning whether the Draghi course of the ECB is compatible with ordoliberal tenets, but let us at least note that Draghi himself claimed just that in an address given in Jerusalem in 2013: "In this context, it is worth recalling that the monetary constitution of the ECB is firmly grounded in the principles of 'ordoliberalism.' . . . Does the fact that our operations include some credit risks on the balance sheet of the central bank imply a violation of our ordoliberal principles? . . . My answer is no. . . . The risks we take onto our balance sheet in the context of our operations are controlled, and they are accepted only insofar as they are strictly necessary for the pursuit of price stability." Of course, we must not be naïve and take Draghi's words at face value, but let us not forget that up to this point, the task of the ECB to pursue price stability, understood as a Eurozone inflation rate of just below 2 percent, has not been compromised by whatever unorthodox policies have been pursued so far. Moreover, contrary to the warnings of Weidmann and others, when the ECB changed its course, there was not even a trace of inflationary tendencies. If anything, there were deflationary ones as the rate dropped from just over 2 percent to as low as –0.5 percent between 2012 and 2015. So it seems that expansionary measures would be in order to counter these tendencies. Finally, and most important, we must consider the timing of the ECB's change of course in 2012. After all, this was a time when all the important structural reforms in countries such as Ireland and Portugal, and to some extent Greece, were under way. And the ECB had not been exactly an innocent bystander. As David Woodruff chronicles, the ECB sent several letters to the various governments demanding that they implement the required reforms. If they refused, the ECB would stop providing direly needed emergency credit lines: "The ECB leadership implicitly or explicitly threatened to withhold its help unless policy or institutional changes implementing Brussels-Frankfurt priorities (especially labor market liberalization and fiscal austerity) were adopted. These threats were made credible by the rigid rules on the ECB's independence and mandate, and the prospect of vigorous German political and legal opposition to exceeding the mandate" (2016, 98). He concludes that the ECB actually played a game of "good cop, bad cop" alongside the German government, and only once both got what they wanted—structural reforms, fiscal compacts, and so on—did the ECB change course. The expansionary policy—and of course the indirect support for states' debt service—was the price to be paid for more and tighter rules: "These institutional changes were, then, entirely in the spirit of Ordoliberalism, restructuring rules and the actors subject to them in ways designed to facilitate the operation of a market economy and make further discretionary interventions both unnecessary and unavailable" (ibid.).

A similar argument can be made about whether the commission's highly specific recommendations mark a departure from a rule-based politics. The recommendations are, in principle, aimed at making themselves superfluous once the various national economies have been restructured so they can compete in the way that the economic constitution has defined and codified desirable competition. It is doubtful whether this can and will ever happen, but this is certainly the thrust of what the ECB and especially the commission endeavor with their push for structural reforms. So if one wants to interpret the recommendations as discretionary interventions, they are still interventions aimed at ensuring that in the future there will be jurisdictional competition according to the rules. The exception to the rule may thus be justifiable as the price for a better functioning of the rules in the future (ibid., 97). The ordoliberalization of Europe is still a work in progress, as the economic constitution remains incomplete in many ways. The interventions by the commission and the existence of the ESM must be interpreted in this context as a consequence of the continued "market failure" produced by this incompleteness: If states refused to restructure their internal politico-economic arrangements, they may run the risk of dwindling competitiveness and, ultimately, default. At the moment, this is still a serious problem from the point of view of the competitive order, because while the ESM is in place to provide conditional financial support in these cases, it is not large enough to bail out an economy such as Italy's, which is the latest source of concern in the Eurozone. There also remains a certain degree of moral hazard, although this is significantly reduced given the considerable strings attached to the support. Accordingly, from the ordoliberal perspective, the problem is that there is still no mechanism in place to let countries like Italy default in an orderly fashion without jeopardizing the existence of the Eurozone. If such a mechanism were in place, countries would not have to be bailed out through the ESM and possibly would not have to be disciplined by EU/Eurozone institutions; the market would take care of it, and the ordoliberalization of Europe would be taken one step further. After all, the ordo-/neoliberal problematic is concerned with the preconditions of functioning markets, and the fundamental one is the possibility of exits from the market, by private actors as well as nation-states. As Eucken wrote, "If one rejects the consequences of collectivism, one must want the laws of competition to rule. *And if the market is to rule one must not refuse to adjust to its requirements*" (1960, 371, my emphasis).

We must conclude that the political theory of neoliberalism, especially the elements on which I have focused, are a far cry from purely theoretical designs with no bearing on the world of actually existing neoliberalism. As has been shown, it is especially the tenets of a Euckenian ordoliberalism that correspond with many elements of the governance of the Eurozone and the EU. However, this does not imply that the structures are incompatible with what other neoliberals were arguing for if one considers, for example, the Fiscal Compact and the constitutional debt brakes it stipulated, which come very close to the kind of constitutional balanced-budget amendment that Buchanan tirelessly advocated. European institutions and politics cannot be reduced to an ordoliberal economic constitution. Political reality does not correspond exactly to theoretical designs because political reality is the site of contestation and rivaling political projects. What I have argued is that there is a discernible tendency toward an ordoliberalization of Europe in the sense of establishing a competitive order for national economies and enforcing the rules of the game, even against the resistance of an individual player. Furthermore, the governance of this competitive order is broadly in line with what ordoliberals and, specifically, Eucken saw as the appropriate role of state, democracy, and science. The response to this tendency cannot be to drum up the need to return powers and competencies to nation-states and dismantle the Eurozone. The competitive order of Europe instead needs to be repoliticized, and, more specifically, it needs to be democratized. In other words, it needs to be less ordoliberal. Discussing the most promising strategies to achieve this would require a study in itself, so I confine myself to the levels of analysis and diagnosis, which leads to this summary: If Europe does not manage to redemocratize its will-formation processes and repoliticize some of its institutions, there is a distinct danger that its ordoliberalization will slowly stagger toward its eventual completion; but in a world of uncertainty, nothing is set in stone.

Notes

Introduction

1. For biographical information on these thinkers, respectively, see Klinckowstroem 2000; Hennecke 2005; Meier-Rust 1993; Friedman and Friedman 1998; Buchanan 2007; Hayek 1994; Caldwell 2003.

2. The neoliberals were keenly aware of this shift, and it was one reason that they thought an alternative version of a "new" liberalism needed to be developed. Because of the terminological ambivalence resulting from this shift, many neoliberals tacitly abandoned the label later. The next chapter deals more extensively with these issues.

3. "The fallacy of identifying neoliberalism exclusively with economic theory becomes apparent when we notice that the historical record teaches that the neoliberals themselves regarded such narrow exclusivity as a prescription for disaster" (Mirowski 2009, 427).

4. I revisit these issues in part 2 and offer more extensive thoughts on how we may conceptualize the influence of (neoliberal) ideas on political practice.

Chapter 1

1. To be precise, the term itself can be found even before this time. In a book from 1925 the Swiss economist Hans Honegger refers to a "theoretical neoliberalism" (13). Even earlier in 1911, somewhat surprisingly, Hans Kelsen uses the term in his *Habilitation*, albeit in a strictly uneconomic meaning. In both instances, however, the term does not refer to the kind of theoretical and political agenda of those who actually called themselves neoliberals. See Kelsen (1923) 1960.

2. Burgin refers to *The Good Society* as "the foundational text of neoliberalism" (2012, 67), but this ignores the fact that several years before the publication of

Lippmann's book, thinkers like Rüstow or Eucken had formulated very similar ideas in the context of the end crisis of the Weimar Republic and thus developed a neoliberalism *avant le lettre*. See particularly Rüstow 2017b; and Eucken 2017a.

3. While Buchanan was a relentless critic of Keynesianism in all its aspects, Friedman may have been strongly opposed to the Keynesian remedies but not necessarily all of its diagnostics. Before turning into a staunch critic of Keynes, the young Röpke still advocated a "jump start" for the economy in case of a "secondary depression" (1936, 119), which is hardly distinguishable from Keynesian demand management. Hayek actually became friends with Keynes during World War II, but while he respected his intellectual opponent (see Hayek 1994, 89–97), Hayek remained convinced that Keynesianism was a thoroughly erroneous view of economics. All translations from German are mine.

4. This is a less trivial statement than particularly English-speaking readers might assume. There has been a long and heated debate, conducted predominantly in German, over the role of ordoliberalism between 1933 and 1945, and the opposition to the Nazis is not as principled as one might have expected in the case of *some* of the ordoliberals, but not Rüstow or Röpke, who went into exile. And while Eucken is a slightly more complicated case, his personal antifascist credentials are beyond doubt. See Ptak 2004; Goldschmidt 2005; Dathe 2010; Biebricher and Vogelmann 2017.

5. Hayek himself confirmed this link in an interview given years later: "It [*The Road to Serfdom*] was aimed against what I would call classical socialism; aimed mainly at the nationalization or socialization of the means of production. Many of the contemporary socialist parties have at least ostensibly given up that and turned to a redistribution/fair-taxation idea—welfare—which is not directly applicable. I don't believe it alters the fundamental objection, because I believe this indirect control of the economic world ultimately leads to the same result, which is a very much slower process . . . destroying the market order and making it necessary, against the will of the present-day socialists, gradually to impose more and more central planning" (1994, 108).

6. I quote this from *A Humane Economy* from the late 1950s, but the criticism dates back to Röpke's *Civitas Humana* from 1944. See particularly Röpke 1949, 250–267.

7. "And some miraculous rediscovery of eighteenth-century political wisdom would scarcely get us out of the woods" (Buchanan 1975, 92).

8. Ignoring this can lead to an ironic déjà vu, as Bruno Amable has pointed out with regard to the discussions following the financial crisis: "The current debate on the financial and economic crisis that focuses on the danger of 'market fundamentalism' and the lack of morals in markets lead to the conclusion that market regulation and morals could save capitalism from its worst tendencies. Unknowingly, most participants in these discussions re-enact the debates of the 1930s that led to the invention of neo-liberalism. Are those who ignore the lessons of economic history condemned to reinvent neo-liberalism?" (2010, 27).

Chapter 2

1. As Foucault puts it in his lectures on ordoliberalism, "Government must accompany the market economy from start to finish" (2008, 121).

2. The hard line of ordoliberal thinkers with regard to monopolies and economic power sets them apart from other varieties of neoliberal thought exemplified in the works of Friedman and Hayek, who are much less concerned about existence and effects of monopolies. See, for example, the later Hayek's oblique critique of the ordoliberal fixation on monopolies (2003, 3:83) and Friedman's judgment that a private monopoly is still better than a public one, both directed at Eucken (2002, 28). This laconic quote from Hayek sums up these positions quite well: "Monopoly is certainly undesirable but only in the same sense in which scarcity is undesirable: in neither case does it mean that we can avoid it" (2009, 231).

3. However, it is important to note that Eucken does not consider the competitive order an end in itself; rather, it is a worthy goal to be pursued because it is the "order that is in accordance with the nature of man and things" (1960, 372). We return to this "natural order" later.

4. The underlying intuition of this criterion is taken up by a number of other neoliberals, especially with regard to social policy issues. See Friedman 2002, 192; Hayek 2002, 39, 124–125.

5. "At the constitutional stage, the state emerges as the enforcing agency or institution, conceptually external to the contracting parties and charged with the single responsibility of enforcing agreed-on rights and claims along with contracts which involve voluntarily negotiated exchanges of such claims" (Buchanan 1975, 68).

6. This is one of the reasons for Buchanan's critique of Friedman's "quantitative" version of a budget rule. See Buchanan 1997b, 132.

7. This should also be read against the backdrop of Buchanan's highly problematic critical stance on desegregation in the Southern states—including Virginia—decided by the Supreme Court and enforced by the federal executive against the resistance of a number of state governments. See MacLean 2017.

8. This would seem to suggest that Hayek is actually a critic of a state that is run like an enterprise. Yet it has become commonplace in some of the literature on the actually existing neoliberal state that it is being assimilated to a private organization and slowly transformed into an enterprise. See particularly Dardot and Laval 2017, 215–254. This may be the case, but the demand for the state to be run in this way is nowhere to be found in Hayek's works or that of any other neoliberal considered here.

9. On the explicitly globalist orientation of *early* neoliberal thought, see Slobodian 2018.

10. Here Röpke emphasizes the conflation of *imperium* and *dominium* as one of the crucial factors in these processes, leading to the economic realm becoming increasingly politicized. See Röpke 1959a, 75.

11. However, in a comment on Europe Buchanan concedes that there is an argument to be made for equalizing grants. See Buchanan and Musgrave 1999, 178.

12. Rüstow is a case in point. While he is an ardent advocate of the strong state in the 1930s, in the 1950s he still refers to a "pluralistic degeneration of the political process" but also writes with regard to the authoritarian state that "such a state no longer exists in Germany, and it will never return" (Rüstow 2014, 463, 470).

13. On the notion of the strong state in ordoliberalism, see also Bonefeld 2012, 2017.

14. "On the contrary, not busyness [*sic*] but independence from group interests and the inflexible will to exercise its authority and preserve its dignity as a representative of the community, mark the really strong state" (Röpke 1950b, 192).

15. "It is all very well to go on explaining . . . that a strong, impartial and enlightened government should break the dominance of organized pressure groups and safeguard the fair rules of competition [but this requires] a change in the pathological condition of society and state themselves" (Röpke 1942, 238).

16. Note that for the moment I will not distinguish systematically between "dictatorship" and "authoritarianism," not the least because neoliberals seem to use the terms interchangeably. However, I revisit the matter of dictatorship in particular in chapter 5.

17. As is well known, Hayek is not the only neoliberal with a controversial relation to Chile and Pinochet. There has been a long debate over Friedman's involvement through the training of the "Chicago Boys," who were to implement economic reforms in Chile, at the University of Chicago and his advice to the regime regarding the feasibility of reforms. For a measured reconstruction of Friedman's role and position on Chile, see Meadowcroft and Ruger 2014. Even Buchanan was willing to associate with the dictatorship on occasion.

18. By now there is a considerable body of scholarship on Hayek's controversial stance on Chile and other military dictatorships at the time, such as Argentina. See, for example, Farrant, McPhail, and Berger 2012; Meadowcroft and Ruger 2014. The focus of this literature tends to be on the model of a transitional dictatorship that paves the way toward a properly liberal democratic order rather than long-term authoritarianism. While I interpret Hayek here as defending the latter, I consider the arguments for a transitional dictatorship later.

19. "Yet anyone who would maintain that the authoritarian direction of state and economic life . . . represents an approximation to the collectivist principle of society, makes it thereby clear that he cannot distinguish between dictatorship and the collectivist state" (Röpke 1942, 256).

Chapter 3

1. Elsewhere I have developed a different account of neoliberal varieties centered on the restriction, replacement, and complementation of representative democracy. See Biebricher 2015.

2. For alternative accounts of Hayek's view on sovereignty that portray it as strongly informed by a Schmittian conceptualization, see Scheuerman 1997; Cristi 1998; and Biebricher 2015.

3. A Pareto optimum is the point in an interactive exchange at which none of the participants can gain a further advantage without putting at least one actor at a disadvantage through continued exchange.

4. "The mass organizations of interested parties dangerously increase the already alarming power of separate interests" (Röpke 1960, 145). Röpke makes the clarification that critique of the state must not imply a principled hostility toward it "because after all the state is the embodiment of the common good that is located above group interests, or at least it should be" (1959a, 45). The postwar Rüstow offers a similar interpretation of the common good: "Of course, one can be of different minds for good reasons over this bonum commune, this common interest, general interest, general welfare, as we should still call it, despite the misuse of this term by the Nazis. These disagreements over the common problem of the state's interest, the general interest; that is the nature of politics and not the representation of particular interests or the compromise between these interests" (1963, 63).

5. There is a brief discussion of democratic matters in a text from 1948, but it does not suggest that Eucken has changed his views. The problem is still that "monopolies exert far more political influence because of their economic power. . . . It then has to be asked whether it is possible to maintain a parliamentary democracy at all in such circumstances" (Eucken 1989, 32).

6. This is also confirmed by the case of Röpke, who bemoans that "the monistic state of democratic doctrine has developed into the pluralistic state of democratic practice." And while he continues to introduce a differentiation between a "sound" and an "unhealthy" pluralism, the first simply amounts to minority rights against the undue use of the majority principle, whereas the second entails what I have characterized as pluralist democracy. See Röpke 1960, 142, 144.

7. Buchanan at times voices similar concerns that are hard to differentiate from neoconservative positions: "Methods, manners, morals, and standards were cavalierly tossed on the junk heap of history. . . . Democracy seemed unable to control its own excesses" (Buchanan and Musgrave 1999, 22).

8. The partial exception to this rule in the form of Hayek's model constitution is discussed later in this chapter.

9. However, this may lead to a fragmentation of the party system and thus increased pluralistic particularism, which the neoliberals find so problematic. See the critical view on proportional representation in Rüstow 1957, 174.

10. It must be noted that Hayek explicitly mentions the potential learning effects stemming from democracy. Yet, as Gamble points out, this point is not pursued further. See Hayek 2009, 96; Gamble 1996, 95.

11. It goes without saying that Buchanan would only like to see constitutional democracy with a strong rule of law *amended* through more direct democratic elements.

12. Buchanan himself at times exhibited this fear and disdain, as his comments on voting rights reforms in the 1990s suggest: "We are increasingly enfranchising the illiterate" (cited in MacLean 2017, 197).

Chapter 4

1. Ascribing a straightforward instrumentalist view to Friedman is a matter of debate to some degree, because at some point he does imply that science has explanatory tasks as well: "A hypothesis is important if it 'explains' much by little" (1953, 14). However, in my view and in much of the literature this is interpreted as a case of imprecise use of terminology—not to mention that the crucial term is put in quotation marks.

2. We should also note that Friedman's monetarism replacing Keynesianism as the dominant paradigm in the "science" of economic policy is hardly that it is more unrealistic or parsimonious in its assumptions but that it has the ability to account for phenomena that could not be adequately captured in the rival paradigm—as Friedman (1977) himself described it in his Nobel lecture.

3. Once again, the salience of this criticism is difficult to determine because Friedman gestures at the possibility of revising assumptions in some passages; in others he seems opposed.

4. I mostly focus on Eucken in this discussion because we know from the letter exchange between him and Rüstow that the latter subscribed almost entirely to Eucken's view of what it meant to practice political economy as a science. See Sala 2011.

5. See also Eucken (1951a, 350n71), where he strongly rejects any relativization of the notion of truth. For Rüstow's equally enthusiastic assessment of political economy's abilities in generating truth see Rüstow (1963, 20).

6. "The competitive order does not implement itself; in this sense it is not a natural order, no *ordre naturel*. . . . But in a different sense it is a natural order or Ordo. It amplifies the tendencies that push toward perfect competition in the industrial economy. . . . We do not find the competitive order, we find its elements in concrete reality. We do not force anything but bring to fruition what exists—alongside other forms—in reality. The remarkably strong tendencies toward perfect competition we find in the things themselves, we aim to bring to fruition" (Eucken 1960, 373–374). See also Hayek's rejection of the "false dichotomy of 'natural' and 'artificial,'" which is completely consistent with Eucken's view (2001, 20).

7. Dardot and Laval offer a perceptive discussion of these matters, but at times they tend to explain away the lingering naturalism in ordoliberal thought without a proper justification (2017, 82).

8. One of Röpke's articles from 1948 even bears the title "The Natural Order."

9. For one of the few explicitly conciliatory remarks on Christian religion and, tellingly, Catholic social thought, see Rüstow 1960, 175–177. Here he also affirms the commitment to natural law theory that is a common denominator among the ordoliberals.

10. Eucken's letters to Rüstow leave little doubt about this. In one of them he writes that the decline of liberalism began "when it lost its religious-metaphysical substance." In another he declares that he could "neither exist nor work, if I did not know that god exists" (cited in Lenel 1991, 12–13).

11. Röpke attacks the "cult of dissection" in science, and even Hayek, somewhat

surprisingly, given his overall stance, points out critically that "although the problem of an appropriate social order is today studied from the different angles of economics, jurisprudence, political science, sociology, and ethics, the problem is one which can be approached successfully only as a whole" (2001, 1:4).

12. This critical stance continues up to the aftermath of the financial crisis of 2008, which turned out to be an embarrassment for the majority of economists, as much of the scientific knowledge they had produced was "exposed as irrelevant and essentially useless" (Buchanan 2009, 151).

13. Friedman returned the favor by submitting that he was an "enormous admirer" of Hayek, "but not for his economics" (Ebenstein 2001, 81).

14. This is not to suggest that Hayek was principally opposed to a science that expressed value judgments, at least in certain contexts and for certain purposes: "An ideal picture of a society, which may not be wholly achievable . . . is nevertheless not only the indispensable precondition of any rational policy, but also the chief contribution that science can make to the solution of the problems of practical policy" (2003, 1:65).

15. "There is little mystery about Keynes's own assumptions concerning the politics of economic policy. Personally, he was an elitist, and his idealized world embodied policy decisions being made by a small and enlightened group of wise people" (Buchanan and Wagner 1977, 78).

16. The Buchanan Center funded by the Koch brothers offered seminars for lawmakers and members of the judiciary on the federal and state levels, and it was only once these activities were made public in a fund-raising effort and the integrity of the center was at stake did Buchanan sever his ties to the Kochs in the late 1990s. See MacLean 2017, 199–204.

17. At one point Röpke refers to "science whose leadership functions and responsibility are obvious [with its] authority of the highest rank" (1960, 133).

18. For a detailed discussion of the role of science, which at least considers the possibility of political consultancy, see Röpke 1953b, 381–382.

Chapter 5

1. See also Hayek 2003, 1:65, 70; Friedman and Friedman 1990, 285; and Eucken 1949, 38. See also Röpke, who approvingly cites Louis de Bonald as suggesting "that ideas are the true masters of the world" (1950b, 40).

2. The choice of an economic system is conceived of as a decision, with slightly Schmittian undertones: "By an 'economic constitution' we mean the decision as to the general ordering of the economic life of a community" (Eucken 1951a, 88).

3. Here it becomes clear that there is some overlap between Röpke's explicit and Eucken's implicit hope for benevolent guardians and Rüstow's notion of a plebiscitary dictatorship—democracy. However, Rüstow obviously opts for a different, institutional strategy, all the difficulties in spelling out its feasibility aside.

4. Röpke does not explicitly endorse transitional dictatorships, but he goes to conspicuously great lengths to differentiate between "modern dictatorships," such as

Turkey, Greece, and Portugal (in the early 1940s), and the modern tyrannies, such as Nazism and communism. See Röpke 1942, 247.

5. I will not systematically investigate Friedman's role with regard to the Chilean military dictatorship. Overall, he seems to have been less favorably inclined toward the regime form than Hayek was. Nevertheless, he did offer economic advice in a letter to Pinochet, not to mention the other "Chicago Boys," or those trained in Chicago who played a vital role in the implementation of the economic reforms. For a measured assessment, see Meadowcroft and Ruger 2014.

6. See also Hayek's own assessment that is difficult to square with the defense of dictatorship: "The powers which modern democracy possesses would be even more intolerable in the hands of some small elite" (2009, 348).

7. Man's tools "consist of what we call 'traditions' and 'institutions,'" which he uses because they are available to him as a product of cumulative growth without ever having been designed by any one mind" (ibid., 25).

8. "Liberalism is not averse to evolution and change; and where spontaneous change has been smothered by government control, it wants a great deal of change of policy" (ibid., 345).

9. "It is at least conceivable that the formation of a spontaneous order relies entirely on rules that were deliberately made" (Hayek 2003, 1:45).

10. For a conciliatory perspective regarding this issue, see Vanberg 1981, 1994.

11. While I will not systematically discuss his case, it should be noted that Friedman is implicitly confronted with a very similar dilemma to the extent that he adopts core tenets of public-choice theory in his works of the 1980s and blames the rigidity of the system on the power of "special interests" in democracies: "Taken together, the three corners of the iron triangle [bureaucrats, politicians, and beneficiaries of governmental policy] guard against dismantling the functions of government. The tyranny of the status quo is strong and difficult to break" (Friedman and Friedman 1984, 51). True, Friedman lays out a strategic path toward a constitutional amendment along his lines—slightly different from what Buchanan envisions—by involving state legislatures, which Buchanan also endorsed in his practical political activities (see MacLean 2017). However, Friedman himself concedes that in the past, all attempts to introduce such amendments have faltered when members of Congress safeguarded their own interests and were pressured by the public. See Friedman and Friedman 1984, 61.

12. Brennan and Munger are therefore entirely correct in their assessment that "Buchanan was always somewhat ambivalent on the *homo oeconomicus* issue" (2014, 339).

13. As his colleagues and collaborators recall, "he was antagonistic toward religion of all kinds. His opposition was not just to 'organized' religion: he was (if possible) even less sympathetic to unorganized populist mystics and new-age spiritualists" (ibid., 331).

14. A similar perspective on the presuppositions of a politics of fundamental change seems to be contained in Hayek's call for a "liberal utopia" mentioned previously.

15. Neoliberal thought is not the only tradition that confronts the challenge of the theorizing change. Various kinds of institutionalism face similar problems, as we see in part 2.

Chapter 6

1. On this regime of "privatized Keynesianism," see Crouch 2009; Streeck 2017.

2. This refers to the director of the Federal Reserve at the time, Paul Volcker, who in the late 1970s dramatically raised interest rates and thus stamped out inflation—at the price of a recession in the United States and a debt crisis in South America.

3. For a succinct overview of the crisis, see Ioannou, Leblond, and Niemann 2015, 156–157. I do not use the conventional term "sovereign debt crisis" because it was not necessarily sovereign debt in itself that caused the crisis. Rather, the exploding sovereign debt in many, if not most, cases was an effect of the preceding banking/financial crisis, the costs of which had to be absorbed by public budgets. We return to this later and see how important the characterization of a crisis is.

4. Seemingly, this possibility was only seriously taken into consideration by investors once Angela Merkel was heard on German TV in February 2010 brusquely saying that "right now we can help Greece by stating clearly that it has to fulfill its duties" (Weisenthal 2010).

5. While there is a notable shift between the Toronto summit and the one in Pittsburgh on the eve of the sovereign debt crisis in September 2009, the Pittsburgh summit's declaration already contained hints of an impending change. See "G20 Leaders Statement" 2009.

6. Consider the Economic Adjustment Programme for Greece from May 2010, authored by the European Commission, which accompanied the very first rescue package and is representative of those to come—for Greece and other countries: "The immediate priority is to contain the government's financing needs and reassure markets of the determination of authorities to do whatever it takes to secure medium- and long-term fiscal sustainability." "In parallel with short-term anti-crisis fiscal measures, there is a need to prepare and implement an ambitious structural reform agenda to strengthen external competitiveness, accelerate reallocation of resources from the non-tradable to the tradable sector [i.e., privatization of public assets], and foster growth" (European Commission 2010, 10, 90). On the adjustment programs administered through ESM and the Troika, see also Stiglitz 2016, 177–213. The actual memoranda of understanding signed by the heads of government of receiving countries can be found on the IMF website.

7. The theory that austerity might actually have expansionary effects is most vehemently defended by Alberto Alesina and Silvia Ardagna (2009). See also Giavazzi and Pagano 1990. For a decidedly more critical look at the possibility of expansionary austerity, see Perotti 2013; and the IMF working paper by Guajardo, Leigh, and Pescatori 2011. For a detailed discussion of the various claims, see Blyth 2013, 205–216.

8. The other major argument floating around in those years came from a now-discredited paper by Reinhardt and Rogoff titled "This Time It's Different," suggesting that beyond a certain threshold public debt had a tangible negative impact on growth. However, it turned out later that they had committed some basic technical errors in reaching their conclusion.

9. This is far from suggesting that the United States (or non-Eurozone countries) was impeccable in its crisis management, but the fact remains that "the eurozone's performance on all accounts has been worse than those countries that do not belong to the eurozone, and worse than in the United States" (Stiglitz 2016, 161–162).

10. For a helpful overview, see, e.g., Pisani-Ferry 2015.

11. The conditionality of the funds was the crucial reason that the ESM, according to the ECJ's *Pringle* ruling (ECJ C-370/12, *Pringle*), does not violate Article 125 of the TFEU. See on this point, and the court's role with regard to the management of the crisis, Hinarejos 2015.

12. In a widely reported referendum in 2015 the Greek population voted against the implementation of further reforms in exchange for financial support, but its government was unable to negotiate better terms. Note also that Portugal and Greece received EFSF funds only once opposition parties had pledged that they would not try to renegotiate the memoranda if they came into power.

13. As Jones notes, "All measures are relative to the accounting practices that underpin them. . . . Deciding whether a government is actually running an excessive deficit is essentially a political choice" (2013, 157).

14. For a more detailed account from a Foucauldian perspective that interprets the scoreboard and the MIP as part of a disciplinary regime, see Biebricher 2017.

15. Two additional reforms (Euro Plus Pact and Banking Union) were passed, but they are of only limited relevance to my argument and therefore are not discussed.

16. On the "deadly embrace" between banks and sovereigns, see, e.g., Acharya, Drechsler, and Schnabl 2014; on the international dimension, see Breckenfelder and Schwaab 2015.

17. On the cultural foundations of Europe, see also Rüstow 1956.

18. For an in-depth account of Röpke's views on European integration, see Wegmann 2002.

19. Razeen Sally lauds what he calls Röpke's "liberalism from below," which, however, seems hardly inclined toward genuine federalism: "To *Röpke*, the cardinal emphasis must be on national-level unilateral action and foreign economic policy . . . *out of which international order emerges as a byproduct*" (1999, 49).

20. We should note that with regard to the power to tax and the related possibility of equalizing transfers from the higher to lower levels, the EU comes much closer to Buchanan's ideal than the United States does.

21. Buchanan also ends up subscribing to this argument in the concrete context of the European Union (1991, 628–629).

22. "Our central suggestion is to deny the European Union the independent power to tax" (Buchanan and Lee 1994, 220).

23. For a more radical critique of central banks, see Friedman 1994.

24. When once asked whether the bank should stick to its mandate or modify it, Friedman (2003) was adamant it should stick with it.

Chapter 7

1. With regard to institutionalist accounts the following would be a concise argument: "It is not just institutions but the very ideas on which they are predicated and which inform their design and development that exert constraints on political autonomy. Institutions are built on ideational foundations that exert an independent path-dependent effect on their subsequent development" (Hay 2010, 69). For a historical institutionalist account of the latest EU restructurings, see Steinberg and Vermeiren 2015.

2. As Hay writes in his ideational institutionalist account of the "crisis" (which, according to him, is derived from the Greek word *Krino*, meaning "a moment of decisive intervention") of Keynesianism in the 1970s: "To make a decisive intervention requires a *perception of the need to make a decisive intervention*" (2001, 203).

3. For a highly informative account of such contesting crisis narratives in the context of the financial crisis in the United States, see Mirowski 2013. On ideas and their various powers, see Carstensen and Schmidt 2016.

4. Although this is also the position shared by Blyth, in his earlier work there were passages that could be read as if ideas did not matter whenever there is no acute crisis. See the critique by Gofas and Hay 2008, 15.

5. For important alternative accounts about what "our neoliberal present is," see especially Brown 2015; Mirowski 2013; Dardot and Laval 2017; Davies 2016; Fraser 2017; MacLean 2017.

6. An EU official complained that "when the German position changes on an issue the kaleidoscope shifts as other countries line up behind them. That's unprecedented in the history of the EU" (*The Economist* 2013, 1).

7. See also Peter Bofinger (2016), who is a (often dissenting) member of the German Council of Economic Experts: "German university students read the same macroeconomic textbooks as students in other countries and at the advanced level the standard DSGE models are taught and applied. But behind the formal theoretical apparatus one can identify a specific paradigm to economic policy, called 'Ordnungspolitik,' which in this form does not exist in other countries. While there are no university courses on this topic, Ordnungspolitik plays an important role in German academic debate on policy issues and actual economic policy."

8. On the European level the Directorate-General for Competition is also considered to be a stronghold of ordoliberal ideas, which is consistent with the scholarship on the ordoliberal influence on European competition policy. See Gerber 1998.

9. On the influence of ordoliberalism on German elites, see also Jacoby 2014; Denord, Knaebel, and Rimbert 2015; Van Esch 2014; and Lechevalier 2015.

10. In this context it is worth noting that this proved to be more than lip service, as the ECB actually *raised* interest rates with reference to its commitment to price stability in the middle of the crisis year of 2011.

11. On the "unintended consequences" of ordoliberal crisis management strategies, see also Nedergaard and Snaith 2015.

12. "Accordingly, there is the primacy of monetary policy for the competitive order" (Eucken 1960, 256).

13. The significance of insolvency law for the functioning of the competitive order is already mentioned in ibid., 282. See also Feld (2012, 13), who notes critically that a sovereign insolvency order was not considered in the Maastricht negotiations.

14. For similar and additional arguments against the significance of ordoliberalism for the current reshaping, see Young (2017), whose views have apparently changed since Young (2014).

15. See Streeck 2015a, 24; Friedman 1997.

16. As Finance Minister Wolfgang Schäuble, who happened to be born in Freiburg and even brings this up occasionally, reminded the readers of the *Guardian* in 2013, all reform efforts were aimed at "improving the competitiveness of all eurozone countries."

17. "Price loses its selective function when all commodities can find a market" (Eucken 1951b, 72).

18. While he concedes that wages are worth protecting for "reasons of social policy," he is still adamant that in order to battle unemployment, it is indispensable to increase profitability through a reduction of the various production costs: "It is self-evident that of these elements [the various costs] wages are the most voluminous" (Rüstow 1930, 1403).

19. For the most recent argument to that effect, see *The Economist* (2017) and its cover story, "The German Problem."

20. That Germany was capable of recovering in part through wage restraint was premised on a certain system of wage bargaining that simply does not exist in other countries. See Höpner and Lutter 2014. As Friedman (1997) had already noted in his discussion of the advantages of devaluation over wage-price adjustments, "If one country is affected by negative shocks that call for, say, lower wages relative to other countries, that can be achieved by a change in one price, the exchange rate, rather than requiring a change in thousands and thousands of separate wage rates."

21. For arguments for a return of "authoritarian liberalism" in Europe, see Streeck 2015b; Wilkinson 2013; Bruff 2014.

22. In 2017 there had been thirteen in-depth country reviews carried out. See European Commission, "In-Depth Reviews," https://ec.europa.eu/info/business-economy-euro/economic-and-fiscal-policy-coordination/eu-economic-governance-monitoring-prevention-correction/macroeconomic-imbalance-procedure/depth-reviews_en.

References

Acharya, Vitali, Itamar Drechsler, and Philipp Schnabl. 2014. "A Pyrrhic Victory? Bank Bailouts and Sovereign Credit Risk." *Journal of Finance* 69 (6): 2689–2739.

Alesina, Alberto, and Silvia Ardagna. 2009. "Large Changes in Fiscal Policy: Taxes versus Spending." National Bureau of Economic Research Working Paper 15438. http://www.nber.org/papers/w15438.pdf.

Amable, Bruno. 2010. "Morals and Politics in the Ideology of Neo-liberalism." *Socioeconomic Review* 9 (1): 3–30.

Art, David. 2015. "The German Rescue of the Eurozone: How Germany Is Getting the Europe It Always Wanted." *Political Science Quarterly* 130 (2): 181–212.

Barber, Benjamin. (1984) 2003. *Strong Democracy: Participatory Politics for a New Age.* Reprint, Berkeley: University of California Press.

Barry, Andrew, Thomas Osborne, and Nikolas Rose, eds. 1996. *Foucault and Political Reason: Liberalism, Neo-liberalism and Rationalities of Government.* London: UCL Press.

Bauer, Michael, and Stefan Becker. 2014. "The Unexpected Winner of the Crisis: The European Commission's Strengthened Role in Economic Governance." *Journal of European Integration* 36 (3): 213–229.

Bellamy, Richard. 1994. "'Dethroning Politics': Liberalism, Constitutionalism and Democracy in the Thought of F. A. Hayek." *British Journal of Political Science* 24:419–441.

Bibow, Jörg. 2004. "Investigating the Intellectual Origins of Euroland's Macroeconomic Policy Regime: Central Banking Institutions and Traditions in West Germany after the War.: The Levy Economics Institute Working Paper 406. https://papers.ssrn.com/sol3/papers.cfm?abstract_id=547122.

Bickerton, Christopher, Dermot Hodson, and Uwe Puetter. 2015. "The New Intergovernmentalism: European Integration in the Post-Maastricht Era." *Journal of
   Common Market Studies* 53 (4): 703–722.

Biebricher, Thomas. 2014. "Sovereignty, Norms, and Exception in Neoliberalism."
   Qui Parle? 23 (1): 77–108.

———. 2015. "Neoliberalism and Democracy." *Constellations* 22 (2): 255–266.

———. 2017. "Disciplining Europe: The Production of Economic Delinquency."
   Foucault Studies 23:63–85.

Biebricher, Thomas, and Frieder Vogelmann, eds. 2017. *The Birth of Austerity:
   German Ordoliberalism and Contemporary Neoliberalism*. London: Rowman and
   Littlefield International.

Birch, Kean, and Vlad Mykhnenko, eds. 2010. *The Rise and Fall of Neoliberalism: The
   Collapse of an Economic Order?* London: Zed Books.

Blyth, Mark. 2002. *Great Transformations: Economic Ideas and Institutional Change in
   the Twentieth Century*. Cambridge: Cambridge University Press.

———. 2010. "Ideas, Uncertainty, and Evolution." In *Ideas and Politics in Social Science Research*, edited by Daniel Béland and Robert Cox, 83–101. Oxford: Oxford
   University Press.

———. 2013. *Austerity: The History of a Dangerous Idea*. New York: Oxford University Press.

Boas, Taylor, and Jordan Gans-Morse. 2009. "Neoliberalism: From New Liberal
   Philosophy to Anti-liberal Slogan." *Studies in Comparative International Development* 44 (2): 137–161.

Bofinger, Peter. 2016. "German Macroeconomics: The Long Shadow of Walter Eucken." *VOX*, June 7. http://voxeu.org/article/german-macroeconomics
   -long-shadow-walter-eucken.

Böhm, Franz, Walter Eucken, and Hans Großmann-Doerth. 1989. "The Ordo-
   Manifesto of 1936." In *Germany's Social Market Economy: Origins and Evo-
   lutions*, edited by Alan Peacock and Hans Willgerodt, 15–25. New York:
   Palgrave.

Bonefeld, Werner. 2012. "Freedom and the Strong State: On German Ordoliberalism." *New Political Economy* 17 (5): 633–656.

———. 2017. *The Strong State and the Free Economy*. London: Rowman and Littlefield International.

Bourdieu, Pierre. "The Essence of Neoliberalism." *Le Monde Diplomatique*, December 1998. https://mondediplo.com/1998/12/08bourdieu.

Breckenfelder, H.-Johannes, and Bernd Schwaab. 2015. "The Bank-Sovereign Nexus
   across Borders." ECB Working Paper. https://pdfs.semanticscholar.org/dce2
   /4a46356db0a5b24a01b699c10c9e69ccdb51.pdf.

Brennan, Geoffrey, and James Buchanan. 1980. *The Power to Tax: Analytical Foundations of a Fiscal Constitution*. Cambridge: Cambridge University Press.

———. 1985. *The Reason of Rules: Constitutional Political Economy*. Cambridge: Cambridge University Press.

Brennan, Geoffrey, and Michael Munger. 2014. "The Soul of James Buchanan?" *Independent Review* 18:331–342.

Brenner, Neil, Jamie Peck, and Nik Theodore. 2010. "Variegated Neoliberalization: Geographies, Modalities, Pathways." *Global Networks* 10 (2): 182–222.

Brenner, Neil, and Nik Theodore. 2002. "Cities and the Geographies of 'Actually Existing Neoliberalism.'" *Antipode* 34 (3): 349–379.

Brown, Wendy. 2015. *Undoing the Demos: Neoliberalism's Stealth Revolution.* New York: Zone Books.

Bruff, Ian. 2014. "The Rise of Authoritarian Neoliberalism." *Rethinking Marxism* 26 (1): 113–129.

Buchanan, James. 1954. "Individual Choice in Voting and the Market." *Journal of Political Economy* 62 (4): 334–343.

———. 1975. *The Limits of Liberty: Between Anarchy and Leviathan.* Chicago: University of Chicago Press.

———. 1979a. "The Potential of Taxpayer Revolt in American Democracy." *Social Science Quarterly* 59:691–696.

———. 1979b. *What Should Economists Do?* Indianapolis, IN: Liberty Press.

———. 1986. *Liberty, Market and State: Political Economy in the 1980s.* Brighton, UK: Harvester Press, 1986.

———. 1991. "An American Perspective on Europe's Constitutional Opportunity." *Cato Journal* 10 (3): 619–630.

———. 1995a. "Federalism and Individual Sovereignty." *Cato Journal* 15 (2–3): 259–268.

———. 1995b. "Federalism as an Ideal Political Order and an Objective for Constitutional Reform." *Publius* 25 (2): 19–27.

———. 1996. "Europe as Social Reality." *Constitutional Political Economy* 7:253–256.

———. 1997a. "The Balanced Budget Amendment: Clarifying the Arguments." *Public Choice* 90:117–138.

———. 1997b. *Has Economics Lost Its Way? Reflections on the Economists' Enterprise at the End of the Century.* Fairfax, VA: Institute for Humane Studies at George Mason University.

———. 2000. "The Soul of Classical Liberalism." *Independent Review* 4:111–119.

———. 2001. "Direct Democracy, Classical Liberalism, and Constitutional Strategy." *Kyklos* 54:235–242.

———. 2004. "Constitutional Efficiency and the European Central Bank." *Cato Journal* 24 (1–2): 13–17.

———. 2007. *Economics from the Outside In: 'Better Than Plowing' and Beyond.* College Station: Texas A&M University Press.

———. 2009. "Economists Have No Clothes." *RMM, Perspectives in Moral Science*, edited by M. Baurmann and B. Lahno. http://www.frankfurt-school-verlag.de/rmm/downloads/010_buchanan.pdf.

Buchanan, James, and Dwight R. Lee. 1994. "On a Fiscal Constitution for the European Union." *Journal des Économistes et des Études Humaines* 5 (2–3): 219–232.

Buchanan, James, and Richard Musgrave. 1999. *Public Finance and Public Choice: Two Contrasting Visions of the State*. Cambridge, MA: MIT Press.

Buchanan, James, Robert Tollison, and Gordon Tullock. 1980. *Toward a Theory of the Rent-Seeking Society*. College Station: Texas A&M University Press.

Buchanan, James, and Richard Wagner. 1977. *Democracy in Deficit: The Political Legacy of Lord Keynes*. London: Academic Press.

Bulmer, Simon. 2013. "Germany and the Eurozone Crisis: Between Hegemony and Domestic Politics." *West European Politics* 37 (6): 1244–1263.

Burgin, Angus. 2012. *The Great Persuasion: Reinventing Free Markets since the Depression*. Cambridge, MA: Harvard University Press.

Cahill, Damien. 2014. *The End of Laissez-Faire? On the Durability of Embedded Neoliberalism*. Cheltenham, UK: Edward Elgar Publishers.

Caldwell, Bruce. 1990. "Critique of Friedman's Methodological Instrumentalism." In *Milton Friedman: Critical Assessments*, edited by John Wood and Ronald Woods, 3:142–153. London: Routledge.

———. 2003. *Hayek's Challenge: An Intellectual Biography of F. A. Hayek*. Chicago: University of Chicago Press.

Caporaso, James, and Sidney Tarrow. 2009. "Polanyi in Brussels: Supranational Institutions and the Transnational Embedding of Markets." *International Organization* 63 (4): 593–620.

Carstensen, Martin, and Vivien A. Schmidt. 2016. "Power over, through and in Ideas: Conceptualizing Ideational Power in Discursive Institutionalism." *Journal of European Public Policy* 23 (3): 318–337.

Chomsky, Noam. 1999. *Profit over People: Neoliberalism and Global Order*. New York: Seven Stories Press.

Cristi, Renato. 1998. *Carl Schmitt and Authoritarian Liberalism: Strong State, Free Economy*. Cardiff: University of Wales Press.

Crouch, Colin. 2009. "Privatized Keynesianism: An Unacknowledged Policy Regime." *British Journal of Politics and International Relations* 11:283–299.

———. 2011. *The Strange Non-death of Neoliberalism*. Oxford: Oxford University Press.

Crozier, Michael, Samuel Huntington, and Jofi Watanuki. 1975. *The Crisis of Democracy: Report of the Ungovernability of Democracies to the Trilateral Commission*. New York: New York University Press.

Dardot, Pierre, and Cristian Laval. 2017. *The New Way of the World: On Neoliberal Society*. London: Verso.

Dathe, Uwe. 2010. *Walter Euckens Weg zum Liberalismus (1918–1934)*. Freiburger Diskussionspapiere zur Ordnungsökonomik 08/10. Freiburg, Germany: Walter-Eucken-Institut.

Davies, William. 2016. "The New Neoliberalism." *New Left Review* 101:121–134.

De Grauwe, Paul. 2011. "The Governance of a Fragile Eurozone." Centre for European Policy Studies Working Paper 346. https://www.ceps.eu/system/files/book/2011/05/WD%20346%20De%20Grauwe%20on%20Eurozone%20Governance.pdf.

Denord, François, Rachel Knaebel, and Pierre Rimbert. 2015. "Germany's Iron Cage." *Le Monde Diplomatique*, August. https://mondediplo.com/2015/08/03ordoliberalism.

Draghi, Mario. 2013. "Opening Remarks at the Session 'Rethinking the Limitations of Monetary Policy.'" European Central Bank, June 18. https://www.ecb.europa.eu/press/key/date/2013/html/sp130618.en.html.

Dullien, Sebastian, and Ulrike Guérot. 2012. "The Long Shadow of Ordoliberalism: Germany's Approach to the Euro Crisis." European Council of Foreign Relations Policy Brief 49. https://www.ecfr.eu/publications/summary/the_long_shadow_of_ordoliberalism_germanys_approach_to_the_euro_crisis.

Duménil, Gerard, and Dominique Lévy. 2011. *The Crisis of Neoliberalism*. Cambridge, MA: Harvard University Press.

Ebenstein, Alan. 2001. *Friedrich Hayek: A Biography*. New York: Palgrave.

The Economist. 2013. "Europe's Reluctant Hegemon: Special Report Germany." *The Economist*, June 13.

———. 2017. "Why Germany's Current Account Surplus Is Bad for the World Economy." *The Economist*, July 8.

Eucken, Walter. 1949. "Die Wettbewerbsordnung und ihre Verwirklichung." *ORDO* 3:1–99.

———. 1951a. *The Foundations of Economics: History and Theory in the Analysis of Economic Reality*. Chicago: University of Chicago Press. Originally published in 1940.

———. 1951b. *This Unsuccessful Age or the Pains of Economic Progress*. London: William Hodge.

———. 1954. *Kapitaltheoretische Untersuchungen*. Tübingen, Germany: Mohr Siebeck.

———. 1960. *Grundsätze der Wirtschaftspolitik*. Tübingen, Germany: Mohr Siebeck.

———. 1989. "What Kind of Economic and Social System." In *Germany's Social Market Economy: Origins and Evolution*, edited by Alan Peacock and Hans Willgerodt, 27–45. London: Macmillan.

———. 2017a. "Structural Transformations of the State and the Crisis of Capitalism." In *The Birth of Austerity: German Ordoliberalism and Contemporary Neoliberalism*, edited by Thomas Biebricher and Frieder Vogelmann, 51–72. London: Rowman and Littlefield International. Originally published in 1932.

———. 2017b. "What Is the Competitive Order?" In *The Birth of Austerity: German Ordoliberalism and Contemporary Neoliberalism*, edited by Thomas Biebricher and Frieder Vogelmann, 99–107. London: Rowman and Littlefield International.

European Commission. 2010. *The Economic Adjustment Programme for Greece*. Directorate-General for Economic and Financial Affairs, Occasional Papers 61. http://ec.europa.eu/economy_finance/publications/occasional_paper/2010/pdf/ocp61_en.pdf.

Farrant, Andrew, Edward McPhail, and Sebastian Berger. 2012. "Preventing the 'Abuses' of Democracy: Hayek, the 'Military Usurper' and Transitional Dictatorship in Chile." *American Journal of Economics and Sociology* 71 (3): 513–538.

Feld, Lars P. 2011. "Für Fehler geradestehen." *Wirtschaftswoche*, October 23.

———. 2012. "Europa in der Welt von heute: Wilhelm Röpke und die Zukunft der Europäischen Währungsunion." Freiburg Discussion Papers on Constitutional Economics 12/2. https://www.eucken.de/en/publications/freiburg -discussion-papers-on-constitutional-economics/.

———. 2014. "James Buchanan's Theory of Fiscal Federalism: From Fiscal Equity to the Ideal Political Order." Freiburg Discussion Papers on Constitutional Economics 14/06. https://www.eucken.de/en/publications/freiburg-discussion -papers-on-constitutional-economics/.

Feld, Lars P., Ekkehard A. Köhler, and Daniel Nientiedt. 2015. "Ordoliberalism, Pragmatism and the Eurozone Crisis: How the German Tradition Shaped Economic Policy in Europe." CESIFO Working Paper 5368. https://econpapers .repec.org/paper/cesceswps/_5f5368.htm.

Feldstein, Martin. 1997. "The Political Economy of the European Economic and Monetary Union: Political Sources of an Economic Liability." *Journal of Economic Perspectives* 11 (4): 23–42.

Follesdal, Andreas, and Simon Hix. 2006. "Why There Is a Democratic Deficit in the EU: A Response to Majone and Moravcsik." *Journal of Common Market Studies* 44 (3): 533–562.

Foucault, Michel. 1989. "What Our Present Is." In *Foucault Live*, edited by Sylvère Lotringer, 407–415. New York: Semiotext(e). Originally published in 1983.

———. 1997. "What Is Enlightenment?" In *Michel Foucault: Ethics, Subjectivity and Truth*, edited by Paul Rabinow, 303–320. New York: New Press.

———. 2008. *The Birth of Biopolitics. Lectures at the Collège de France 1978–79*. New York: Palgrave.

Fraser, Nancy. 2017. "The End of Progressive Neoliberalism." *Dissent Magazine*, January 2. https://www.dissentmagazine.org/online_articles/progressive -neoliberalism-reactionary-populism-nancy-fraser.

Friedman, Milton. 1951. "Neo-liberalism and Its Prospects." *Farmand*, February 17, 89–93.

———. 1953. "The Methodology of Positive Economics." In *Essays in Positive Economics*, by Milton Friedman, 3–43. Chicago: University of Chicago Press.

———. 1955. "Liberalism." In *1955 Collier's Year Book*, edited by William Couch, 360–363. New York: P. F. Collier and Son.

———. 1960. *A Program for Monetary Stability*. New York: Fordham University Press.

———. 1977. "Nobel Lecture: Inflation and Employment." *Journal of Political Economy* 85 (3): 451–472.

———. 1994. "Do We Need Central Banks?" In *Monetary Management in Hong Kong*, 44–47. Hong Kong: Hong Kong Monetary Authority.

———. 1997. "The Euro: Monetary Unity to Political Disunity?" *Project Syndicate*, August 28. https://www.project-syndicate.org/commentary/the-euro —monetary-unity-to-political-disunity.

————. 2002. *Capitalism and Freedom*. Chicago: University of Chicago Press.

————. 2003. "Should the European Central Bank Change Its 'Two Percent Inflation Ceiling'?" *International Economy* 17 (1): 46.

Friedman, Milton, and Rose Friedman. 1984. *Tyranny of the Status Quo*. San Diego: Harcourt Brace Jovanovich. Originally published in 1983.

————. 1990. *Free to Choose: A Personal Statement*. Orlando, FL: Harvest Books.

————. 1998. *Two Lucky People: Memoirs*. Chicago: University of Chicago Press.

Furet, François. 1999. *The Passing of an Illusion: The Idea of Communism in the Twentieth Century*. Chicago: University of Chicago Press.

"G20 Leaders Statement: The Pittsburgh Summit." 2009. G20 Information Centre, September 24–29. http://www.g20.utoronto.ca/2009/2009communique0925.html.

"The G-20 Toronto Summit Declaration." 2010. G20 Toronto, June 26–27. https://www.oecd.org/g20/summits/toronto/g20-declaration.pdf.

Galbraith, James K. 2016. *Welcome to the Poisoned Chalice: The Destruction of Greece and the Future of Europe*. New Haven, CT: Yale University Press.

Gamble, Andrew. 1996. *Hayek: The Iron Cage of Liberty*. Cambridge: Polity Press.

Gerber, David. 1998. *Law and Competition in Twentieth-Century Europe: Protecting Prometheus*. Oxford: Oxford University Press.

Giavazzi, Francesco, and Marco Pagano. 1990. "Can Severe Fiscal Contractions Be Expansionary? Tales of Two Small European Countries." NBER Working Paper 3372. http://www.nber.org/papers/w3372.

Giles, Chris, and Christian Oliver. 2010. "G20 Drops Support for Fiscal Stimulus." *Financial Times*, June 6. https://www.ft.com/content/786776b4-708f-11df-96ab-00144feabdco.

Gofas, Andreas, and Colin Hay. 2008. "The Ideas Debate in International and European Studies: Towards a Cartography and Critical Assessment." IBEI Working Paper 2008/11. ttps://www.ibei.org/en/the-ideas-debate-in-international-and-european-studies-towards-a-cartography-and-critical-assessmen_20677.

Goldschmidt, Nils. 2001. *Entstehung und Vermächtnis ordoliberalen Denkens: Walter Eucken und die Notwendigkeit einer kulturellen Ökonomik*. Münster, Germany: LIT.

————. 2005. "Die Rolle Walter Euckens im Widerstand: Freiheit, Ordnung und Wahrhaftigkeit als Handlungsmaximen." In *Wirtschaft, Politik und Freiheit: Freiburger Wirtschaftswissenschaftler und der Widerstand*, edited by Nils Goldschmidt, 289–314. Tübingen, Germany: Mohr.

Goldstein, Judith, and Robert Keohane. 1993. *Ideas, Interests and American Trade Policy*. Ithaca, NY: Cornell University Press.

Gray, John. 1984. *Hayek on Liberty*. Oxford: Blackwell.

Green, Donald, and Ian Shapiro. 1994. *Pathologies of Rational Choice Theory: A Critique of Applications in Political Science*. New Haven, CT: Yale University Press.

Guajardo, Jamie, Daniel Leigh, and Andrea Pescatori. 2011. "Expansionary Austerity: New International Evidence." IMF Working Paper 11/158. https://www.imf.org/external/pubs/ft/wp/2011/wp11158.pdf.

Guggenberger, Bernd, and Claus Offe, eds. 1984. *An den Grenzen der Mehrheits-demokratie. Politik und Soziologie der Mehrheitsregel*. Opladen, Germany: West-deutscher Verlag.

Habermas, Jürgen. 1992. *Between Facts and Norms: Contributions to a Discourse Theory of Law and Democracy*. Cambridge, MA: MIT Press.

———. 2015. *The Lure of Technocracy*. London: Polity.

Hahn, Roland. 1993. *Sozialromantik und Marktwirtschaft: Die programmatische Er-neuerung des Liberalismus in Deutschland unter dem Einfluss der Ideen Wilhelm Röpkes und Alexander Rüstows*. Frankfurt: Hänsel-Hohenhausen, 1993.

Hall, Peter, and Rosemary Taylor. 1996. "Political Science and the Three New Institutionalisms." *Political Studies* 44 (5): 936–957.

Hartwich, Oliver Marc. 2009. "Neoliberalism: The Genesis of a Political Swear-word." CIS Occasional Paper 114. https://www.cis.org.au/app/uploads/2015/07/op114.pdf.

Harvey, David. 2005. *A Brief History of Neoliberalism*. New York: Oxford University Press.

Haselbach, Dieter. 1991. *Autoritärer Liberalismus und Soziale Marktwirtschaft: Ge-sellschaft und Politik im Ordoliberalismus*. Baden-Baden, Germany: Nomos, 1991.

Hay, Colin. 1996. "Narrating Crisis: The Discursive Construction of the 'Winter of Discontent.'" *Sociology* 30 (2): 253–277.

———. 2001. "The 'Crisis' of Keynesianism and the Rise of Neoliberalism in Brit-ain." In *The Rise of Neoliberalism and Institutional Analysis*, edited by John Campbell and Ove Pedersen, 193–218. Princeton, NJ: Princeton University Press.

———. 2007. "The Genealogy of Neoliberalism." In *Neoliberalism: National and Regional Experiments with Global Ideas*, edited by Ravi K. Roy, Arthur T. Denzau, and Thomas D. Willett, 51–70. London: Routledge, 2007.

———. 2010. "Ideas and the Construction of Interests." In *Ideas and Politics in Social Science Research*, edited by Daniel Béland and Robert Cox, 65–82. Oxford: Oxford University Press.

Hayek, Friedrich August. 1960. "The Intellectuals and Socialism." In *The Intel-lectuals: A Controversial Portrait*, edited by George Huszar, 371–384. Glencoe, IL: Free Press.

———. 1967a. "The Principles of a Liberal Social Order." In *Studies in Philosophy, Politics and Economics*, by F. A. Hayek, 160–177. London: Routledge. Originally published in 1966.

———. 1967b. "The Theory of Complex Phenomena." In *Studies in Philosophy, Politics and Economics*, by F. A. Hayek, 22–42. London: Routledge.

———. 1978a. "The Campaign against Keynesian Inflation." In *New Studies in Philosophy, Politics, Economics and the History of Ideas*, by F. A. Hayek, 191–231. London: Routledge.

———. 1978b. "Liberalism." In *New Studies in Philosophy, Politics, Economics and the History of Ideas*, by F. A. Hayek, 119–151. London: Routledge. Originally published in 1973.

———. 1978c. "The Pretence of Knowledge." In *New Studies in Philosophy, Politics, Economics and the History of Ideas*, by F. A. Hayek, 23–34. London: Routledge.

———. 1980. *Individualism and the Economic Order*. Chicago: University of Chicago Press.

———. 1988. *The Fatal Conceit: The Errors of Socialism*. London: Routledge.

———. 1992. "Opening Address to a Conference at Mont Pèlerin." In *The Fortunes of Liberalism: Essays on Austrian Economics and the Ideal of Freedom*, edited by Peter G. Klein, 237–248. Indianapolis, IN: Liberty Fund.

———. 1994. *Hayek on Hayek: An Autobiographical Dialogue*. Edited by Stephen Kresge and Leif Wenar. Indianapolis, IN: Liberty Fund.

———. 2001. *The Road to Serfdom*. London: Routledge.

———. 2002. "Competition as a Discovery Procedure." *Quarterly Journal of Austrian Economics* 5 (3): 9–23.

———. 2003. *Law, Legislation and Liberty: A New Statement of the Liberal Principles of Justice and Political Economy*. 3 vols. London: Routledge. Originally published in 1982.

———. 2009. *The Constitution of Liberty*. London: Routledge.

———. 2010a. "Individualism: True and False." In *Studies on the Abuse and Decline of Reason*, by F. A. Hayek, 47–76. Chicago: University of Chicago Press.

———. 2010b. *Studies on the Abuse and Decline of Reason*. Chicago: University of Chicago Press.

Heipertz, Martin, and Amy Verdun. 2010. *Ruling Europe: The Politics of the Stability and Growth Pact*. Cambridge: Cambridge University Press.

Heller, Hermann. (1933) 2015. "Authoritarian Liberalism?" *European Law Journal* 21 (3): 295–301.

Hennecke, Hans Jörg. 2005. *Wilhelm Röpke: Ein Leben in der Brandung*. Stuttgart: Schäffer-Pöschel.

Hinarejos, Alicia. 2015. *The Euro Area Crisis in Constitutional Perspective*. Oxford: Oxford University Press.

Hobsbawm, Eric. 1987. *The Age of Empire 1875–1914*. London: Weidenfeld and Nicholson.

———. 1994. *Age of Extremes: The Short Twentieth Century, 1914–1991*. London: Michel Joseph.

Höpner, Martin. 2014. "Wie der Gerichtshof und die europäische Kommission Liberalisierung durchsetzen: Befunde aus der MPIfG-Forschungsgruppe zur politischen Ökonomie der europäischen Integration." MPIfG Discussion Paper 14/8. http://www.mpifg.de/pu/mpifg_dp/dp14-8.pdf.

Höpner, Martin, and Mark Lutter. 2014. "One Currency and Many Modes of Wage Formation: Why the Eurozone Is Too Heterogeneous for the Euro." MPIfG Discussion Paper 14/14. www.mpifg.de/pu/mpifg_dp/dp14-14.pdf.

Höpner, Martin, and Florian Rödl. 2011. "Illegitim und rechtswidrig: Das neue makroökonomische Regime im Euroraum." *Wirtschaftsdienst* 92:219–225.

Höpner, Martin, and Armin Schäfer. 2010. "Polanyi in Brussels? Embeddedness and the Three Dimensions of European Economic Integration." MPIfG Discussion Paper 10/8. http://www.mpifg.de/pu/mpifg_dp/dp10-8.pdf.

Howarth, Ben, and Lucia Quaglia. 2015. "The Political Economy of the Euro Area's Sovereign Debt Crisis: Introduction to the Special Issue of the Review of International Political Economy." *Review of International Political Economy* 22 (3): 457–484.

Ioannou, Demosthenes, Patrick Leblond, and Arne Niemann. 2015. "European Integration and the Crisis: Practice and Theory." *Journal of European Public Policy* 22 (2): 155–176.

Jackson, Ben. 2010. "At the Origins of Neo-liberalism: The Free Economy and the Strong State, 1930–1947." *Historical Journal* 53 (1): 129–151.

Jacoby, Wade. 2014. "The Politics of the Eurozone Crisis: Two Puzzles behind the German Consensus." *German Politics and Society* 34:70–85.

Jessop, Bob. 2016. "Neoliberalismen, kritische politische Ökonomie und neoliberale Staaten." In *Der Staat des Neoliberalismus*, edited by Thomas Biebricher, 123–152. Wiesbaden, Germany: Nomos.

Joerges, Christian. 2014. "Law and Politics in Europe's Crisis: On the History of the Impact of an Unfortunate Configuration." *Constellations* 21 (2): 249–261.

———. 2015. "The Legitimacy *Problématique* of Economic Governance in the EU." In *The Governance Report 2015*, edited by Mark Dawson, Henrik Enderlein, and Christian Joerges, 69–95. Oxford: Oxford University Press.

Jones, Erik. 2013. "The Collapse of the Brussels-Frankfurt Consensus and the Future of the Euro." In *Resilient Liberalism in Europe's Political Economy*, edited by Vivien A. Schmidt and Mark Thatcher, 145–170. Cambridge: Cambridge University Press.

Kelsen, Hans. (1923) 1960. *Hauptprobleme der Staatsrechtslehre: Entwickelt aus der Lehre vom Rechtssatze*. Reprint, Aalen, Germany: Scientia.

Keynes, John Maynard. (1944) 1980. "Letter to Hayek." In *Collected Writings*, vol. 27, *Activities 1940–1946*, edited by Elizabeth Johnson and Donald Moggridge, 385–388. Reprint, Cambridge: Cambridge University Press.

Kirchgässner, Gebhard. 1988. "Wirtschaftspolitik und Politiksystem: Zur Kritik der traditionellen Ordnungstheorie aus der Sicht der Neuen Politischen Ökonomie." In *Ordnungspolitik*, edited by Dieter Cassel, Bernd-Thomas Ramb, and Jörg Thieme, 53–75. Munich: Vahlen.

Klinckowstroem, Wendula Gräfin von. 2000. "Walter Eucken: Eine biographische Skizze." In *Walter Eucken und sein Werk: Rückblick auf den Vordenker der sozialen Marktwirtschaft*, edited by Lüder Gerken, 53–116. Tübingen, Germany: Mohr Siebeck.

Kolev, Stefan. 2013. *Neoliberale Staatsverständnisse im Vergleich*. Stuttgart: Lucius and Lucius.

Krugman, Paul. 2012. *End This Depression Now!* New York: W. W. Norton.

Larner, Wendy. 2000. "Neo-liberalism: Policy, Ideology, Governmentality." *Studies in Political Economy* 63:5–25.

Leblond, Patrick. 2006. "The Political Stability and Growth Pact Is Dead: Long Live the Economic Stability and Growth Pact." *Journal of Common Market Studies* 44 (5): 969–990.

Lechevalier, Arnaud. 2015. "Eucken under the Pillow: The Ordoliberal Imprint on Social Europe." In *Social Europe: The Dead End. What the Eurocrisis Is Doing to Europe's Social Dimension*, edited by Arnaud Lechevalier and Jan Wielghos, 49–102. Copenhagen: Djof Publishing.

Lenel, Hans Otto. 1991. "Walter Euckens Briefe an Alexander Rüstow." *ORDO* 42:11–14.

Linz, Juan J. 2000. Totalitarian and Authoritarian Regimes. Boulder, CO: Lynne Rienner.

Lippmann, Walter. 1937. *The Good Society*. Boston: Little, Brown.

MacLean, Nancy. 2017. *Democracy in Chains: The Deep History of the Radical Right's Stealth Plan for America*. New York: Viking.

Majone, Giandomenico. 1994. "The Rise of the Regulatory State in Europe." *West European Politics* 17 (3): 77–101.

———. 2014. "From Regulatory State to a Democratic Default." *Journal of Common Market Studies* 52 (6): 1216–1223.

Marneffe, Wim, Bas van Aarle, Wouter van der Wielen, and Lode Vereeck. 2011. "The Impact of Fiscal Rules on Public Finances in the Euro Area." *CESifo DICE Report* 3:18–25.

Matthijs, Matthias. 2016. "Powerful Rules Governing the Euro: The Perverse Logic of German Ideas." *Journal of European Public Policy* 23 (3): 375–391.

Meadowcroft, John, and William Ruger. 2014. "Hayek, Friedman, and Buchanan: On Public Life, Chile, and the Relationship between Liberty and Democracy." *Review of Political Economy* 26 (3): 358–367.

Mehta, Jal. 2011. "From 'Whether' to 'How': The Varied Role of Ideas in Politics." In *Ideas and Politics in Social Science Research*, edited by Danile Béland and Robert Cox, 23–46. Oxford: Oxford University Press.

Meier-Rust, Kathrin. 1993. *Alexander Rüstow: Geschichtsdeutung und liberales Engagement*. Stuttgart: Klett-Cotta.

El Mercurio. 1981. "Friedrich von Hayek: Lider y maestro de liberalismo económico." *El Mercurio*, April 12, D8–9.

Merkel, Angela. 2011. "Regierungserklärung vom Bundeskanzlerin." Die Bundesregierung, December 2. https://www.bundesregierung.de/Content/DE/Bulletin /2010-2015/2011/12/131-1-bk-bt.html.

Mirowski, Philip. 2009. "Postface: Defining Neoliberalism." In *The Road from Mont Pèlerin: The Making of the Neoliberal Thought Collective*, edited by Philip Mirowski and Dieter Plehwe, 417–455. Cambridge, MA: Harvard University Press.

———. 2013. *Never Let a Serious Crisis Go to Waste: How Neoliberalism Survived the Financial Meltdown*. London: Verso.

Mirowski, Philip, and Dieter Plehwe, eds. 2009. *The Road from Mont Pèlerin: The Making of the Neoliberal Thought Collective*. Cambridge, MA: Harvard University Press.

Mudge, Stephanie Lee. 2008. "What Is Neo-liberalism?" *Socio-Economic Review* 6:703–731.

Mundell, Robert. 1961. "A Theory of Optimum Currency Areas." *American Economic Review* 51 (4): 657–665.

Nedergaard, Peter, and Holly Snaith. 2015. "'As I Drifted on a River I Could Not Control': The Unintended Ordoliberal Consequences of the Eurozone Crisis." *Journal of Common Market Studies* 53 (5): 1094–1109.

Nientiedt, Daniel, and Ekkehard A. Köhler. 2016. "Liberalism and Democracy—a Comparative Reading of Eucken and Hayek." *Cambridge Journal of Economics* 40:1743–1760.

North, Douglass. 1990. *Institutions, Institutional Change and Economic Performance*. Cambridge: Cambridge University Press.

Offe, Claus. 1984. "Ungovernability: On the Renaissance of Conservative Theories of Crisis." In *Observations on the "Spiritual Situation of the Age,"* edited by Jürgen Habermas, 67–88. Cambridge, MA: MIT Press.

Osborne, George. 2010. "Statement on the Emergency Budget." *The Telegraph*, June 22. http://www.telegraph.co.uk/finance/budget/7846849/Budget-2010-Full -text-of-George-Osbornes-statement.html.

Peck, Jamie. 2008. "Remaking Laissez-Faire." *Progress in Human Geography* 32 (1): 3–43.

———. 2010. *Constructions of Neoliberal Reason*. New York: Oxford University Press.

———. 2014. "Pushing Austerity: State Failure, Municipal Bankruptcy and the Crises of Fiscal Federalism in the USA." *Cambridge Journal of Regions, Economy and Society* 7:17–44.

Perotti, Roberto. 2013. "The 'Austerity Myth': Gain without Pain?" In *Fiscal Policy after the Financial Crisis*, edited by Alberto Alesina and Francesco Giavazzi, 307–358. Chicago: University of Chicago Press.

Pisani-Ferry, Jean. 2015. "Rebalancing the Governance of the Euro Area." In *Beyond the Crisis: The Governance of Europe's Economic, Political, and Legal Transformation*, edited by Mark Dawson, Henrik Enderlein, and Christian Joerges, 62–82. Oxford: Oxford University Press.

Plant, Raymond. 2009. *The Neo-liberal State*. Oxford: Oxford University Press.

———. 2016. "Friedrich August von Hayek: Der (neo-)liberale Staat und das Ideal des Rechtsstaats." In *Der Staat des Neoliberalismus*, edited by Thomas Biebricher, 73–97. Baden-Baden, Germany: Nomos.

Polanyi, Karl. 2001. *The Great Transformation: The Political and Economic Origins of Our Time*. New York: Beacon Press. Originally published in 1944.

Ptak, Ralf. 2004. *Vom Ordoliberalismus zur Sozialen Marktwirtschaft: Stationen des Neoliberalismus in Deutschland*. Wiesbaden, Germany: VS-Verlag.

Reinhoudt, Jurgen, and Serge Audier. 2018. *The Walter Lippmann Colloquium: The Birth of Neo-liberalism*. New York: Palgrave.

Röpke, Wilhelm. 1936. *Crises and Cycles*. London: William Hodge. Originally published in 1932.

———. 1942. *International Economic Disintegration*. London: William Hodge.

———. 1948. "Die natürliche Ordnung: Die neue Phase der wirtschaftspolitischen Diskussion." *Kyklos* 2 (3): 211–232.

———. 1949. *Civitas Humana: Grundfragen der Gesellschafts- und Wirtschaftsreform*. Erlenbach-Zürich, Switzerland: Eugen Rentsch Verlag. Originally published in 1944.

———. 1950a. *Maß und Mitte*. Erlenbach-Zürich, Switzerland: Eugen Rentsch.

———. 1950b. *The Social Crisis of Our Time*. Chicago: University of Chicago Press.

———. 1953a. "Europäische Wirtschaftsgemeinschaft." In *Aufbau eines neuen Europa: Fünf Aufsätze über wirtschaftliche Zusammenarbeit*, 7–33. Berlin: Grunewald Verlag.

———. 1953b. Der wissenschaftliche Ort der Nationalökonomie." *Studium Generale* 6:374–382.

———. 1954. *Internationale Ordnung—heute*. Erlenbach-Zürich, Switzerland: Eugen Rentsch, 1954.

———. 1955. "Europäische Investitionsplanung: Das Beispiel der Montanunion." *ORDO* 7:71–102.

———. 1958. "Political Enthusiasm and Economic Sense: Some Comments on European Economic Integration." *Modern Age* 2 (2): 170–176.

———. 1959a. *International Order and Economic Integration*. Dordrecht, Netherlands: Reidel Publishing.

———. 1959b. "Die Massengesellschaft und ihre Probleme." In *Masse und Demokratie*, edited by Louis Baudin and Albert Hunold, 13–38. Erlenbach-Zürich, Switzerland: Eugen Rentsch.

———. 1960. *A Humane Economy: The Social Framework of the Free Market*. Chicago: Henry Regnery. Originally published in 1958.

———. 1963. *Economics in the Free Society*. Chicago: Henry Regnery.

———. 1964. "European Economic Integration and Its Problems." *Modern Age* 8 (3): 231–244.

———. 1987. *Two Essays by Wilhelm Röpke: The Problem of Economic Order / Welfare, Freedom and Inflation*. Lanham, MD: University Press of America.

Roubini, Nouriel, and Stephen Mihm. 2010. *Crisis Economics: A Crash Course in the Future of Finance*. New York: Allen Lane.

Roy, Ravi K., Arthur T. Denzau, and Thomas D. Willett. 2007. "Introduction: Neoliberalism as a Shared Mental Model." In *Neoliberalism: National and Regional Experiments with Global Ideas*, edited by Ravi K. Roy, Arthur T. Denzau and Thomas D. Willett, 3–13. London: Routledge.

Rüstow, Alexander. (1929) 1959. "Diktatur innerhalb der Grenzen der Demokratie: Dokumentation des Vortrags und der Diskussion von 1929 an der Deutschen Hochschule für Politik." *Vierteljahreshefte für Zeitgeschichte* 7 (1): 85–111.

———. 1930. "Selbstkostensenkung, Lohnabbau und Preisabbau." *Der deutsche Volkswirt* 4 (2): 1403–1406.

———. 1940. "Zu den Grundlagen der Wirtschaftswissenschaft." *Revue de la Faculté des Sciences Economiques de l'Université d'Istanbul* 2:105–154.

———. 1942. "General Sociological Causes of the Economic Disintegration and Possibilities of Reconstruction." In *International Economic Disintegration*, by Wilhelm Röpke, 267–283. London: William Hodge.

———. 1949. "Politik und Moral." *Zeitschrift für die gesamte Staatswissenschaft* 105:575–590.

———. 1956. "Geistige Grundlagen des Bewußtseins der europäischen Einheit." In *Europa—Erbe und Aufgabe*, edited by Martin Göhring, 3–13. Wiesbaden, Germany: Franz Steiner Verlag.

———. 1957. *Ortsbestimmung der Gegenwart: Eine universalgeschichtliche Kulturkritik. Dritter Band: Herrschaft oder Freiheit?* Erlenbach-Zürich, Switzerland: Eugen Rentsch.

———. 1960. "Paläoliberalismus, Kollektivismus und Neoliberalismus in der Wirtschafts- und Sozialordnung." In *Christentum und Liberalismus*, edited by Karl Forster, 149–178. Munich: Karl Zink.

———. 1963. *Rede und Antwort*. Ludwigsburg, Germany: Martin Horch.

———. 2009. *Die Religion der Marktwirtschaft*. Münster, Germany: LIT.

———. 2014. *Freedom and Domination: A Historical Critique of Civilization*. Edited by Dankwart Rustow and Salvator Attanasio. Princeton, NJ: Princeton University Press.

———. 2017a. "Social Policy or Vitalpolitik (Organic Policy)." In *The Birth of Austerity: German Ordoliberalism and Contemporary Neoliberalism*, edited by Thomas Biebricher and Frieder Vogelmann, 163–177. London: Rowman and Littlefield International. Originally published in 1951.

———. 2017b. "State Policy and the Necessary Conditions for Economic Liberalism." In *The Birth of Austerity: German Ordoliberalism and Contemporary Neoliberalism*, edited by Thomas Biebricher and Frieder Vogelmann, 143–149. London: Rowman and Littlefield International. Originally published in 1932.

Sala, Roberto. 2011. "Methodologische Positionen und soziale Praktiken in der Volkswirtschaftslehre: Der Ökonom Walter Eucken in der Weimarer Republik." WZB Discussion Paper No. SP IV 2011-401. https://www.econstor.eu/handle/10419/71267.

Sally, Razeen. 1999. "Wilhelm Röpke and International Economic Order: 'Liberalism from Below.'" *ORDO* 50:47–51.

Sandbu, Martin. 2015. *Europe's Orphan: The Future of the Euro and the Politics of Debt*. Princeton, NJ: Princeton University Press.

Savage, James. 2007. *Making the EMU: The Politics of Budgetary Surveillance and the Enforcement of Maastricht*. Oxford: Oxford University Press.

Savage, James, and Amy Verdun. 2015. "Strengthening the European Commission's Budgetary and Economic Surveillance Capacity since Greece and the Euro Area Crisis: A Study of Five Directorates-General." *Journal of European Public Policy* 23 (1): 101–118.

Sayer, Andrew. 2008. *Realism and Social Science*. Thousand Oaks, CA: Sage.

Scharpf, Fritz. 1999. *Governing in Europe: Effective and Democratic?* Oxford: Oxford University Press.

———. 2010. "The Asymmetry of European Integration, or, Why the EU Cannot Be a 'Social Market Economy.'" *Socio-Economic Review* 8:211–250.

———. 2011. Monetary Union, Fiscal Crisis and the Preemption of Democracy. MPIfG Discussion Paper 11/11.

———. 2016. "Forced Structural Convergence in the Eurozone—or a Differentiated European Monetary Community." MPIfG Discussion Paper 16/15. www .mpifg.de/pu/mpifg_dp/dp16-15.pdf.

Schäuble, Wolfgang. 2010. "Nachhaltiges Wachstum durch nachhaltiges Sparen— die deutsche Finanzpolitik ist auf dem richtigen Weg." *Handelsblatt*, June 24. https://www.bundesfinanzministerium.de/Content/DE/Reden/2010/2010-06 -24-handelsblatt.html.

———. 2013. "We Germans Don't Want a German Europe." *The Guardian*, July 19. ttps://www.theguardian.com/commentisfree/2013/jul/19/we-germans -dont-want-german-europe.

Scheuerman, William. 1997. "The Unholy Alliance of Carl Schmitt and Friedrich A. Hayek." *Constellations* 4 (2): 172–188.

Schimmelfennig, Frank. 2015. "Liberal Intergovernmentalism and the Euro Area Crisis." *Journal of European Public Policy* 22 (2): 177–195.

Schmidt, Vivien A. 2008. "Discursive Institutionalism: The Explanatory Power of Ideas and Discourse." *Annual Review of Political Science* 11:303–326.

Schmidt, Vivien A., and Cornelia Woll. 2013. "The State: The Bête Noire of Neo-liberalism or Its Greatest Conquest?" In *Resilient Liberalism in Europe's Political Economy*, edited by Vivien A. Schmidt and Mark Thatcher, 112–141. Cambridge: Cambridge University Press.

Schmitt, Carl. 1998. "Appendix: Carl Schmitt, Strong State and Sound Economy: An Address to Business Leaders." In *Carl Schmitt and Authoritarian Liberalism: Strong State, Free Economy*, by Renato Cristi, 212–232. Cardiff: University of Wales Press.

Skocpol, Theda. 1985. "Bringing the State Back In: Strategies and Analysis in Current Research." In Bringing the State Back In, edited by Peter B. Evans, Friedrich Rueschemeyer, and Theda Skocpol, 3–37. Cambridge: Cambridge University Press.

Slobodian, Quinn. 2018. *Globalists: The End of Empire and the Birth of Neoliberalism*. Cambridge, MA: Harvard University Press.

Stark, Jürgen. 2008. "Monetary, Financial and Fiscal Stability in Europe." Speech delivered at 11th Euro Finance Week, Frankfurt, November 18.

Steger, Manfred B., and Ravi K. Roy. 2010. *Neoliberalism: A Very Short Introduction*. Oxford: Oxford University Press.

Steinberg, Federico, and Mattias Vermeiren. 2015. "Germany's Institutional Power and the EMU Regime after the Crisis: Towards a Germanized Euro Area?" *Journal of Common Market Studies* 54 (2): 388–407.

Stiglitz, Joseph. 2008. "The End of Neo-liberalism?" *Project Syndicate*, July 2. https://www.project-syndicate.org/commentary/the-end-of-neo-liberalism?barrier=true.

———. 2010. *Freefall: Free Markets and the Sinking of the Global Economy*. New York: Allen Lane.

———. 2016. *The Euro: How a Common Currency Threatens the Future of Europe*. New York: W. W. Norton.

Streeck, Wolfgang. 2015a. "Heller, Schmitt and the Euro." *European Law Journal* 21 (3): 361–370.

———. 2015b. "Why the Euro Divides Europe." *New Left Review* 95:5–26.

———. 2017. *Buying Time: The Delayed Crisis of Democratic Capitalism*. London: Verso.

Trichet, Jean-Claude. 2010a. "Interview with *La Repubblica*." *La Repubblica*, June 24. https://www.bis.org/review/r100625a.pdf.

———. 2010b. "Stimulate No More—It Is Time for All to Tighten." *Financial Times*, July 27. https://www.ft.com/content/1b3ae97e-95c6-11df-b5ad-00144feab49a.

Turner, Rachel S. 2007. "The 'Rebirth of Liberalism': The Origins of Neo-liberal Ideology." *Journal of Political Ideologies* 12 (1): 67–83.

Van Esch, Femke. 2014. "Exploring the Keynesian-Ordoliberal Divide: Flexibility and Convergence in French and German Leaders' Economic Ideas during the Euro-Crisis." *Journal of Contemporary European Studies* 22 (3): 288–302.

Vanberg, Viktor. 1981. *Liberaler Evolutionismus oder vertragstheoretischer Konstitutionalismus? Zum Problem institutioneller Reformen by F. A. von Hayek und J. M. Buchanan*. Tübingen, Germany: Mohr.

———. 1994. "Cultural Evolution, Collective Learning and Constitutional Design." In *Economic Thought and Political Theory*, edited by David Reisman, 171–204. Boston: Kluwer.

———. 2014. "Liberalismus und Demokratie: Zu einer vernachlässigten Seite der liberalen Tradition." HWWI Policy Paper 85. http://www.roepke-institut.org/fileadmin/roepke/roepke-dokumente/8_Roepke_Vorlesung_Viktor_Vanberg.pdf.

Walpen, Bernhard. 2004. *Die offenen Feinde und ihre Gesellschaft: Eine hegemonietheoretische Studie zur Mont Pèlerin Society*. Hamburg: VSA.

Weaver, Kent. 1986. "The Politics of Blame Avoidance." *Journal of Public Policy* 6 (4): 371–398.

Wegmann, Milène. 2002. *Früher Neoliberalismus und europäische Integration: Interdependenz der nationalen, supranationalen und internationalen Ordnung von Wirtschaft und Gesellschaft (1932–1965)*. Baden-Baden, Germany: Nomos.

Weidmann, Jens. 2013. *Crisis Management and Regulatory Policy*. Walter Eucken Lecture, February 11. http://www.bundesbank.de/Redaktion/EN/Reden/2013/2013_02_11_weidmann_eucken.html. https://www.bis.org/review/r130214c.pdf.

———. 2016. "Fiscal Rules Need More Bite." *BILD*, December 26. https://www.bild.de/geld/mein-geld/jens-weidmann/lohnt-sich-sparen-ueberhaupt-noch-49488690.bild.html.

———. 2017. "Prospects for the Economy." Speech delivered at the Jahresempfang der Wirtschaft, February 7. https://www.bundesbank.de/Redaktion/EN/Reden/2017/2017_02_07_weidmann.html.

Weisenthal, Joe. 2010. "Merkel: There Is 'No Possibility' of Bailing Out Greece." *Business Insider*, February 28. http://www.businessinsider.com/angela-merkel-denies-greek-bailout-2010-2?IR=T.

Wilkinson, Michael. 2013. "The Specter of Authoritarian Liberalism: Reflections on the Constitutional Crisis of the European Union." *German Law Journal* 14 (5): 527–560.

Woodruff, David. 2016. "Governing by Panic: The Politics of the Eurozone Crisis." *Politics & Society* 44 (1): 81–116.

Young, Brigitte. 2014. "German Ordoliberalism as Agenda Setter for the Euro Crisis: Myth Trumps Reality." *Journal of Contemporary European Studies* 22 (3): 276–287.

———. 2017. "Is Germany's and Europe's Crisis Politics Ordoliberal and/or Neoliberal?" In *The Birth of Austerity: German Ordoliberalism and Contemporary Neoliberalism*, edited by Thomas Biebricher and Frieder Vogelmann, 221–237. London: Rowman and Littlefield International.

Index

CURRENCIES

New Thinking for Financial Times
Melinda Cooper and Martijn Konings, Editors

In the wake of recent events such as the global financial crisis, the Occupy Wall Street Movement, and the rise of anti–student-debt activism, the need for a more sophisticated encounter between economic theory and social and political philosophy has become pressing. The growth of new forms of money and finance, which has only accelerated since the financial crisis, is recognized as one of the defining developments of our time. But even as finance continuously breaches limits and forces adjustments, much scholarly commentary remains focused on the limits of the market and the need to establish some prior state of political stability, thus succumbing to a nostalgia that blunts its critical edge. Not content to adopt a defensive posture, books in this series move beyond well-rehearsed denunciations of out-of-control markets and seek to rethink the core institutions and categories of financial-ized capitalism. *Currencies* will serve as a forum for work that is situated at the intersection of economics, the humanities, and the social sciences. It will include conceptually driven historical or empirical studies, genealogies of economic ideas and institutions, and work that employs new or unexplored theoretical resources to rethink key economic categories and themes.

Lisa Adkins, *The Time of Money*

Martijn Konings, *Capital and Time: For a New Critique of Neoliberal Reason*

The authorized representative in the EU for product safety and compliance is:
Mare Nostrum Group
B.V Doelen 72
4831 GR Breda
The Netherlands

www.ingramcontent.com/pod-product-compliance
Lightning Source LLC
Chambersburg PA
CBHW020845270326
41928CB00006B/555